# Making Sense of Advance Directives

# CLINICAL MEDICAL ETHICS

## Editors

H. TRISTRAM ENGELHARDT, JR., The Center for Ethics, Medicine and Public Issues, Baylor College of Medicine, Houston, Texas

KEVIN WILDES, S.J., Department of Philosophy, Georgetown University, Washington, D.C.

## Editorial Advisory Board

## Previous Books in the Series

# Making Sense of
# Advance Directives

*Revised Edition*

Nancy M. P. King, J.D.

GEORGETOWN UNIVERSITY PRESS / WASHINGTON, D.C.

Georgetown University Press, Washington, D.C.   20007
© 1996 by Georgetown University Press. All rights reserved.
Printed in the United States of America.
10  9  8  7  6  5  4  3  2  1     1996
THIS VOLUME IS PRINTED ON ACID-FREE OFFSET BOOKPAPER.


**Library of Congress Cataloging-in-Publication Data**

King, Nancy M. P.
    Making sense of advance directives / Nancy M. P. King. — Rev. ed.
        p.     cm.   —   (Clinical medical ethics)
    Includes bibliographical references and index.
    1.  Right to die.   2.  Right to die—Law and legislation.   3.  Do-not
-resuscitate orders.   I. Title.   II. Series: Clinical medical
ethics (Washington, D.C.)
    R726.K5   1996
    174'.24—dc20
    ISBN 0-87840-605-0 (pbk. : alk. paper)
                                                                95-42746

*To my family*

# Contents

## 4
## Advance Directives: Current Forms, Legal Fears, Moral Goals     108

## 5
## Directions for Decision: When Documents Don't Do It All     184

# Preface to the Revised Edition

As the first edition of this book was going to press in late 1990, three important things were happening. The Nancy Cruzan case (*Cruzan v. Director* 1990) had just been decided by the United States Supreme Court; the Patient Self-Determination Act (PSDA 1990) had passed; and a new end-of-life decision-making issue, the problem of "futile treatment," was just beginning to be widely discussed in the literature of medical ethics and medical jurisprudence. Although only the PSDA appeared to bear directly on the meaning and status of written advance directives, these three developments, and others that they have spawned, have in several respects greatly changed the decision-making climate in which advance directives must be considered and understood (Danis 1994).

First, the *Cruzan* decision, because of what it did not say rather than what it did say, touched off an explosion of legislative activity in the states. As a result, not only do nearly all states now have living will statutes but even more have health care proxy statutes, which provide a formal means of designating surrogate decision-makers for decisionally incapable patients. Health care proxies are now more popular than living wills.

Moreover, the deaths in mid-1994 of Richard Nixon and Jacqueline Kennedy Onassis focused renewed attention on advance directives ("Patients Ask" 1994). Both of these public figures might have had their lives prolonged with terminal illness. Both had living wills refusing such treatment. The decisions of both were honored by the same New York City teaching hospital: New York Hospital–Cornell Medical Center. New York is one of the few remaining states without a living will statute. It is also home to Choice in Dying, the most prominent patient advocacy organization for end-of-life choices, which received thousands of phone calls daily after the deaths of Mr.

Nixon and Mrs. Onassis from people seeking information about advance directives.

Next, the PSDA's required information and inquiry about health care decision-making focused enormous attention on the logistics of encouraging the expression of treatment preferences. The law and its implementation have begun to spawn extensive quantitative research on patients' preferences and whether and how they are honored in hospitals and other inpatient settings. In addition, a period of great controversy about the law's form and substance has given way to attempts to develop educational and other efforts to increase its effectiveness (see the discussion in chapter 4).

Finally, the problem of futility has swiftly and thoroughly changed the climate for end-of-life decision-making. Although few patients execute formal "request directives," much research has shown that many patients express preferences for more rather than less treatment at the end of life. This discovery and the extensive discussion of several cases (especially *In re Conservatorship of Wanglie* 1991 and *In re Baby K* 1994) in both academic and popular literature have had several consequences. First, the cultural and social determinants of end-of-life preferences are beginning to be examined. Second, the nature of medical judgments about "futile" treatment is being explored in an attempt to make sense of the opposition between the physician's judgment against further treatment and the patient's choice to have "everything" done—just as the opposition between the "integrity of the medical profession" and the patient's autonomy was reconciled in court decisions where patients and their families refused treatment that physicians sought to continue. The question whether there is medical consensus about futility is being probed, and the role of power and authority in health care decision-making is being revisited (Macklin 1993). Third, requesting futile treatment has raised questions about the relationship between health care delivery and payment for care—questions that have never before been posed so starkly. As a result, the boundaries of permissible decision-making are becoming sharper, and what will happen to patients without advance directives is quite likely to become better defined, or even prescribed, as health care providers and institutions move to clarify their responsibilities and limit their obligations (Angell 1994).

Most interestingly, however, the resurgence of medical judgment to limit futile treatment continues to coexist with many bitter battles by patients, their surrogates, and their families to cease unwanted end-of-life treatment. It seems that for every Helga Wanglie, whose family wants treatment to continue despite unanimous medical judgment to the contrary (*In re Conservatorship of Wanglie* 1991), there is a Jean Elbaum, whose husband must fight for years to convince the nursing home to cease treatment—and then must pay for the treatment his wife refused by valid advance directive (*Elbaum v. Grace Plaza of Great Neck, Inc.* 1989; *Grace Plaza of Great Neck, Inc. v. Elbaum* 1993). This seemingly contradictory pair of model disputes brackets the issue of advance directives as we move toward the end of the 1990s, and virtually guarantees the persistence of the questions this revised volume sets out to address.

# Acknowledgments

I am grateful for the thoughtful critical commentary of Richard Robeson, Carol Leininger, Larry Churchill, and Arlene Davis; for all I've learned from colleagues and students through trying to make sense of advance directives; and for the patient secretarial expertise of Angie Boudwin, Deborah Eakins, Carolyn McIntyre, and most especially Jackie Jones.

# Notice

Except for cases that have been reported in the public media or have become public through court hearings, all identifiable information used in case examples has been changed, and the structure of the case example altered, to protect the identities of the individuals and institutions involved. Instead, case examples have been constructed out of numerous clinical experiences to illustrate general problems in bioethics, health care delivery, or health care policy. Any similarity to actual individuals living or dead is purely coincidental.

Also, though this volume examines legal cases and principles, it does not intend to provide legal advice. For legal advice there is no substitute for directly consulting the legal profession.

# 1

# Introduction

The first time I read the medical consent and authorization, it had registered in my mind simply as a legal document. Now I began to understand what it meant. It was a letter of ultimate love and trust. (Schucking 1985, 268)

Ever since Karen Ann Quinlan slipped into permanent unconsciousness in 1975 and her father agonized publicly over whether she should remain indefinitely on a respirator (*In re Quinlan* 1976), the desires of patients, their families, and their friends to limit the application of apparently limitless medical technology have been a pressing concern for ethics, law, and public policy. Ms. Quinlan's case contained nearly all the elements of the problems we still face: vague, general, but sincere prior oral statements suggesting that she would not want continued treatment; a family attempting to do what they saw as best for her; and physicians uncertain whether to use medical judgment alone (and if so, what the "right" medical decision was), to preserve her life at all costs, or to honor the family's interpretation of their daughter's choice. Most ironically, once she was removed from her respirator, she did not die.

Karen Quinlan—like dozens of other names made famous by court decisions, newspaper stories, and television evening news—has come to symbolize a tangled knot of issues surrounding the end of life and who controls it. Of all the contenders for that control—patients, their families, their doctors, ethics committees, legislatures, and courts—patients themselves have an overwhelmingly strong claim to make end-of-life health care decisions about their own bodies, lives, and futures. Much of the time, however, the health care choices patients make will not be effectuated until they have lost their decisional capacity, their ability to ratify prior choices, and their ability to consider their current condition. To rely on patients' choices

1

under these circumstances means to give effect to their advance directives about medical treatment.

This book is for clinicians and others who wish to understand and make use of advance directives as a primary vehicle for end-of-life decisions that concern the health care of patients. It addresses why patients' advance directives are a better means of making such decisions than reliance on other possible decision-makers, and it examines how advance directives should be written, interpreted, and implemented. Though directed primarily to clinicians, this book will also help persons wishing to write their own advance directives to make sense of the issues that make these health care choices so highly charged.

An advance directive is a written statement [1] that is intended to govern health care decision-making for its author, should he or she lose decisional capacity in the future. Though by this definition advance directives can apply to any health care decision, they are almost always addressed to end-of-life issues, and it is in this context that they are best known. As "living wills" (directives giving lists of instructions), "health care proxies" (durable powers of attorney naming proxy decision-makers, or agents, for health-related decision-making), or both, advance directives are becoming commonplace. Attorneys and advocacy groups often counsel the elderly and the chronically ill to write advance directives in order to ensure that physicians will honor their wishes for "death with dignity." And courts deciding the ever-increasing number of "right to die" cases often express the wish that the patient had written an advance directive instead of just telling family and friends, "I hope I never become another Karen Ann Quinlan" or, "I would not want to live as a vegetable"—as did Paul Brophy (*Brophy v. New England Sinai Hospital* 1986) and perhaps now the most famous name of all, Nancy Beth Cruzan (*Cruzan v. Director* 1990). The implication is that advance directives provide needed—and wanted—guidance, certainty, and legal and moral protection for certain kinds of important, value-laden health care decisions.

But what are advance directives really? How should physicians view them and what should they accomplish? Should everyone have one? And above all, when should an advance directive be honored? Many patients believe strongly that advance directives give them the only possibility of dignity and control at the end of life. At the same time, however, many caregivers, sometimes from an excess of caution but often through bitter experience, see advance directives as barriers to doing what is best for patients, engendering a false sense of certainty and promoting misunderstandings between health care providers and the patient's friends and family.

For the clinician, making sense of advance directives means (1) understanding how to help a patient prepare a directive and how to discuss a patient's directive with the patient and the patient's family or friends so that it contains what the patient wants and can be understood by caregivers, and (2) knowing how to respond to an advance directive: how to read it, apply it, and decide whether and how it should be honored. Ideally, the doctor and the patient will write the patient's advance directive together—a directive that the doctor will later honor. But many clinicians will also help patients write directives that others will have to honor, and will also face the question of honoring existing advance directives that they have not helped prepare. Thus, all clinicians must have a sound understanding of what advance directives are and what it means to write them, so that all directives may be read and judged practically and fairly.

## MAKING SENSE OF ADVANCE DIRECTIVES

The basis for the moral (and legal) validity of advance directives is the patient's right of autonomy or self-determination. To understand why advance directives are desirable and should be implemented, it is necessary to understand the patient's right of autonomy or self-determination as it applies to health care decisions that are intended to be acted upon both contemporaneously and in the future. Establishing the validity of advance directives does not end the matter, however—or responsible caregivers would not have the concerns they do about implementing directives. Yes, the patient's right of autonomy implies a duty of others—physicians and other caregivers in particular—not to interfere with its exercise. Yet this duty of noninterference by itself does not help guide physicians in interpreting and implementing directives or in helping patients to formulate and articulate their wishes by means of directives.

The enforceability of directives depends on more than just their basis in autonomy; it also depends, in an important way, upon *community*: upon the willingness of patients and doctors to talk together about health care choices, to share values and goals, confront differences, and make true efforts at understanding. The values of community—trust and respect for others—give content and workability to the requirement that patients' directives be honored, by providing a basis for (1) requiring patients to make good-faith efforts to write directives that others can interpret and apply without undue difficulty and confusion, and (2) requiring caregivers and others to make good-faith efforts to understand patients' directives so that they may be implemented as they were intended, regardless of personal disagreement with the patient's values and choices. Patients' most significant choices about treatment are, at the same time, in one sense truly private and in another sense necessarily social, shared, the products of a community. Recognizing the duality and tension in these difficult choices is essential. In order to understand and use directives well, therefore, this book must address three distinct but related issues: the patient's right of choice, the meaning of that right for choices that will be applied in the future, and concerns of fairness and practicality in the interpretation and application of directives.

### The First Issue: The Extent of Consent

First, we must look at patients' legal right of consent. What health care choices may patients with decisional capacity make? Are there any limits to their power to decide? (For example, are their rights greater when they are dying, or perhaps less because death is an irrevocable and socially disfavored choice?) Do they have less right to refuse treatments when death could be readily avoided with treatment (for example, refusal of blood transfusions or antibiotics) or when the refusal seems like suicide? In addition to their legal right to refuse, may patients *request* any treatments? And may physicians morally or legally refuse to comply with patients' decisions?

This book argues that patients have a strong and clear moral interest and legal right to act as the ultimate decision-makers about their own medical care. The interest extends to any and all decisions, including decisions viewed by others as wrong, that are made by persons who have the ability to make autonomous choices.

When a patient refuses medical interventions intended to preserve or prolong his or her life, health professionals and others may often quite reasonably question the authenticity of the patient's choice. We are at pains to assure ourselves that such patients are not speaking solely out of fear, pressure from family, financial worries, delirium, or despair. We want to know that the choice represents the will of the patient, as free, knowledgeable, and unimpaired as possible. In serious illness, with its attendant impairments and constraints, decisions may be less authentic, more pressured; they will certainly be suspected of being so. Nonetheless, patients may still make valid choices at difficult times—including decisions to refuse treatment. Indeed, the more consequential the decision, the more expressive of important personal values and human ends it may be, so that honoring patients' wishes may become more necessary than ever. This issue is examined in chapter 2.

## The Second Issue: Past Choices, Future Consequences

Second, we must look at the future factor. Once we have gained some understanding of the choices decisionally capable patients may make, what basis is there for applying these choices when the patients have irretrievably lost their decisional capacity? Why do patients want their wishes honored at a time when they often cannot perceive their circumstances and have certainly lost their ability to understand their own past preferences and reasoning? Why should caregivers not simply be empowered to act in the patient's best interests once the patient can no longer make decisions? And if the patient has in a directive named someone else to decide on his or her behalf, why should we not limit such a proxy's power to decide, since the patient cannot dissent from the proxy's decision?

This book argues that the patient's right to choose extends also to choices that are meant to affect medical care in the future, in anticipation of future decisional incapacity. There are several reasons for extending the patient's right of choice to include prospective choices. In practical terms, to recognize only contemporaneous choices would permit caregivers to alter an agreed-upon plan of care as soon as a patient became unable to reaffirm previously made care choices. This could result in decisions, by persons other than the patient, to administer recently refused treatments on the patient's deathbed.

To avoid this obvious unfairness, a decision-making standard labeled "substituted judgment" has been identified as a primary means of determining how decisions should be made for a patient no longer capable of making them. Substituted judgment requires a reconstruction of the prior competent self in an effort to determine what this patient would have wanted. Evidence of the patient's prior wishes and views is assembled, and only if the evidence available is insufficient to enable such a reconstruction should outside decision-makers, acting on behalf of the incompetent patient, turn instead to a more objective "best interests" standard, which may, if necessary, rest heavily on medical judgment.

Some have argued, however, that prospective decisions can never be sufficiently informed to be valid, that persons who have not yet experienced the circumstances about which they are deciding cannot sufficiently appreciate them, and that genuine uncertainties about consciousness and the end of life make it impossible, even theoretically, to dismiss the possibility of disagreement between the present, deciding self and the future, decided-about self. The issue is not whether unconscious, demented, dying patients have value or whether they experience their existence as valuable but whether the possibility, or even the certainty, that the future self might have such value precludes anyone in the present from choosing death instead of a diminished future existence.

The argument in support of the validity of prospective choices rests upon an understanding of the continuity of the self and of the individual's right to make choices that reflect a valuation of the self. An individual's self-definition depends upon embracing and developing a certain set of attributes while refusing or discouraging the adoption of others. Recognizing prospective choices requires not only that individuals be permitted to prefer some attributes over others but also that individuals be permitted to reject some attributes that are partially unknown and even unknowable.

Making decisions that include unknowns of all kinds, as well as considerations about the future, is nothing new in medical decision-making or in decision-making about anything else. Thus, the "future factor" does not represent a barrier to acceptance of advance directives. This issue is examined in chapter 3.

## The Third Issue: Practicalities and Particulars

Third and finally, we must read and use particular directives well. Having established a basis for honoring a patient's previously expressed wishes, we face the very central and practical questions of certainty in advance directives:

Does/did the author have decisional capacity? How do we test for that, and what is our standard? How thoughtful and reasonable and persuasive must patients be for their directives to be honored?

Is/was the person informed? What does it mean to be informed about situations that do not yet exist and may never come to pass? How much uncertainty can patients be permitted to deal with? Is there a point at which it becomes unreasonable to ask caregivers to apply a directive to a given decision, either because we cannot be sure what the patient meant or perhaps even because we can't be sure that the patient has not changed his/her mind?

And lastly, what is the difference between answering these essentially practical concerns in the *writing* of a directive—with patient and physician talking together—and addressing them in the directive's *application*—when the patient can no longer be consulted? If every clinician who cares for a patient is tempted anew to second-guess the patient's advance directive, no certainty at all can exist for patients. Yet if we do not scrutinize advance directives and require patients to take some care to make them clear and unambiguous, the adverse consequences could be significant for the patient.

If advance directives are valid in theory, should individuals who wish their choices to be known and honored think carefully and deeply about them? Of course they should. Everyone who decides to write an advance directive must take into account that each of us can only imperfectly understand the future; and everyone who must decide whether to honor a directive must understand that it represents a free choice in the face of an uncertain future, a choice between what we know ourselves to want and the chance that with new information what we want could diverge from what is morally best for us. Writing, assessing, and implementing directives, then, is a matter of weighing their goals against their effects, their benefits against their risks, and making choices about them that are both personal and principled. If the directive is valid, it is also, in at least some sense, binding on others. Thus, individuals executing directives have some duty to others to provide circumstantial guarantees of a directive's validity—simply in order to be able to expect that the directive will be implemented. A crucial concern of this book, then, is an inquiry into what gives a directive sufficient apparent validity that it ought to be honored.

Advance directives should not be primarily intended to protect physicians who implement them from legal liability. Such a goal would be futile no matter what; *there is no "suit-proof" living will.* Directives should seek to memorialize patients' prospective decisions, for reasons of evidence, certainty, and clarity. If caregivers are willing to implement only directives executed in accordance with narrowly drawn state living will statues—or if they believe that only such statutory directives are legally valid—the patient's interest in decision-making is jeopardized. In contrast, a directive that is intended to facilitate the mutual decisional progress of the physician-patient relationship is far more likely to provide physicians with the opportunity to satisfy themselves about the patient's mental state, decision-making character, level of appreciation of the facts and issues at hand, and relevant personal values. The physician-patient relationship provides the physician with the opportunity to encourage a high degree of reflection in the patient and to assist the patient in writing an advance directive that demonstrates the patient's seriousness of consideration.

How far does the physician's duty to trust the patient's expression of choice extend? And how far may patients' trust in others' obedience to their choices extend? These questions may not be possible to answer with any precision in general terms. Physicians must be willing to consider each situation closely and carefully, and patients may have to accept the practical necessity of persuading others of the validity of their directives. But once the patient's interest in prospective decision-making is recognized as valid, the guiding principles underlying that recognition will order and ease the practical difficulties that remain. Chapters 4, 5, and 6 further address these concerns.

## EASY CASES, HARD CASES, AND
## ADVANCE DIRECTIVES IN PERSPECTIVE

Advance directives are not usually treated as an isolated matter; instead, they are often considered as one of the many available means of caring for "hopelessly ill patients" (Wanzer et al. 1984, 1989) or of addressing the problem of "life-sustaining treatment" (Hastings Center 1987). Living wills and health care powers of attorney, do-not-resuscitate orders and hospital ethics committees, and reasoning based on the patient's autonomy, the patient's best interests, the needs of the family, and the interests of society are often considered all together in analyzing decision-making at the end of life. As a result, there is at least some societal agreement about "easy" cases involving terminally ill patients and refusal of invasive life-sustaining treatments like artificial ventilation, resuscitation, and chemotherapy. And there is a redundancy of reasoning about these cases as well: there are many good reasons to support the decision to stop treatment. Both patients' rights and patients' best interests can justify treatment withholding and withdrawal in these cases. Treatment cessation can be supported by an advance directive, a verbal declaration, a family request, a statute, a hospital policy, or a medical decision.

So many reasons come together in these easy cases that we can get fuzzy and fail to distinguish among them. The result is that when we go beyond the easy cases and consider the hard ones—namely, refusals of treatments that are clearly life-saving or life-preserving and refusals of treatment when patients are not terminally ill—we are less than certain about which of these reasons, if any, can still apply. (Harder still are *requests* for end-of-life treatment that appears to care-givers to be futile, excessive, or ill-advised, where the patient's rights are thought to conflict with the patient's best interests in the opposite way from treatment refusals and the reasoning is even more tangled.)

This book is primarily concerned with *written documents*. This helps to distinguish the discussion of advance directives from the potentially more difficult practical problems of determining what a patient with no written document would have wanted, as well as from the theoretical question whether trying to make such a determi-nation for patients is a better approach than trying to determine their best interests. The written expression of wishes (in the form of instructions, the naming of a proxy decision-maker, or both) estab-lishes the patient's seriousness of purpose and at least begins to show *that* the patient wanted his/her wishes honored and *what* those wishes were at the time of writing (Cohen 1991). Problems of the meaning and application of written directives may still exist, but these problems will usually not be as severe as the problems that arise when nothing is in writing and when caregivers must make decisions with little or no information about the patient's prior views. (The focus on written documents also bypasses much of the current futility controversy. Although many patients say they would want aggressive treatment in the future and many families request "every-thing" on behalf of decisionally incapable patients, few patients actu-ally write "request directives.")

Moreover, discussion here will not be limited to the class of writ-ten advance directives that appear in state legislation. It is true that the form, content, and application of such statutory directives are suf-ficiently narrow and particular to provide solutions to some of the potential problems raised by directives. Statutory directives are writ-ten to describe and define the "easy" cases. They also offer a small amount of legal insulation for physicians who honor them, and sometimes even the hint of a remedy for patients whose physicians fail to do so. This book is also concerned with advance directives that are not statutorily prescribed, and seeks to promote the use of directives that are more detailed and extensive than those prescribed by statute. This distinguishes the discussion here from that of many legally oriented articles and advocacy group publications, whose focus is on the documents approved by the various states. Though these statutes serve as useful starting points for writing directives and may be sufficient for many people, concentrating on statutes obscures both the general issue of the basis of the patient's authority to write directives—which is not merely statutory in *any* state—and the particular question of how to deal with directives that do not fit the template provided by the relevant statute.

Many patients seek to make choices that statutory directives do not address. More and more patients are attempting to refuse treatments when they are not terminally ill. Many state statutes now address treatment refusal in persistent vegetative state, but there are other serious and progressive conditions, such as severe Alzheimer's dementia, in which patients may live for many years and the prospect of which may prompt advance refusal of treatment. More and more patients are attempting to refuse food and water when they are supplied by artificial means, ranging from nasogastric tube feeding to total parenteral nutrition. In the mid-1980s many states attempted by statute to preclude refusal of artificial nutrition and hydration. More recently, however, most state statutory directives permit its refusal, though many states place it in a category of its own, separate from all other treatments.[2]

There are many other treatment decisions patients might make that are not contemplated by narrowly drawn advance directive statutes. The importance of these most difficult decisions highlights the problem of how to think about advance directives. Are they legal documents? Or are they fundamentally something else? Are directives "letters of trust"? Binding contracts? Non-binding documents? Legal protection for caregivers? Moral statements? Or just a way to begin a conversation about health care choices and expectations? Which of these effects are intended by an advance directive's author, which are looked for by those responding to a directive, and which of them all should be decisive? By examining the legal foundations of treatment refusal as well as statutory forms of advance directives, chapters 2 and 4 consider the legal status of advance directives, conclude that they are not primarily legal documents, and suggest ways they can secondarily fulfill that role while remaining faithful to their primary purpose of *effectuating patients' previously expressed wishes within the patient's decisional community of caregivers, family, and friends.*

The following case examples are meant to illustrate some of the ways in which advance directives appear in medical practice and the ways in which the issues they address are interwoven with many other issues for patients and for doctors. Discussion of these cases is far from exhaustive and is intended to stimulate the reader's reflection.

### Example 1: Thinking about Directives

The Carpenters have been your patients for three years, since retirement brought them south from New Jersey, where Betty, a school librarian, and Herman, a middle manager in light industry, raised three children. Herman's arthritis is mildly disabling; Betty is recovering from cataract surgery. Today they have come for a routine visit, a check on their medications, and prescription renewals. They also have some questions.

"We went to see a lawyer recently," Herman explains. "One of our daughters was divorced last year, and we've also become grandparents again, so we decided to update our wills for the first time in about twenty years. The lawyer told us we should also make out 'living wills' to make certain that we will be able to control the care we receive in case of some serious illness."

"This lawyer was recommended to us by a friend we met at a Weekend Retirement College seminar," Betty explained. "He was quite helpful and professional, but he wasn't really able to answer our questions about this 'living will.' He left the impression that if we didn't have one of these documents, we would have difficulty in dealing with doctors and hospitals; but he wasn't clear on how we should use it to avoid those problems. So we decided to ask you," Betty concludes, handing you a one-page photocopied form. You recognize it as the Standard Living Will that is contained in the Natural Death Act for your state; unsuccessfully you try to recall what the continuing education lecturer said about it in the Practice Update keynote speech last year.

The lawyer who proposed to the Carpenters that they needed living wills meant well, but his advice did not help the Carpenters much. The brief standard directives contained in most state statutes tend to be both vague and narrowly applicable; therefore they are potentially quite difficult for caregivers to interpret and apply. In order to know what it is they are signing, patients must know what the terms of such documents mean: What is included in "lifesaving treatment?" When is a person "terminally ill?" and so forth. Legal definitions can help make this clearer, certainly; but because directives will be interpreted and applied by caregivers, it seems necessary to know how they, too, would define such terms. Moreover, a directive that has been left in a lawyer's hands along with family wills, or placed in a safe-deposit box, or even filed with important personal papers at home is unlikely to be available when it is needed. Anyone who writes a directive must think about ways of bringing it to caregivers' attention. The best way for patients to address both of these concerns is to discuss them with their physicians.

The answers to the Carpenters' questions may, under the circumstances, be easy to give. As their physician of several years, you may assure them that you intend to act in their best interests in any instance of serious illness. You might explain that if one of them were unable to express choices, you would consult the other to help decide what is best; you might emphasize your commitment to keeping them well informed and honoring their wishes. Because they currently have no serious health problems that could trigger the need for an advance directive, you might advise the Carpenters that a living will is probably not necessary so long as you can be contacted when needed. If they are concerned about relying on other caregivers to contact you in an emergency, an advance directive might be only one of several appropriate mechanisms to deal with that situation.

### Example 2: Discussing Directives

A year later, the Carpenters are back in your office. Six months ago, Herman was diagnosed as having amyotrophic lateral sclerosis (ALS, or Lou Gehrig's disease); his disease has progressed during that time, but he is still able to care for himself, with substantial assistance from Betty. His principal complaints are increasing difficulty in getting up out of chairs and into and out of the car, and shortness of breath, which he confesses he finds frightening. Herman and Betty have been seeing you regularly to keep up with Herman's illness, to plan for changes in his care, and to discuss what can be expected in the future. On this visit, it is Betty who brings up the subject of advance directives—she has written one for herself, and it is several pages long.

"I've joined one of those groups that help people to control their own health care," she announces. "I brought you my living will, so that we can discuss it; I've thought a lot about this lately, and I just don't want to be dependent. I want to die with dignity. I don't want, ever, to be resuscitated, to be on a ventilator, to have radiation therapy or chemotherapy, or to be fed intravenously or by a tube. If I am not able to make my own rational choices and my mental capacity can't be restored, I don't want any treatment except to keep me comfortable. I've prepared a health care power of attorney, too, and I'm naming my sister Clara to make these decisions for me. Herman says he could never do that—could never tell a doctor not to do something that would help keep me living a little longer. Well, I think that's barbaric; I guess I see why he feels that way, but I know Clara will stand up for me and do what I want. What do you think, doctor; will this living will make certain that I die the way I choose?"

While devoutly wishing Betty had not asked you such a loaded question, you scan her document, which fairly bristles with instructions, explanations, and philosophical statements. Gently you suggest that Betty's concerns are more likely to be well addressed if you and she talk about what she wants and why than if she attempts to present an ironclad contract to every potential caregiver. You steer Herman and Betty into a discussion of their difference of opinion over the health care power of attorney, explaining that many caregivers would be troubled by such a disagreement unless they could be assured that Herman understood his wife's position and would not object to Clara's role. You debate with yourself whether you should ask Herman whether he would also like to write an advance directive, and decide to do three things instead:

1. You strongly suggest that Herman and Betty begin talking separately, with a counselor you recommend, about how they are coping with Herman's diagnosis. Because you suspect that some of the stress of Herman's illness has influenced Betty's thinking, you would like to be sure that the influence is productive.

2. You make an appointment to discuss with Herman and Betty how you intend to cope with Herman's increasing respiratory problems; you will instruct them about what to do in a crisis, and explain the likelihood that Herman could require temporary ventilatory assistance in the near future.

3. A month from now, after they have had some counseling sessions, you will return to the topic of advance directives. You intend to emphasize the importance of discussing the future, sharing decisions, and respecting others' wishes and needs. You want both Herman and Betty to be able to express their choices and to count on your support and each other's, even though their choices may differ. And finally, you cross your fingers and hope you know enough now to help them make decisions if the need arises before the month is out!

### Example 3: Reading Directives

Brenda Harmon has just arrived by ambulance to the critical care nephrology unit where you are the chief resident.[3] Her private physician is a division chief in the hospital; you do not know him personally. He is not in the hospital now; he has called and left word that Mrs. Harmon appears to be infected. You know that she is an insulin-dependent diabetic who has been on home dialysis for eight years and that she has been treated at your hospital in the past. Now she is somnolent and is not responding to questions. Her husband, who has arrived with her, has given you what information he can about her condition over the past thirty-six hours. He appears upset and agitated, and you have asked him to wait outside the unit; he stands in the doorway as you begin to examine Brenda and draw blood for tests.

Before you have gotten very far, she suffers an arrest and you begin resuscitation. Suddenly her husband rushes into the room brandishing a sheaf of papers: Brenda Harmon's living will and a health care power of attorney naming him as her decision-maker. Professor Harmon demands that the resuscitation cease, claiming that the documents show that Brenda has specifically expressed a wish not to be resuscitated in circumstances like this.

You leave the bedside, ordering the team to continue the resuscitation, and examine Professor Harmon's papers. They seem perfectly authentic, combining a statutory living will form, handwritten notarized instruction statements, and a statutory health care power of attorney. But what are you to do with them now? Should you stop the resuscitation, or continue?

Although you do not know Brenda Harmon or her husband, perhaps you can verify the authenticity of these documents and begin to determine how they should be applied by contacting her physician immediately to see whether he knows of their existence. (It is also possible that copies of the documents could have been made part of her medical record already, since she has been treated here before. Unfortunately, even if this has been done, the documents could still go unnoticed during emergencies.) In this case, Mrs. Harmon's doctor knows about the documents and informs you that Brenda has strong opinions and is indeed deeply opposed to any resuscitative efforts. He points out, however, that because an infection is potentially curable, he would not have discouraged or opposed resuscitation if consulted before it was begun. You are puzzled and a bit annoyed at this: Who would think of consulting about an emergency resuscitation before beginning it, unless previously alerted to a patient's potential objections? If her physician knew of her objections and did not convey them when Mrs. Harmon was admitted, is it not true that he has refused to honor her wishes—in a way that leaves you with the responsibility?

Professor Harmon certainly thinks so. He is furious when you convey to him the substance of your conversation with the division chief and explain that you are obligated to continue the resuscitation until it either is effective in restoring function or shows itself to be futile. He claims that his wife does not care whether her infection is treatable; she wants no resuscitation *no matter what.* You wish that Professor Harmon had showed you these documents half an hour ago, when you were asking him about his wife's medical history; to be fair, however, if *you* did not know they would be relevant, how could he? And even then, you do not know how you could avoid an emergency resuscitation anyway; maybe they should not have come to the hospital at all. Mrs. Harmon's reasoning sounds like a suicide wish to you, but if she had stayed home, at least you would not be involved.

Returning to the bedside, you find that heartbeat has been restored and that the patient has been placed on ventilatory support. But Professor Harmon wants the ventilator withdrawn; he wants no further resuscitation, cardiac drugs, or intervention of any sort. In response, you call the hospital administrator, the chaplain, and the unit social worker to an emergency care conference. Professor Harmon will have to live with the fact that until he can explain his wife's views to these people and to you, her care will go forward. You cannot see that you have any other choice right now.

These case examples were crafted to describe some of the implications that advance directives have in the different settings in which they may be discussed or employed. Our discussion of them has not been exhaustive, but it should be clear that advance directives can apply to situations ranging from home care to nursing home care to hospitals; to critical or to chronic care; to choices ranging from "do not resuscitate" and "do not hospitalize" to "do not tube-feed" and "do not give antibiotics"; and to a variety of treatment goals. Every situation is further modified by the involvement, and the perspectives, of the patient's family or intimate friends, all of the patient's caregivers, institutions in which the patient is residing or to which the patient wishes to go, and even the patient's insurer. We are just at the beginning.

## FIVE MODELS OF ADVANCE DIRECTIVES

For a long time, "advance directive" was popularly understood as synonymous with "living will"—a short official document, in a form either legally prescribed or prepared and distributed by some prominent organization, that refuses treatments that impede "death with dignity." This popular portrait has begun to change considerably over the last five years, however. It has been amplified to include the naming of a proxy decision-maker authorized to refuse treatments on the patient's behalf, and it is beginning to be viewed as a flexible documentation of patients' preferences. Virtually all states now have some form of advance directive statute that provides residents with a "pre-approved" model form. This legislation is discussed in some detail in chapter 4. Before state living will laws were common, however, a variety of model advance directives were drafted and promulgated by health law scholars, patient advocacy groups, and other organizations. The styles, contents, and philosophies of these models greatly influenced state lawmakers in the 1970s and 1980s. In turn, patients' experiences in using statutory advance directives provided useful information to be reflected in both new and revised model documents.

Although the use of model advance directive forms has decreased considerably now that state legislation is so common, much can be learned from examining some model forms. Five models of advance directives demonstrate both a core understanding of what advance directives are and some of the bewildering array of points and variations that have given rise to confusion about the legal, practical, and moral significance of different forms. The first directive is model legislation drafted by a law school project; the second directive is distributed by Choice in Dying;[4] the third was developed by physicians in response to problems they saw in existing models; the fourth is from the new Uniform Health-Care Decisions Act; and the fifth was recently developed by the American Association of Retired Persons, the American Bar Association, and the American Medical Association.

In addition to these models, persons interested in promoting the effective use of advance directives may consult many other sources of exemplary documents, such as Cantor's excellent "annotated living will" (1990) and the model legislation drafted by the Concern for Dying Legal Advisors Committee (1983). These and other models are discussed further in chapter 4.

## DECLARATION
(President's Commission, 1983, p. 314)

Declaration made this _____ day of _____ (month, year). I, _____ being of sound mind, willfully and voluntarily make known my desire that my dying shall not be artificially prolonged under the circumstances set forth below, do hereby declare:

If at any time I should have an incurable injury, disease, or illness certified to be a terminal condition by two physicians who have personally examined me, one of whom shall be my attending physician, and the physicians have determined that my death will occur whether or not life-sustaining procedures are utilized and where the application of life-sustaining procedures would serve only to artificially prolong the dying process, I direct that such procedures be withheld or withdrawn, and that I be permitted to die naturally with only the administration of medication or the performance of any medical procedure deemed necessary to provide me with comfort care.

In the absence of my ability to give directions regarding the use of such life-sustaining procedures, it is my intention that this declaration shall be honored by my family and physician(s) as the final expression of my legal right to refuse medical or surgical treatment and accept the consequences from such refusal.

I understand the full import of this declaration and I am emotionally and mentally competent to make this declaration.

Signed _____

City, County and State of Residence _____

The declarant has been personally known to me and I believe him or her to be of sound mind.

Witness _____

Witness _____

This living will was drafted as part of model legislation, the Medical Treatment Decision Act, in a Yale Law School Legislative Services Project in the early 1980s. Both its style (short, general, and legal-sounding) and its very narrow application (to terminal illness where death will occur *whether or not* life-sustaining treatment is employed) are typical of model directives appearing in state statutes in the 1980s. As part of model legislation, this directive is not meant to be self-explanatory; its key terms are defined outside the document itself. And as was common at that time, there is no provision for appointment of a substitute decision-maker.

$$* \quad * \quad *$$

## Choice in Dying
## Living Will

**Instructions**

————

**Print Your Name**

I, _____
being of sound mind, make this statement as a directive to be followed if I become permanently unable to participate in decisions regarding my medical care. These instructions reflect my firm and settled commitment to decline medical treatment under the circumstances indicated below.

I direct my attending physician to withhold or withdraw treatment if I should be in an **incurable or irreversible mental or physical condition with no reasonable expectation of recovery.**

These instructions apply if I am a) **in a terminal condition**; b) **permanently unconscious**; or c) **if I am minimally conscious but have irreversible brain damage and will never again regain the ability to make decisions and express my wishes.**

I direct that treatment be limited to measures to keep me comfortable and to relieve pain, including any pain that might occur by withholding or withdrawing treatment.

While I understand that I am not legally required to be specific about future treatments, **if I am in the condition(s) described above I feel especially strongly about the following forms of treatment:**

**Cross out any statements that do not reflect your wishes**

I do not want cardiac resuscitation (CPR).

I do not want mechanical respiration.

I do not want tube feeding.

I do not want antibiotics.

However, **I do want** maximum pain relief, even if it may hasten my death.

**Add personal instructions (if any)**

Other directions (insert personal instructions):

These directions express my legal right to refuse treatment, under federal and state law. I intend my instructions to be carried out, unless I have rescinded them in a new writing or by clearly indicating that I have changed my mind.

**Sign and date the document and print your address**

Signed: _____ Date: _____

Address: _____

_____

I declare that the person who signed this document is personally known to me and appears to be of sound mind and acting of his or her own free will. He or she signed (or asked another to sign for him or her) this

**Witnessing Procedure**

document in my presence.

**Two Witnesses**   Witness: _____
**Must Sign and**   Address: _____
**Print Their**
**Addresses**       _____


Witness: _____

Address: _____

_____

| |
|---|
| 1994 Choice in Dying, Inc.          1/94 |
| 200 Varick Street, New York, NY 10014    1-800-989-WILL |

Choice in Dying is a national not-for-profit organization advocating patients' rights to make their own decisions about medical treatment and to receive compassionate and dignified care at the end of life. Choice in Dying distributes advance directives that conform to each state's specific legal requirements and maintains a national Living Will Registry for completed documents. Choice in Dying's living will is the latest in a long line of model directives drafted by it and its two parent organizations, Concern for Dying and Society for the Right to Die. It attempts to combine readability and generality with persuasive formalities and room for specificity, and it is meant to stand on its own. Choice in Dying distributes this document, however, only to residents of New York, Massachusetts, and Michigan, the states that have no living will statutes, advising everyone who can to use state statutory directives in order to reduce confusion and maximize the likelihood that all directives will be honored by health care providers.

＊　＊　＊

Next, the Medical Directive is a comprehensive document also meant to stand alone. Developed by Drs. Linda and Ezekiel Emanuel of Harvard Medical School (Emanuel and Emanuel, 1989, 1990), the Directive is complex and has undergone several major revisions, but it usefully focuses decisions upon desired and unwanted life and health outcomes. Its explanatory statement, which opens the document, is simple and straightforward: "This Medical Directive shall stand as a guide to my wishes regarding medical treatments in the event that illness should make me unable to communicate them directly. I make this Directive, being 18 years or more of age, of sound mind, and appreciating the consequences of my decisions."

The centerpiece of the Medical Directive is a matrix of boxes that allow Directive writers to check clearly whether they want, do not want, want a trial of, or are undecided about a list of nine commonly discussed treatments: cardiopulmonary resuscitation, major surgery, mechanical breathing, dialysis, blood transfusions or blood products, artificial nutrition and hydration, simple diagnostic tests, antibiotics, and pain medications, "even if they dull consciousness and indirectly shorten my life." They make these choices in the context of six "situations," each of which is described in terms of its health outcomes "in the opinion of my physician and two consultants." The six situations are as follows:

*SITUATION A:* If I am in a coma or a persistent vegetative state, and have no known hope of regaining awareness and higher mental functions no matter what is done.

*SITUATION B:* If I am near death and in a coma and have a small but uncertain chance of regaining higher mental functions, a somewhat greater chance of surviving with permanent mental and physical disability, and a much greater chance of not recovering at all.

*SITUATION C:* If I have brain damage or some brain disease that cannot be reversed and that makes me unable to recognize people, to speak meaningfully to them, or to live independently, *and I also have a terminal illness.*

*SITUATION D:* If I have brain damage or some brain disease that cannot be reversed and that makes me unable to recognize people, to speak meaningfully to them, or to live independently, *but I have no terminal illness.*

*SITUATION E:* This situation offers writers the opportunity to describe a situation "that is important to you and/or your doctor believes you should consider in view of your current medical situation."

*SITUATION F:* If I am in my current state of health (a brief description is solicited here) and then have an illness that is life threatening but reversible, and I am temporarily unable to make decisions.

Each situation statement concludes: "then my goals and specific wishes—if medically reasonable—for this and any additional illness would be:
- prolong life; treat everything
- attempt to cure, but reevaluate often
- limit to less invasive and less burdensome interventions
- provide comfort care only
- other (*please specify*) _____

This general list of preferences can be checked off in addition to or instead of the box matrix with its list of specific treatments. The next page of the Directive provides space for a personal statement, with the following directions, also focused on outcomes: "Please mention anything that would be important for your physician and your proxy to know. In particular, try to answer the following questions: 1) What medical conditions, if any would make living so unpleasant that you would want life-sustaining treatment *withheld*? (Intractable pain? Irreversible mental damage? Inability to share love? Dependence on others? Another condition you would regard as intolerable?) 2) Under what medical circumstances would you want to *stop* interventions that might have already been started?"

After the space for the personal statement, the writer is invited to determine which component of the Directive should be given greater weight in case there are differences: the choices checked off in the box matrix, the checkoff list of general goals, or the personal statement. The writer may also indicate a preference for the site of terminal care: home/hospice, nursing home, hospital, or other. There is an organ donation form, and the Medical Directive concludes with a health care proxy appointment.

The proxy's authority becomes effective when the writer's attending physician determines in writing that the writer lacks the capacity to make or communicate health care decisions. The proxy appointment form directs the proxy to make decisions "based on his/her assessment of my personal wishes" or, if these are unknown, "based on his/her best guess as to my wishes." There is a space within which to indicate any desired limitations on the proxy's authority, a statement allowing the writer to indicate whether the proxy or the written statements in the Directive shall have binding authority in case there is disagreement, and the opportunity to choose which proxy shall have final authority if more than one has been appointed and they disagree. The Directive closes with signature lines for the writer and two witnesses, and an optional statement for the writer's physician to sign indicating that the physician has seen the document, discussed the writer's end-of-life preferences, and understands the "duty to interpret and implement the preferences contained" therein.

✳   ✳   ✳

The Medical Directive is interesting because it focuses on choosing or refusing specific treatments and on both current conditions and possible outcomes, including different capabilities and different chances of recovery. The authors view as particularly significant its equal emphasis on requests "if medically reasonable" and refusals (Emanuel and Emanuel 1990). Equally significant is the inclusion of the trial-of-treatment choice: "I want treatment tried. If no clear improvement, stop." Making this option explicit can greatly advance understanding between patients and physicians.

The Medical Directive attempts to bring together issues of concern for both caregivers and patients. It was drafted as a response to the conceptual and practical failings of model and statutory directives like the first one reproduced above. Its obvious advantages may be offset by its complexity, but the Model Directive is a document very much worth considering.[5]

Next, the elaborate optional form in the Uniform Health-Care Decisions Act attempts to address all the problems raised by the current bewildering variety of state laws:

## ADVANCE HEALTH-CARE DIRECTIVE
### Explanation

You have the right to give instructions about your own health care. You also have the right to name someone else to make health-care decisions for you. This form lets you do either or both of these things. It also lets you express your wishes regarding donation of organs and the designation of your primary physician. If you use this form, you may complete or modify all or any part of it. You are free to use a different form.

Part 1 of this form is a power of attorney for health care. Part 1 lets you name another individual as agent to make health-care decisions for you if you become incapable of making your own decisions or if you want someone else to make those decisions for you now even though you are still capable. You may also name an alternate agent to act for you if your first choice is not willing, able, or reasonably available to make decisions for you. Unless related to you, your agent may not be an owner, operator, or employee of [a residential long-term health-care institution] at which you are receiving care.

Unless the form you sign limits the authority of your agent, your agent may make all health-care decisions for you. This form has a place for you to limit the authority of your agent. You need not limit the authority of your agent if you wish to rely on your agent for all health-care decisions that may have to be made. If you choose not to limit the authority of your agent, your agent will have the right to:

(a) consent or refuse consent to any care, treatment, service, or procedure to maintain, diagnose, or otherwise affect a physical or mental condition;

(b) select or discharge health-care providers and institutions;

(c) approve or disapprove diagnostic tests, surgical procedures, programs of medication, and orders not to resuscitate; and

(d) direct the provision, withholding, or withdrawal of artificial nutrition and hydration and all other forms of health care.

Part 2 of this form lets you give specific instructions about any aspect of your health care. Choices are provided for you to express your wishes regarding the provision, withholding, or withdrawal of treatment to keep you alive, including the provision of artificial nutrition and hydration, as well as the provision of pain relief. Space is also provided for you to add to the choices you have made or for you to write out any additional wishes.

Part 3 of this form lets you express an intention to donate your bodily organs and tissues following your death.

Part 4 of this form lets you designate a physician to have primary responsibility for your health care.

After completing this form, sign and date the form at the end. It is recommended but not required that you request two other individuals to sign as witnesses. Give a copy of the signed and completed form to your physician, to any other health-care providers you may have, to any health-care institution at which you are receiving care, and to any health-care agents you have named. You should talk to the person you have named as agent to make sure that he or she understands your wishes and is willing to take the responsibility.

You have the right to revoke this advance health-care directive or replace this form at any time.

## PART 1
## POWER OF ATTORNEY FOR HEALTH CARE

(1) DESIGNATION OF AGENT: I designate the following individual as my agent to make health-care decisions for me:

_____

(name of individual you choose as agent)

_____

(address)          (city)          (state)          (zip code)

_____

(home phone)                    (work phone)

OPTIONAL: If I revoke my agent's authority or if my agent is not willing, able, or reasonably available to make a health-care decision for me, I designate as my first alternate agent:

_____

(name of individual you choose as first alternate agent)

_____

(address)          (city)          (state)          (zip code)

_____

(home phone)                    (work phone)

OPTIONAL: If I revoke the authority of my agent and first alternate agent or if neither is willing, able, or reasonably available to make a health-care decision for me, I designate as my second alternate agent:

_____

(name of individual you choose as second alternate agent)

_____

(address)          (city)          (state)          (zip code)

_____

(home phone)                    (work phone)

(2) AGENT'S AUTHORITY: My agent is authorized to make all health-care decisions for me, including decisions to provide, withhold, or withdraw artificial nutrition and hydration and all other forms of health care to keep me alive, except as I state here:

_____

_____

_____

(Add additional sheets if needed.)

(3) WHEN AGENT'S AUTHORITY BECOMES EFFECTIVE: My agent's authority becomes effective when my primary physician determines that I am unable to make my own health-care decisions unless I mark the following box. If I mark this box [ ], my agent's authority to make health-care decisions for me takes effect immediately.

(4) AGENT'S OBLIGATION: My agent shall make health-care decisions for me in accordance with this power of attorney for health care, any instructions I give in Part 2 of this form, and my other wishes to the extent known to my agent. To the extent my wishes are unknown, my agent shall make health-care decisions for me in accordance with what my agent determines to be in my best interest. In determining my best interest, my agent shall consider my personal values to the extent known to my agent.

(5) NOMINATION OF GUARDIAN: If a guardian of my person needs to be appointed for me by a court, I nominate the agent designated in this form. If that agent is not willing, able or reasonably available to act as guardian, I nominate the alternate agents whom I have named, in the order designated.

## PART 2
## INSTRUCTIONS FOR HEALTH CARE

If you are satisfied to allow your agent to determine what is best for you in making end-of-life decisions, you need not fill out this part of the form. If you do fill out this part of the form, you may strike any wording you do not want.

(6) END-OF-LIFE DECISIONS: I direct that my health-care providers and others involved in my care provide, withhold, or withdraw treatment in accordance with the choice I have marked below:

[ ] (a) Choice Not To Prolong Life

I do not want my life to be prolonged if (i) I have an incurable and irreversible condition that will result in my death within a relatively short time, (ii) I become unconscious and, to a reasonable degree of medical certainty, I will not regain consciousness, or (iii) the likely risks and burdens of treatment would outweigh the expected benefits, OR

[ ] (b) Choice To Prolong Life

I want my life to be prolonged as long as possible within the limits of generally accepted health-care standards.

(7) ARTIFICIAL NUTRITION AND HYDRATION: Artificial nutrition and hydration must be provided, withheld, or withdrawn in accordance with the choice I have made in paragraph (6) unless I mark the following box. If I mark this box [ ], artificial nutrition and hydration must be provided regardless of my condition and regardless of the choice I have made in paragraph (6).

(8) RELIEF FROM PAIN: Except as I state in the following space, I direct that treatment for alleviation of pain or discomfort be provided at all times, even if it hastens my death:

_____

_____

(9) OTHER WISHES: (If you do not agree with any of the optional choices above and wish to write your own, or if you wish to add to the instructions you have given above, you may do so here.) I direct that:

_____

_____

(Add additional sheets if needed.)


**PART 3**
**DONATION OF ORGANS AT DEATH**
(OPTIONAL)

(10) Upon my death (mark applicable box)

[ ] (a) I give any needed organs, tissues, or parts, OR

[ ] (b) I give the following organs, tissues, or parts only

(c) My gift is for the following purposes (strike any of the following you do not want)

    (i)  Transplant
  (ii)  Therapy
 (iii)  Research
 (iv)  Education

## PART 4
## PRIMARY PHYSICIAN
(OPTIONAL)

(11) I designate the following physician as my primary physician:

_____
(name of physician)

_____
(address)        (city)        (state)      (zip code)

_____
(phone)

OPTIONAL: If the physician I have designated above is not willing, able, or reasonably available to act as my primary physician, I designate the following physician:

_____
(name of physician)

_____
(address)        (city)        (state)      (zip code)

_____
(phone)

(12) EFFECT OF COPY: A copy of this form has the same effect as the original.

(13) SIGNATURES: Sign and date the form here:

_____    _____
(date)                    (sign your name)

_____    _____
(address)               (print your name)

_____
(city)        (state)

(Optional) SIGNATURES OF WITNESSES:

| First witness | Second witness |
|---|---|
| _____ | _____ |
| (print name) | (print name) |
| _____ | _____ |
| (address) | (address) |
| _____ | _____ |
| (city)          (state) | (city)          (state) |
| _____ | _____ |
| (signature of witness) | (signature of witness) |
| _____ | _____ |
| (date) | (date) |

This directive clearly announces itself to be optional, and despite its length, it is only a small part of a very extensive uniform law, drafted in 1993 to replace the revised Uniform Rights of the Terminally Ill Act.[6] In accordance with the current trend, this directive's centerpiece is not a living will expressing treatment choices but a proxy designation naming a substituted decision-maker. And even a brief perusal of this directive's provisions reveals in its proposed solutions a catalogue of the interpretive problems posed by advance directives in the late 1980s and early 1990s.

Finally, a new comprehensive model document called the Health Care Advance Directive has been developed by the AARP, ABA, and AMA. It is distributed in a booklet entitled _Shape Your Health Care Future with Health Care Advance Directives_, which includes commentary and directions for completing the form, information about resources to consult with questions, and advice about how to use the model document to satisfy state law.[7] It also includes a wallet card alerting health care providers to the existence of a directive.

This new model directive attempts to address many of the same problems as the Uniform Act's "Advance Health-Care Directive." It is, however, a little less elaborate and a little more accessible. Moreover, the advice provided along with the form is very clear and very sound.

The first section of the booklet explains the reasons to have an advance directive, the reasons to appoint a health care agent, and when it might be preferable to do one without the other. It asks directive writers to think about their health care choices in terms of the goals of treatment, lists some questions to consider to aid in doing that, and discusses the need for specificity, health care providers' obligations to honor directives, and what happens to patients who do not have directives. It addresses who should be involved in helping to create directives, and explains the directive's important evidentiary role.

The second section of the booklet contains the model directive, with commentary explaining how to complete each section. It opens with the following caution: "This Health Care Advance Directive is a general form provided for your convenience. While it meets the legal requirements of most states, it may or may not fit the requirements of your particular state. Many states have special forms or special procedures for creating Health Care Advance Directives. Even if your state's law does not clearly recognize this document, it may still provide an effective statement of your wishes if you cannot speak for yourself."

Part I of the directive is the appointment of a health care agent. It names an agent "to make health and personal care decisions for me as authorized in this document." Space is provided for the naming of two alternate agents. The agency appointment is effective upon, and only during, a period in which the writer cannot make or communicate health care decisions. Incapacity is to be determined by the agent, the attending physician, and any other necessary experts. The statement of the agent's powers is a page long, and very broad and detailed, including consent and refusal to "any and all types of health care," access to records, admission and discharge, contracting for care, hiring and firing of support personnel, broad authorization for pain relief, anatomical gifts, and any other actions necessary to do what is authorized (including signing waivers and pursuing legal actions). There are no limitations related to particular interventions or physical conditions or diagnoses, but a place is provided (in Part II, but referenced here) for the writer to include special instructions, including any limitations or modifications of the agent's powers.

Part II is the instruction directive. The writer can initial one of several statements, including:

- a directive that states "My agent knows my values and wishes, so I do not wish to include any specific instructions here;"

- a "directive to withhold or withdraw treatment," containing a philosophical statement explaining that the writer does not want life prolonged if the result will be (1) permanent unconsciousness, (2) some consciousness with irreversible loss of ability to think or communicate, or (3) some ability to think and communicate but where the risks and burdens of treatment outweigh the expected benefits (the benefit-burden calculation is to include length and quality of life, dignity, privacy, and finances);

- a "directive to receive treatment" that states "I want my life to be prolonged as long as possible, no matter what my quality of life;" and

- a "directive about end-of-life treatment in my own words."

The directive also includes a liability limitation for those relying on the directive in good faith; an organ donation statement; a nomination of the named agent as guardian should that be necessary; a revocation of prior directives; a statement that the directive "is intended to be valid in any jurisdiction in which it is presented;" and a statement that copies have the same effect as the original. Finally, there is a signature statement ("By signing here I indicate that I understand the contents of this document and the effect of this grant of powers to my agent"), a witness statement with space for the signatures, names, addresses, and phone numbers of two witnesses, and a notarization statement. Both the witness statement and the commentary to it explain what witnesses are for and who is usually statutorily excluded from witnessing advance directives.

The Health Care Advance Directive is somewhat similar to the directive provided in the Uniform Act. It is a bit less detailed and complete, in part because it is not included in a statutory scheme but stands alone, and therefore does not address some issues of interpretation and application that can readily be addressed in legislation. Perhaps also because it is not legislative in nature, this directive uses clearer and more accessible language than the Uniform Act's Advance Health-Care Directive. Like that directive, however, it prioritizes the appointment of a health care agent over the instruction directive.

This directive is also similar to the Medical Directive in its attempt at comprehensiveness. Its directions to writers admirably serve to promote thoughtfulness, but the directive itself fails to provide the same range of choices. Most notably, it does not consider the trial of treatment option. Nor does it limit its request option by any reference to appropriateness or reasonableness according to medical standards. A source of potential confusion is its direction, in the instructions section (Part II; see the list of statements enumerated above), to initial *only* one statement. Some of the statements in that list are indeed mutually exclusive, but not all of them are. A writer could easily initial all three options within the "directive to withhold or withdraw treatment," and many people will want to do so. In addition, a writer might also want to supply a directive "in my own words," to give more information and reinforcement for the directive, or to list more choices, or both.

A signal advantage of the Health Care Advance Directive is its clear directions to writers and users about how it should be viewed and honored, and how it may be reconciled with state law. Also significant is its breadth. This directive has the broadest potential applicability and fewest stated limitations of all the model directives—a design in keeping with its intended flexibility and emphasis on deliberate and thoughtful choices by its users. An additional advantage of this directive is its endorsement by three large, prestigious, and influential organizations with interests in health care decision-making. This directive stands a chance of being well-disseminated and well-recognized. Happily, it is also well worth the recognition.

✳   ✳   ✳

These five directives are intended to be formal documents, supplementing their formality of tone with witness statements and even notary seals, after the fashion of a last will and testament. Four specifically assert the writer's soundness of mind at the time of writing, in the same way a last will and testament does. All of the directives state, with varying directness, that they expect physicians, family, and others to honor them; all assert that they are based upon rights: legal, moral, or both. In addition, one points out that directives serve as guides to physicians and should be discussed with them; another encourages discussion with the patient's named agent. Three explicitly claim to be based upon the patient's understanding, careful consideration, or settled values.

Significantly, only one of these directives—the oldest—limits its applicability to terminal illness; the others apply whenever the patient is unlikely to recover from extreme disability, which could include nonterminal conditions such as coma, persistent vegetative state, or even severe dementia from Alzheimer's disease. The first two directives are designed to facilitate the refusal of treatment; the last three also permit patients to request treatments or to choose to prolong life. Artificial nutrition and hydration is treated specifically and separately from other treatments in only two.

Finally, three of these directives feature a proxy designation. Linked as they are to the patient's expressed wishes, which can be made quite specific in these directives, these proxy designations require the proxy to make decisions based on those wishes, rather than solely on what the proxy thinks is best for the patient, unless the patient's wishes and values are unknown.

These five model advance directives—quite different in some ways, quite similar in others—reflect many of the issues that have appeared, disappeared, and persisted over the brief but complex history of advance directives and their use. The concerns they address will be touched on throughout this book. Some of these concerns are essentially conceptual, others are fundamentally practical, and many stem from ambivalence about whether advance directives are properly to be viewed as legal documents or as moral guides for difficult choices.

## ADVANCE DIRECTIVES IN CONTEXT

Advance directives, as substitutes for patients' own contemporaneous decisions, could potentially authorize *any* decisions that decisionally incapable patients might make if they still had decision-making capacity. Thus, advance directives could go well beyond their popular association with drastically diminished existence and dying, to apply to any treatment choice about which a patient feels strongly enough. For example, as more permanently unconscious patients survive longer, advance directives are more often employed in the absence of terminal illness. Advance directives can specify decisions or categories of decisions to be made, or name values and preferences that should influence decision-making on the patient's behalf, or appoint a substitute decision-maker, or all of the above. Advance directives are meant to perpetuate patients' preferences and values whenever patients cannot speak for themselves. They presume that individuals have the right, while capable of making choices, to decide about their own futures. Finally, directives may either refuse or request treatment, or specific treatments, or temporary trials of treatments; the same power of personal decision underlies both types of directive. As requests to "do everything" become increasingly common and increasingly controversial, however, the moral and legal status of "request directives" is being closely scrutinized.[8]

The potentially broad reach of advance directives, combined with the softness and generality of the language employed, as in our four models, to convey the patient's sense of self and value and reasons for refusing treatments, may result in a paradox. The more clearly and poignantly detailed are the patient's values, the harder it may be for the patient's caregivers to apply those values to the particular decisions faced. Thus, advance directives work best when addressed to common and commonly understood disabilities and treatments at the end of life, and proxy directives appointing contemporaneous, decision-makers—which shift the responsibility of applying a directive away from caregivers—have gained much favor in recent years. These two solutions, however—sticking to certain kinds of easy cases and requiring the appointment of a proxy decision-maker—do not answer the paradox, however. Nor do they address the wishes of patients in different circumstances or patients who do not have available to them a suitable candidate for proxy decision-maker. Therefore, the task of making sense of advance directives belongs to the caregiver—both by default and by the nature of the caregiver's role. Because the legal, moral, and practical meaning of each directive is different, it is the clinician's task to attempt to understand what the patient expects from the directive. Yet the patient's wishes are not the only factor. Because every person and institution affected by a directive has expectations, needs, interests, and duties with regard to the directive, all of these concerns must also be placed in perspective.

Making sense of advance directives for the clinician is not the same as determining when nontreatment should be considered or recommended. It is not the same as understanding hospital policy on do not resuscitate orders or trying to decide what to do for nursing home patients or patients in the intensive care unit. These are questions of overwhelming importance that must be addressed; but they are also questions that may become less necessary, in many instances, if discussion of advance directives is initiated and taken seriously with decisionally capable adult patients, including those apparently not at risk of decisional incapacity or serious illness. Much literature is available on terminating treatment for incompetent dying patients, including extensive guidelines for clinicians and institutions (President's Commission 1983; Wanzer et al. 1984, 1989; Hastings Center 1987; Angell 1994). Law and policy alike address the question of appropriate care for persons whose wishes are unknown. Here we should principally be concerned with patients who seek to make their wishes known through some form of directive, and with the clinicians who seek to assist them and who are charged with honoring their wishes.

Every institution should have a treatment termination policy in place and, as part of that policy, should make provision for honoring advance directives. All clinicians should have some familiarity with the applicable law in their states: case law and statutes on advance directives and termination of treatment. It is vital, however, for clinicians in all jurisdictions to recognize that implementing an advance directive that does not perfectly mirror institutional policy or state law is not wrong, nor is it unduly risky, either legally or morally. Advance directives, besides responding to patients' most important rights and interests in making their own decisions, provide clinicians with the best available means of avoiding the postponement of crucial choices. They assist caregivers both by substituting for and by supplementing patients' decisions when their decisional capacity is uncertain. When we wait until the patient is in intensive care, or until somebody brings up the question of a do not resuscitate order, or until the patient is incapable and the family in disagreement, time is short, and clear evidence of the patient's wishes is often unavailable. The results of such postponement are often disastrous—physically, psychologically, and financially—for the patient, the family, all of the caregivers, and the institution. Lawsuits start here, not when foresight is encouraged and reflection facilitated by timely discussion of the patient's choices.

Clinicians should prepare to understand and use advance directives by taking the following general steps:

1. Identify the most pressing questions addressed by the model directives given in this chapter and by the statutory directive provided by the law of your state.

2. Determine the kind of information necessary to answer these questions so that you are prepared to obtain this information from patients, if possible, from their named proxies, or from their families and friends.

3. Be ready to suggest to patients that they consider the difficult choices they may face, and be ready to discuss directives and difficult choices fully and frankly with them or with their proxies, friends, and family.

4. Acknowledge that when patients have tried, in a directive, to make known wishes about the future direction of their lives and deaths, you must try in good faith to understand and implement those wishes.

Similarly, persons wishing to write their own directives should talk with their clinicians about their wishes in order to identify and address the kinds of questions that health care providers may have about interpreting and implementing directives. Whatever the form or content of an advance directive, it will work best when its potential problems are anticipated so that others who read it are assured that its writer was thoughtful and serious in considering its implications.

Family, friends, policy, and the values of others have a place and a meaning when there is a directive, though the place is lesser and the meaning is diminished, because the patient's wishes are known. Advance directives depend for their validity first on the value of the individual, which entails recognition of individuals' rights to shape their own goals, values, and lives. But they further depend for their enforcement upon the values of community—mutual trust and respect for the choices of others. Advance directives are, unavoidably, social documents. To understand and use them well is to make explicit the assumptions and obligations entailed in acknowledging ourselves members of a society that recognizes advance directives as valid expressions of these important values. Such an understanding will enable clinicians to assist their patients by discussing, preparing, and implementing advance directives.

# 2

# Treatment Refusal and the Patient's Choice: Foundations in History, Law, and Ethics

This chapter addresses the first of the three central issues for advance directives: the nature and extent of the patient's right of choice. What kinds of health care decisions should patients be permitted to make? The chapter provides a general foundation in the moral and legal basis for informed consent and refusal of treatment, a brief look at the impact of technology upon how patients' choices are regarded, and an examination of what it means to say that a patient has—or lacks—the capacity to make his or her own health care decisions, especially decisions that will or may result in death.

## REFUSING TREATMENT AND DYING WELL

Even though advance directives embody such a broad range of possible forms, most advance directives are written to refuse treatment in the case of terminal illness or permanent unconsciousness. Their popular identification with the refusal of treatment has associated advance directives with newly emerging concerns for the acceptance and compassionate management of dying.

For as long as we humans have concerned ourselves with the good life and how to lead it, we have also hoped for a good death. Dying well may in the past have meant dying in battle, or after a long life of service to family, or with one's soul free of blemish. It might entail purification through suffering, or time enough to settle accounts, or just a swift and painless end. Whatever the good death may be, we have wished for it, prayed for it, reasoned about it, and sung about it throughout history. In this respect, a good death is an integral component of a good life.

Before the healing arts developed to a degree genuinely able to affect the course of illness, disease and death were simply things to be borne. Living and dying well meant accepting disease and facing death in ways that accorded with cultural and religious views of nobility and virtue. Essentially, these views instructed us to shoulder whatever was our lot, because there was no choice.

Things are different now, in some ways; in others, not different at all. Medicine now has more power, both to heal and to harm. Choices abound—choices of ends (e.g., restoration vs. enhancement of performance or of appearance) as well as choices of means (e.g., surgery, drugs, diet, exercise, radical therapies, conservative therapies). And choosers and advisers often disagree—even among themselves— about a choice to be made and its basis. It is this availability of choice that unmasks the fundamental possibility of disagreement between patients and caregivers about health care treatment.

Disagreement about the management of illness can be an unwelcome surprise. We are often not prepared to expect disagreement in medicine, either among healers, who are after all people of science, or between healers and their patients, who presumably wish nothing but to be healed. Even if we realize that medicine not only is an imperfect science but also contains value choices, we may be surprised at the range of values held by patients and the number of courses of action they might therefore select. Each offer of health care entails, at the very least, acceptance or refusal of that offer; often there are further choices, and a process of negotiation unfolds between healer and patient.

Refusing an offer of treatment is a particularly sensitive situation. By approaching a physician, a patient enters into a setting and a relationship designed for healing, in which refusal may scarcely seem credible. Many times patients, instead of stating their decision to refuse, simply remove themselves from the relationship entirely. At other times, anticipating the need to negotiate extensively or to refuse, they may never seek treatment at all, or they may put off seeking treatment until they feel they have no choices.

Some refusals of treatment carry a double burden. These are the refusals that form part of the process of "dying well." These refusals of treatment are the least amenable to the bureaucracies of healing that exist in modern society, because they decline services that may offer at least some benefit. They are also the least amenable to management by means of withdrawal from relationship with those bureaucracies, because they concern patients who cannot refuse treatment without the cooperation of their caregivers.

## TECHNOLOGY AND TREATMENT REFUSAL

Lewis Thomas (1975, 35–42) has divided medical technology into three categories: nontechnologies, halfway technologies, and decisive technologies. Nontechnology, or supportive care, has always been a mainstay of healers. Provision of supportive care was the aim of almshouses and early hospitals, and it underlay the founding of the nursing profession. Supportive care is comparatively painless, nonintrusive, and inexpensive. Nobody seems to have made much of an issue out of refusal of supportive care, and current institutional policies for the withholding or withdrawal of other levels of treatment from patients generally provide that such "comfort care" will always be given. This is not to say that refusals of supportive care are invalid or likely to be viewed as invalid; they are simply uncommon.[1]

Decisive, or effective, technology is a phenomenon both recent and rare. Thomas cites immunizations and antibiotics as prime examples. The essential characteristic of decisive technology is a genuine understanding of the mechanisms of disease; Thomas claims that with such an understanding this technology is relatively inexpensive and easy to deliver. Refusal of effective technology is not rare. It is often based on religious or idiosyncratic reasons (*Application of President and Directors of Georgetown College* 1964).

"Halfway technology"—a term now well entrenched in the vocabulary of medicine—is a label most often applied to innovative procedures, techniques, and treatments that have entered the medical armamentarium only recently. Prime examples, for Thomas, of halfway technologies are organ transplants, artificial organs, and most of the treatment of heart disease and cancer. Renal dialysis, treatment of AIDS and diabetes, and psychotropic medication for mental illness are other examples. The essential characteristic shared by these technologies is lack of understanding of the underlying disease mechanisms sufficient to prevent or cure the disease itself.

This characteristic ineffectiveness is shared by nontechnology, or supportive care, as well. What makes halfway technologies different is that, in addition, they are generally expensive and intrusive and are very often risky, unpleasant, or harmful in themselves. Sometimes it is said—as has been said of dialysis and organ transplantation—that a halfway technology merely replaces one chronic disease with another.

Although the term has had an almost exclusively modern application, "halfway technology" is an appellation that is surprisingly apropos for most early medical treatment that was not mere supportive care. Amputations, many tuberculosis treatments, bleeding, purging, medications containing heavy metals and other extremely dangerous ingredients, hysterectomies as treatment for nervous conditions—all these treatments, commonly employed at different times up through the nineteenth century, fit the definition of halfway technology extremely well. By recognizing that halfway technologies have been employed for most of the history of medicine, we can identify and understand the refusal of treatment throughout most of the history of medicine as well.

It has been said that not until the twentieth century did patients have a better than even chance of benefiting from an encounter with a physician (Stevens 1971, 135). If treatment is likely to be ineffective, costly, risky, and painful, refusal of treatment should not be surprising; and certain treatments historically enjoyed a very high rate of refusal. Amputations and other major surgical procedures were often refused, both because of the pain in the era before anesthesia and because of the high risk of fatal infection in the era before asepsis and antisepsis. Resistance to the assault on body image represented by amputation, as well as fear of being rendered handicapped and unemployable at a time when limb prostheses were very primitive, also figured into many refusals of amputation (Pernick 1982).

In the nineteenth century, when medical cultism was at its height in the United States, popular rejection of harsh and harmful treatments was evidenced by the many medical movements that challenged the theories of prevailing allopathic medicine. The best example of such movements is homeopathy, whose gentle, almost infinitely diluted herbal remedies certainly must have seemed a pleasant alternative to the bleeding, purging, mercury-containing compounds, and other drastic measures favored by allopaths of the day. Popular accusations of deception by physicians in connection with surgery and drug dispensation also support concern about refusal of surgery and of some other treatments (Pernick 1982).

Further evidence of treatment refusal for reasons of pain, risk, and expense comes from an unusual and much earlier source: religious writings from Europe, dating from as early as the sixteenth century, in which theologians explain the nature of the individual's duty to preserve his or her own life in the case of illness. These writings agree that especially where cure is not entirely certain, patients need not undertake surgical, drug, or dietary treatment if so doing would cause excessive and overbearing pain, disgust, or even financial hardship. Cardinal De Lugo, an influential seventeenth-century Catholic theologian, seems to capture aptly the problem of halfway technology by supposing a situation in which a person is condemned to death by fire. While surrounded by the flames, he notices that he has sufficient water to extinguish some of the fire but not all of it. Must he use this water? De Lugo says no, and gives his reason:

> "[I]f a man condemned to fire, while he is surrounded by the flames, were to have at hand water with which he could extinguish the fire and prolong his life, while at the same time other wood is being carried forward and burned, he would not be held to the obligation to conserve his life for such a brief time because the obligation of conserving life by ordinary means is not an obligation of using means for such a brief conservation—which is morally considered nothing at all" (De Lugo 1868).

This reasoning would seem to apply generally to decisions refusing treatment that is likely to be ineffective or that merely prolongs dying in the case of terminal illness. Theologians of this era, however, also held that patients could be permitted to refuse certain treatment even where cure is possible, stating that "no one can be forced to bear the tremendous pain in the amputation of a member or in an incision into the body: because no one is held to preserve his life with such torture" (Soto 1582).

Theological discussions of the individual's duty to preserve life even included consideration of the propriety of forgoing changes in diet and place of habitation. These discussions are especially interesting because the most healthful foods and climates recognized at the time were also the most costly, without being risky or unpleasant. Religious authority held that it was not sinful to choose not to spend one's entire income on a drug, a diet, or a move to a new place, despite the fact that one's life would be shortened as a result. Similarly, health policy-makers in the twentieth century have recognized that patients are often forced for financial reasons to choose between food and medication, supporting their families and consulting a specialist, caring for their own health and caring for the health of their spouse or children (Stevens 1971, 135–37).

It seems abundantly clear, therefore, that in the days before medicine was so effective, refusals of harsh, costly, dangerous, or ineffective treatment were far from unknown. By the end of the nineteenth century in the United States, however, the circumstances that had created the climate of skepticism and vigilance that supported such refusals had changed. Medicine was being transformed, in the popular view, into a noble science; physicians were being trusted as scholarly professionals rather than scrutinized as tradesmen and quacks; hospitals were growing in number and becoming oriented toward acute care, technologically sophisticated, and safer (Starr 1982; Stevens 1971, 145).

On the one hand, these developments seemed to undo many of the early reasons for refusal of treatment. Surgery was less painful and less risky; better chances of cure were available for many ailments. On the other hand, technology greatly increased the expense of treatment, and the shift to the hospital eliminated many lower-cost, low-technology alternatives, like midwifery and home birth (Stevens 1971, 179), leaving many other reasons for treatment refusal intact. At the same time, the growth of institutional medicine, with its employment of new technologies, its greater numbers of providers and support staff, and its large facilities, made treatment refusal more difficult to initiate and to sustain.[2]

The full flowering of the high-technology acute-care hospital did not come until the 1950s and 1960s. It was in the 1950s that the first intensive-care units were established, premature nurseries began to use intensive care, open heart surgery was begun, and mechanical ventilation was first used extensively for polio patients and others. In the 1960s kidney dialysis and kidney transplants became generally available, cardiopulmonary resuscitation became a hospital routine, coronary care options grew by leaps and bounds to include coronary artery bypass surgery, heart transplants, and cardiac care units, and radiotherapy and chemotherapy for cancer were introduced (U.S. Congress, Office of Technology Assessment 1987, 40).

By no coincidence, it was precisely during this period of burgeoning technical capability that the legal doctrine of informed consent was given its name and became notorious—most notably in the 1957 *Salgo* case (*Salgo v. Leland Stanford* 1957) and the 1960 *Natanson* case (*Natanson v. Kline* 1960), which dealt with complications arising from new technology: in *Salgo* a new diagnostic procedure, lumbar aortography, and in *Natanson* cobalt therapy as an adjunct to mastectomy for breast cancer.

The legal doctrine of informed consent does not merely require that doctors provide information to patients. Patients in informed consent cases make the claim that although they agreed to the physician's treatment, "if I had the right information, I would have refused treatment." Thus, beginning in the 1950s, law and society implicitly approved of treatment refusals through the developing doctrine of informed consent, even though patients in informed consent cases have not refused treatment.

At the same time, the unique circumstances of high-technology catastrophic medicine made it unlikely that the informed consent doctrine could be successfully applied to many patients' circumstances. Many of the traditional exceptions to the informed consent doctrine (*Canterbury v. Spence* 1972, Meisel 1979) were present in cases where patients might have sought to refuse treatment. The patient was often considered incapable of making decisions because of unconsciousness, dementing conditions, depression, or stress. In addition, many situations calling for high-technology intervention developed as emergencies: By the time consent was needed, there was no time to obtain it. Resuscitation efforts, artificial ventilatory support, and the like were usually instituted on an emergency basis. Thus, the issue of informed consent was often sidestepped when life-prolonging treatment was at stake.

This brief history shows us two things. First, it is apparent that treatment refusal is a familiar occurrence historically. Patients have always refused treatments, sought forms of treatment of their own choosing, and generally acted independently of the advice of recognized caregivers of all eras; for it is the patient who ultimately controls health care choices about his or her body. Second, in all eras philosophers, theologians, and jurists have attempted to probe for moral guidance about treatment refusals.

Such guidance is most likely to be found by placing the issue of the patient's treatment decisions within a larger context of discussion: the principles that properly underlie morally and legally justifiable decision-making in health care. In the remainder of this chapter, we will examine the development of informed consent and the philosophical foundations of the patient's choice.

## THE NATURE AND HISTORY OF INFORMED CONSENT

Informed consent is the name for a doctrine of twentieth-century American common law that upholds a patient's moral and legal right to make choices about recommended medical therapies (Faden and

Beauchamp with King 1986). As a byword of the patients' rights movement, informed consent is a primary means of ensuring every patient's autonomy in health care decision-making. A brief examination of the doctrine is useful for understanding the scope of patients' power to control their treatment.

First, it should be recognized that truth telling in medicine, though a necessary prerequisite to informed consent, is not the same issue as informed consent. The question of what patients should or should not be told about their health has historically been viewed as distinguishable from questions about patients' decisions whether to seek treatment and whether to accept or reject their physicians' recommendations about treatment (Faden and Beauchamp with King 1986). Before the nineteenth century, truth telling generally was viewed by physicians as counterproductive, largely because, in what was often a highly competitive atmosphere, patients were accustomed to doctor shopping according to whether they liked what they heard. Because therapeutic alternatives were few, diagnosis and prognosis were all-important, and accuracy warred with optimism as the approach most likely to help patients.

The lack of effective therapy similarly severed any potential connection between information and choices. Truth telling might be seen as beneficent because it enabled the dying patient to put his affairs in order and compose himself to face death well, or as harmful because it destroyed hope and thus might hasten the patient's decline (Pernick 1982); but it was not considered relevant to the patient's choice among therapies, for usually there was no such choice.

Nonetheless, the choice between therapy and no therapy has always existed, even when no other choices did. The Hippocratic physician was enjoined to refuse to treat those who were "overmastered" by their diseases (Hippocrates 1977), thus indicating early recognition by physicians that there was a time to stop. Moreover, to refrain from treating the hopelessly ill was a professional choice, designed to improve medical practice (Amundsen 1978). It was not until centuries later, when heroic measures like bleeding, purging, and amputation became commonplace, that significant attention began to be paid to patients' decisions, since many chose not to pursue these extreme but potentially "lifesaving" treatment alternatives (Pernick 1982). And it was not until the recent advent of scientific medicine that it became professionally acceptable to intervene in hopeless cases (Loewy 1987). Thus, there has always been one choice available—acceptance or refusal of whatever might be offered. Sometimes in the past there have been other alternatives as well. Until recently, however, the giving of information was not generally viewed as related to patients' choices.

What we now know as informed consent is essentially a twentieth-century idea (Appelbaum, Lidz, and Meisel 1987; Faden and Beauchamp with King 1986; Katz 1984; Pernick 1982). It developed along two separate paths, both of which had important histories and significant implications. One of the two paths of development of informed consent was the human-rights concerns that arose during the midtwentieth century, particularly in connection with abuses of human subjects during medical and scientific research (Faden and Beauchamp with King 1986). The 1947 Nuremberg trial of *United States v. Karl Brandt* (Katz 1972, 292–306) brought to light the work of the Nazi "experimenters" in World War II, and the Nuremberg Code, which emerged in 1948 from that trial, became the first widely known statement of research principles to require the informed and voluntary consent of all human subjects. The Nuremberg Code's first principle provides in part:

> The voluntary consent of the human subject is absolutely essential. . . . [T]he person involved . . . should be so situated as to be able to exercise free power of choice, without the intervention of any element of force, fraud, deceit, duress, over-reaching, or other ulterior form of constraint or coercion; and should have sufficient knowledge and comprehension of the elements of the subject matter involved as to enable him to make an understanding and enlightened decision. This . . . requires that . . . there should be made known to him the nature, duration, and purpose of the experiment; the method and means by which it is to be conducted; all inconveniences and hazards reasonably to be expected; and the effects upon his health or person which may possibly come from his participation in the experiment. (Katz 1972, 305)

In 1964 the World Medical Association's Declaration of Helsinki also required physicians engaged in nontherapeutic research to obtain the subject's "freely given informed consent" (World Medical Assembly 1964). These influential pronouncements began to focus attention on the rights of human subjects of research—that is, upon the nature of their humanity and the obligations of researchers to respect that humanity.

Deception in research received great attention in the mid-twentieth century, further reinforcing public and professional consciousness of what is owed by researchers to subjects. In the Tuskegee Syphilis Study, subjects were led to believe that they were receiving treatment, when in fact effective treatment was withheld (Faden and Beauchamp with King 1986, 165–67). In the Jewish Chronic Disease Hospital case, subjects were given injections of cancer cells without their consent (Faden and Beauchamp with King 1986, 161–62); the injections were considered by the investigators to be harmless, but the word "cancer" was not. And in Stanley Milgram's obedience experiments, subjects were allowed to believe they were seriously injuring another who was posing as a subject (Faden and Beauchamp with King 1986, 174–77).

All of these notorious cases helped set the stage for federal regulation of federally funded research. Regulations issued by the FDA and DHEW (now DHHS) imposed relatively stringent informed consent requirements that contained "laundry lists" of the material to be disclosed, including a statement that the study constitutes research, a description of the research itself, its risks, discomforts, possible benefits, and alternatives, confidentiality protection if any, injury compensation if any, names of persons to contact with questions, and the subject's right to refuse or withdraw from participation.[3]

In all of these concerns for informed consent in research, the connection between information and choice was clear: For a subject's consent to have meaning, he or she must know that the consent is for research rather than for therapy. The nature of the research and its potential risks must be known. This information is necessary for choice—the choice to participate or not.

The role of informed consent in therapy, however, is not necessarily the same as its role in research. Research and therapy are not the same. Indeed, in much of the notoriously deceptive research mentioned above, the deception lay in permitting research to be understood by the subjects as therapy. The promise of benefit is a strong inducement to consent to therapy, so that if research not expected to benefit the subject is presented as therapy, potential subjects might be more likely to consent. It is surprising to no one that this form of deception should be thought wrong. By the same token, it should not be surprising that it is still occasionally questioned whether informed consent is necessary or desirable in the ordinary, therapeutically oriented doctor-patient relationship,[4] where benefit to the patient is the physician's goal.

The second path of development for the informed consent doctrine focuses on the patient's role in the therapeutic relationship. Entering into the physician-patient relationship is a matter of mutual quasi-contractual consent for physician and patient, even when both seek the patient's benefit. There is a sort of presumption that the goals of physicians and patients tend in the same direction; after all, the relationship is a therapeutic alliance, and physicians generally treat only patients who have voluntarily sought their services. The patient's decision to seek treatment is usually not an issue discussed between them, and patient and physician begin their relationship with at least some expectation of agreement. It seems reasonable to assume that a patient who knowledgeably chooses a physician because of that physician's superior skill and knowledge should be prepared to trust the physician's judgment and embark upon the proffered treatment in reliance upon that judgment. Surely we generally expect people to consider favorably what is offered for their therapeutic benefit; that is exactly why patients go to doctors, and also exactly why we are concerned that research not masquerade as treatment.

Yet there are limits to the scope of any consent to become a physician's patient. Physicians are required, under the threat of malpractice, to treat patients according to the custom of the profession, delivering care that meets at least minimal standards of effectiveness and safety. Patients are understood to consent only to treatment that is according to custom. They may not consent to treatment so inferior as to be negligent or to unheard-of or outlandish procedures, even those claimed to be beneficial.[5] Whatever the precise limits of the physician-patient relationship may be, it is clearly wrong to assume that the patient, in entering into one, implicitly consents to everything offered by the physician for ever after (*Mohr v. Williams* 1905; *Pratt v. Davis* 1906).

Furthermore, it has always been acknowledged that patients may sever their relationships with physicians at will (*Carpenter v. Blake* 1871). A patient who knows what the physician proposes to do may avoid it by dismissing the physician entirely—an effective but unwieldy protection against unwanted treatment. The fact that the patient can terminate the physician-patient relationship at will, without "good reason" or even "against medical advice," illuminates the central moral tenet of that relationship: Its purpose is not simply the best interest of the patient but the patient's own determination of his or her best interest—even to the point where the patient refuses to accept continued care.

If, then, the physician conceals his or her treatment intentions from the patient in order to preclude the patient from severing the relationship, the physician is practicing deception. Such deception may be rectified by recognizing the patient's right to select a new physician when he or she wishes to refuse a proffered treatment or by acknowledging the patient's interest in making choices directly about the proffered treatments themselves. The dilemma remaining for physicians is how to maintain relationships with patients who make treatment choices that do not accord with their physicians' recommendations. This is a dilemma that is often at the heart of the clinician's ambivalence and confusion about advance directives.

Informed consent in the therapeutic relationship has its conceptual origins in the bare right to be left alone—a fundamental principle of the common law, or judge-made law, of England and the United States (*Satz v. Perlmutter* 1978). According to the law of battery, to make any intentional physical contact with someone without that person's consent is offensive, and the offended party may be entitled to collect civil damages in court (*Schloendorff v. Society of New York Hospitals* 1914).

The root premise of "bodily integrity," dignity, autonomy, independence, or self-direction upon which the offense of battery is based is treated simply as a given by law. If consent is obtained, then there is no battery. (As a matter of social policy, consent is implied in many circumstances, from social handshaking and kissing to emergency medical treatment for unconscious persons.) According to the law of battery, it is the patient who initiates the physician-patient relationship; the relationship can begin only when the patient consents to the physician's touch.

Battery also makes clear that because it is the *touch* that is consented to, the patient's consent to the relationship does not automatically encompass all treatments. Each recommendation must be examined on its own terms; that first consent cannot reasonably be construed as a consent to anything the physician recommends unless the patient understands it in precisely that way (*Mohr v. Williams* 1905; *Pratt v. Davis* 1906). Sometimes patients do so understand their consents: "I know you will do what is best for me, Doctor, so whatever you recommend is fine with me." When patients consent on these terms, the operative factor for them is the doctor's judgment of their best interest. Even under these circumstances, they understand their consent as being for a particular purpose, their best medical interest, even though that purpose may encompass a very broad range of recommended procedures.

All consents are therefore born of some understanding of what is consented to. Patients may consent to particular "touchings" by their physicians, or they may consent to any touchings necessary to accomplish a particular purpose, their well-being. The law of battery holds that a consent given without any such understanding of what is consented to is not valid. A touching that follows upon a consent obtained by deception or by withholding of crucial information is still a battery. Early cases where patients consented to a particular treatment and received a different one, or more than they asked for, thus paralleled cases in the 1950s where patients claimed they were given an incomplete understanding of their treatments.

The importance of the patient's self-determination in informed consent (*Canterbury v. Spence* 1972) is a reminder that in the physician-patient relationship, the purpose of the touching is the crucial determinant of what makes a consent informed. Patients consent to medical treatment not for the sake of the touching itself or as part of the rules of the encounter, as we consent to being touched while dancing or playing basketball, but for its benefits. Informed consent is an issue because benefits are offered and because a choice is available.

Self-determination is also a reminder that it is the *patient's* view of benefits that matters. It is the patient's autonomy, dignity, and independence that are protected by informed consent, and it is the patient's own judgment and understanding of the situation that turn what would otherwise be a battery into a permitted intrusion. Informed consent gives to patients the right to receive information relevant to decisions about therapy, and to physicians the opportunity to educate and advise patients in order to bring the patient's and physician's views of benefit into closer alignment. Ultimately, though, the patient's decision controls.

Informed consent acknowledges patients' control of their own bodies and their control of caregivers' access to their bodies for treatment purposes. This control furthers patients' interests in making life choices, including medical choices, that serve their own views of their best interests. The information in informed consent comes from physicians, in the form of recommendation and advice. In addition, patients often decide with the help and consultation of family and friends. The patient's process of decision is a process of reasoning, just as other decisions in life—small and large, common and uncommon—reflect a reasoning process. The variety of decision-making processes engaged in by ordinary people is staggering. Still, patients and physicians alike lead ordinary lives that have at least some things in common—enough to engage in discussion of a decision and gain some degree of understanding of each other's views.

The first reported cases requiring the physician to obtain consent to medical treatment appeared around the turn of this century. These were cases based on battery. They simply required the physician to obtain consent before performing a procedure and to remain within the bounds of the consent given unless there was some emergency which made delaying for consent unsafe (*Mohr v. Williams* 1905; *Pratt v. Davis* 1906).

Later cases, still using the reasoning of battery, began to enumerate the information that patients need to have (and that therefore physicians are required to give them) in order to give a valid consent with some understanding of what they are consenting to. The issue of information disclosure is the focus of modern legal action based on informed consent, and there has come to be a legal laundry list for it: Physicians must disclose to patients the nature of the procedure, its expected consequences, the significant risks associated with it, the expected benefits, and the available alternatives to it—always including the alternative of no treatment at all. To know what you are consenting to, say the courts, you need to know what it is and what it is for, which includes what the chances are that it will work, what might go wrong, and what other choices there are (*Berkey v. Anderson* 1969; *Cooper v. Roberts* 1971; *Gray v. Grunnagle* 1966).

Once the cases began to be concerned with disclosure of so much information to patients, the legal theory of informed consent began to undergo a subtle shift away from its simple vision of the patient's right of choice. This happened for a very simple reason: The disclosure physicians were required to make had to be measured largely according to medical standards. Even though the patient's judgment of benefit ultimately guided the treatment decision, only the medical profession could say what the proffered procedure entailed, what risks and benefits were likely to arise from it, and what alternatives were medically feasible.

The modern laundry list of disclosure was to be given to patients regardless of whether the medical profession thought that was a good idea, but the standards of the medical profession had to be applied to determine the precise content of this required disclosure. Many courts soon decided to treat informed consent as a form of professional negligence—as medical malpractice, an injury of carelessness in disclosure rather than an intentional contact without valid consent. This shift was probably a matter of judicial convenience, but it served misleadingly to overemphasize the physician's judgment about the patient's benefit (Comment 1967; McCoid 1957; *Natanson v. Kline* 1960; Note 1970; Plant 1968; Waltz and Scheuneman 1970).

Despite this shift in emphasis, informed consent has preserved its focus on the patient's autonomy in a number of ways. Most significant is its recognition of the patient's right to refuse treatment regardless of whether nontreatment is a medically acceptable option. The physician's obligation to disclose alternative treatments need not include a complete discussion of treatment refusal, but any patient's refusal will always trigger an obligation to disclose the risks and consequences of refusal (*Truman v. Thomas* 1980). The doctrine of informed consent thus acknowledges that nontreatment is always an option the patient may consider—that the patient's judgment of his or her own best interests might be best served by nontreatment even though such a choice runs counter to good medical judgment.[6]

In this way, informed consent raises the possibility that the patient may make a choice that runs counter to the physician's medical judgment. Informed consent raises the question of the physician's freedom (or obligation) to respond to the patient's choice—but it alone cannot answer it. The question whether physicians may be required to support patients in the making of decisions against medical advice goes beyond informed consent and into the related but still distinct issue of the patient's right to refuse treatment.

## CONTEMPORANEOUS CHOICE: AUTONOMY VERSUS BENEFICENCE

Many health professionals who think about health care decision-making tend to view informed consent as no more than a means of arriving at more accurate determinations of the patient's best interests (Pernick 1982). The basis for informed consent, the patient's interest in autonomy or self-determination, is by this reasoning protected and honored because patients know themselves better than doctors do. These caregivers consider the patient's autonomy interest only as a means to the right decision, and when they are reluctant to honor patients' choices, they may explain their reluctance as a disagreement about whose judgment is better—theirs or their patient's.

This weak view of autonomy is in reality a version of the this-is-for-your-own-good reasoning characteristic of the principle of beneficence. Though willing to allow patients to make many disapproved choices, some courts and caregivers wrongly believe that the patient's right of autonomy has substantive limits—that patients do not have the right to make choices that will result, or are highly likely to result, in death. They reason that death cannot, by definition, be in anyone's best interest.

Although many moral and religious traditions hold that continued existence is in the individual's best interests, the assertion that the principle of beneficence outweighs the principle of autonomy whenever the patient's autonomous choice would result in death cannot be sustained. The duty to preserve one's life always has limits.

A patient who makes a choice to refuse treatment, even if it will result in death, may have many reasons for doing so. All of these reasons in some sense reflect that patient's own view of his or her best interests, but some of them may stray far afield from what health care providers are accustomed to consider in their determination of what is best for the patient. Patients may wish to avoid pain or disfigurement or loss of dignity, or to spare spouse and family from emotional pain or financial hardship; or patients may make particular choices just because health is not the same issue for them as it is for their doctors.

The patient's decision-making autonomy is important not because patients may be best at determining what is best for them but because they are the only ones who can say who they are and what matters to them (Dworkin 1986). The uneasiness that some caregivers feel in the face of patients' decisions to refuse treatment provides a basis for discussion with the patient and perhaps even for moral persuasion; by itself, however, this uneasiness does not provide a basis for interference with autonomous choice (Annas and Glantz 1986; Buchanan and Brock 1986; Faden and Beauchamp with King 1986).

The principle of autonomy is a powerful one—so powerful that modern philosophers are properly alert to the risk that an autonomy-based theory of health care decision-making could become atomistic and compassionless (Veatch and Callahan 1984). Yet this risk is greatly minimized with a proper and responsible recognition of the true meaning of autonomy for patients, including the proper and responsible exercise of that autonomy (Childress 1990).

Beauchamp and Childress describe the core idea of personal autonomy as the extension of political self-rule by governments to self-governance by individuals. Autonomous persons rule themselves while remaining "free from both controlling interferences by others and from personal limitations that prevent meaningful choice, such as inadequate understanding." They explain that autonomous persons are able to act in accordance with informed and freely chosen plans, whereas persons of diminished autonomy are, in at least some respects, controlled by others or incapable of deliberating or acting on the basis of their plans (Beauchamp and Childress 1994, 121).

Two figures in the history of philosophy, Immanuel Kant and John Stuart Mill, have shaped our understanding of autonomy as, respectively, freedom of the will and freedom of action. For Kant, autonomy is governing oneself, including making one's own choices, in accord with moral principles that are one's own but that can be willed to be universally valid for everyone. In Kant's view, respect for autonomy is a part of perceiving persons as "ends in themselves," able to determine their own destiny, rather than treating them merely as means to the ends of others. Moral relationships, for Kant, are essentially characterized by mutual respect for autonomy.

Mill's concern was about autonomy of action. In his *On Liberty*, Mill argues that social and political control over individual actions is legitimate only if necessary to prevent harm to other individuals affected by those actions. All citizens should be free to develop their potential according to their own convictions, as long as they do not interfere with a like expression of freedom by others (Beauchamp and Childress 1994, 125).

Respect for autonomy is a societal obligation imposed on each of us to recognize the autonomy of others and to respect their judgments even when we believe them mistaken. Beauchamp and Childress state this as a principle: *"Autonomous actions should not be subjected to controlling constraints by others."* (Beauchamp and Childress 1994, 126).

No reasonable argument can be made to support the position that either the autonomy of the patient or the authority of health care providers or of society is absolute, that is, capable of outweighing *all* other principles, rights, interests, and reasons in all cases. As Beauchamp and Childress point out, the moral principle of respect for autonomy, like all others, has only prima facie standing. There are some circumstances in which "others can justifiably restrict our exercises of autonomy. The justification must, however, rest on some competing and overriding moral principles" such as beneficence or justice (Beauchamp and Childress 1994, 126).

Legitimate moral authorities provide reasons to explain and justify their commands; legitimate exercises of autonomy are similarly reflective and therefore explainable. The expectation of communication about moral choices is critical: Moral beliefs arise from shared experiences and perceptions, and moral conflicts between autonomous patients and beneficent medical authorities properly take place within a community able to share traditions and examine commonly held values. As Beauchamp and Childress observe, in medical contexts the principle of respect for autonomy establishes "the positive obligation of respectful treatment in disclosing information and fostering autonomous decisionmaking" (Beauchamp and Childress 1994, 126). For advance directives, questions must be asked about what sort of communication about patients' decisions is necessary, and what is sufficient, for those decisions to be recognized and honored as autonomous.

## Arguments against Refusal

It cannot be said that there are no grounds at all for questioning a patient's autonomous decision. In law, autonomous choices may be curtailed for significant public policy reasons or to prevent harm to others. Moral reasoning about whether treatment may or may not be refused is closely related to legal reasoning in this area, though some of the argument structure is dissimilar. Legal reasoning provides a relatively clear and handy model for moral reasoning about treatment choice, and it will be so used here.

We have already discussed the law's battery-based concept of autonomy or self-determination in the context of informed consent. This legal concept is a matter of common (judge-made) law; it has evolved from court decisions in the various states over the years and rests upon basic principles inherited from early Anglo-Saxon legal traditions. In the law of treatment refusal, the right of autonomy also has an additional basis: the federal Constitution. Many courts have looked to the constitutional right of privacy as the source of legal protection for the patient's autonomy (e.g., *Gray v. Romeo* 1988). The U.S. Supreme Court, however, has chosen instead to identify patients' autonomy with a Fourteenth Amendment liberty interest (*Cruzan v. Director* 1990).

The right of privacy has a controversial constitutional history and origin (Tribe 1988, 1302–12, 1362–71). Beginning in the 1960s, privacy was viewed as an expansive right of personal decision and control, carrying implications of dignity and intellectual sophistication not yet shared by the common-law self-determination basis of informed consent. Informed consent cases, as a rule, arise after the claimed injury has occurred; the only remedy is money damages. Constitutional privacy instead paved the way for preventing injury by controlling actions prospectively. Currently the two rights are viewed as fundamentally similar in nature, though not in origin (Faden and Beauchamp with King 1986, 39–42). The U.S. Supreme Court's reliance, in the *Cruzan* case, on "liberty" rather than "privacy" appears to focus the constitutional analysis more on the physical intrusion of unwanted treatments than on a broader freedom from state interference with decisions. Nonetheless, there is at least no doubt that both Constitution and common law support the right of treatment refusal.

## Nancy Cruzan and the Supreme Court

Nancy Cruzan, like Karen Quinlan, was a healthy young person who had written no advance directive before the accident that left her in a persistent vegetative state. Like Karen, Nancy had had conversations with friends about treatment refusal and was supported by a loving family determined to do what they judged she would want. Unlike the Quinlan family, however, the Cruzans had access to more than a decade's worth of new medical knowledge about PVS, and they focused on artificial nutrition and hydration as the unwanted treatment.

Nancy Cruzan had been in PVS for five years when the supreme court of her home state, Missouri, refused to recognize her family's authority to decline treatment on her behalf based on what she would have wanted. Only her own specific advance directive would satisfy that court's desire for "clear and convincing evidence" of the patient's wishes to overcome its strong presumption in favor of preserving life.

When the United States Supreme Court agreed to hear the case, its decision was eagerly awaited. Right-to-die advocates hoped for a definitive statement by the high court about the constitutional nature of the right to refuse treatment and for clarification of the status of artificial nutrition and hydration. Although very few state courts had taken positions like Missouri's, a growing number of state living will statutes contained very restrictive language. Some states, in their statutory living will forms, attempted to prohibit anyone from refusing artificial nutrition and hydration; some states also declared advance directives invalid during pregnancy, in order to preserve the life of the fetus. If artificial nutrition and hydration were a treatment and if the right to refuse treatment had constitutional status, state laws like these would be unconstitutional.

The U.S. Supreme Court's opinion in *Cruzan* can be said with equal accuracy to have pleased everyone and disappointed everyone. In a five-to-four decision, the Court upheld Missouri's right to require both a high standard of proof and a subjective standard (Meisel 1992), that is, direct evidence of the patients' expressed wishes rather than "substituted judgment." The Court did not distinguish between artificial nutrition and hydration and any other medical treatment, nor did it view PVS as distinguishable from terminal illness. The majority opinion rested on a liberty interest in refusing unwanted medical treatment, rather than on the right of privacy. But a majority of the court—the four dissenting justices and one in the majority, Justice Sandra Day O'Connor—explicitly acknowledged that the right to refuse treatment is fundamental. Thus, the *Cruzan* decision resolved no unsettled questions and changed virtually nothing about end-of-life jurisprudence (Annas et al. 1990). It presented some risks, sounded some warnings, and (as Justice O'Connor's concurring opinion emphasized) threw the impetus for change squarely back to the states (Gostin 1991; Areen 1991; Annas 1993, 85–97).

In the aftermath of the *Cruzan* decision, several important things happened. States did not leap to copy Missouri by setting high evidentiary standards. Instead, many state legislatures moved in the opposite direction, amending living will statutes to encompass PVS as a reason for refusing treatment and making it easier to refuse artificial nutrition and hydration. The states also followed Justice O'Connor's suggestion and passed a great many new health care proxy laws or added proxy designation clauses to their existing advance directive statutes. Thus, in the few years since *Cruzan*, state common-law doctrines and legislation have advanced a great deal in their vision of health care decision-making rights. Despite the *Cruzan* decision's disappointing and ambiguous aspects, however, it is important to preserve an understanding of the depth and breadth of treatment refusal according to common law and the Constitution by examining traditional constitutional analysis of the right.

One advantage of thinking in constitutional terms is that constitutional rights are ranked according to how powerful they are. The right of privacy is in the most powerful category: It is a *fundamental* right. Decades of discussion about the constitutional dimensions of self-determination in state and federal courts have reinforced society's understanding of the importance of the right to refuse treatment.

Once the right to refuse treatment is established, legal reasoning examines the nature and strength of the countervailing interests that may be present. The rights and interests on both sides are balanced in a sort of cost-benefit calculation in order to reach a conclusion about whose should prevail. In order to overcome the patient's right to refuse treatment, the countervailing interests asserted by the state on behalf of its citizens must be very powerful (Tribe 1988, 1362–73). The power of these state interests depends on the particular facts of each case, but the interests themselves are constants, and there are four of them that are regularly discussed in the cases (President's Commission 1983, 31–32; *Satz v. Perlmutter* 1980; *Superintendent of Belchertown State School v. Saikewicz* 1977). They are

- the preservation of life
- the prevention of suicide
- the protection of innocent third parties
- safeguarding the integrity of the medical profession

The *protection of innocent third parties* is in some ways the easiest of these four interests to analyze. The analysis should be a straightforward weighing of the harms anticipated from alternative courses of action. It is a staple of moral reasoning that if one person's actions harm others and if those others can be protected best by controlling that individual's actions, then control may be appropriate. A classic example of this reasoning is the state's exercise of its public health power to isolate or treat persons suffering from contagious diseases. Another example is the state's power of compulsory vaccination, which was justified by the U.S. Supreme Court in the early part of this century on the grounds that persons who refuse to be vaccinated present a risk to others who are not yet, or cannot be, vaccinated (*Jacobson v. Massachusetts* 1905). Modern legal analysis requires that

the risk to others be comparatively great and not reasonably avoidable except by curbing the actor's rights, and that these rights be curtailed to the minimum extent needed to effectively remove the risk to
others.

In refusal of treatment cases, the innocent third parties whose
interests are at issue are the born and unborn children of the refusing
patient (who in the cases is usually, but not always, female). An early
decision, once influential but now recognized as having been hastily
decided and poorly reasoned, was the Georgetown College case (Application of President and Directors of Georgetown College 1964), in which
the court ordered a blood transfusion for the mother of an infant
because of the infant's interest in the mother's continued support.
The mother was a Jehovah's Witness, who according to the beliefs of
that sect faced the possibility of eternal damnation from receiving
blood.

There are now many decisions upholding refusal of transfusions
by Jehovah's Witnesses (Fosmire v. Nicoleau 1990; In re Jamaica Hospital
1985; In re Melideo 1976; In re Osborne 1972). Such decisions reject the
reasoning of the Georgetown College case as it applies to already born
children. Though parents may have a moral duty to their children not
to risk their own lives unnecessarily, judgment about the acceptabil-
ity of the risk should be left to the parents, and the state should not
seek to interfere except in extreme circumstances.

Already born children can be supported emotionally and financially by others if a parent's treatment decision results in death.
Unborn children, however, are dependent upon their mothers and
usually cannot be safely separated from that dependence, even if
they are viable, without contravention of the mother's right to refuse
treatment. A highly controversial body of case law and commentary
has addressed the rights of pregnant women to refuse treatment
when the decision affects the fetus. There is no other situation in
which one individual can be required to perform a risky act for the
benefit of another, even when the other will die without it. For example, where a patient in need of a bone marrow transplant locates an
unwilling potential donor, the courts have declined to order the transplant, even when the potential donor is related to the patient and is
the patient's only hope (McFall v. Shimp 1978). Nonetheless, treatment
refusal in pregnancy is debated with considerable heat, though recent
well-publicized cases may be focusing attention on better legal reasoning and sensitive communication without resort to the courtroom

(Annas 1986, 1993; *In re A.C.* 1990; *In re Baby Boy Doe v. Mother Doe* 1994; Mathieu 1991; Rhoden 1987; Scott 1994).

End-of-life treatment refusals such as those addressed by advance directives do sometimes arise with pregnant women. The belief that some permanently unconscious or dying pregnant women might possibly be kept alive until their fetuses are viable and can be delivered has led some legislatures to hold that a dependent fetus's interests can override a mother's decision to refuse treatment. As of mid 1995, living will statutes in some thirty-four states purport to preclude the withholding or withdrawal of treatment during pregnancy, and health care proxy legislation in fourteen states purports to prevent health care agents from ordering treatment abatement for pregnant patients (Choice in Dying 1995). These restrictions are certainly unconstitutional (Note 1990), but the issues are startling and emotional enough that they will no doubt continue to be reexamined as new cases arise.

The other interests potentially running counter to the patient's right to refuse treatment do not directly weigh the patient's right against the interests of other identifiable individuals. Instead they raise broader societal concerns about the appropriateness of treatment refusals.

Two of these remaining interests, the *prevention of suicide* and the *preservation of life*, at first may seem to amount to the same thing, but they are distinguishable. Social, moral, and legal prohibitions against suicide historically stemmed, at least in part, from the principle of beneficence; that is, the individual's suicide is prevented for his or her own good. Suicide is no longer a crime in the United States. Disapproval of suicide persists, however, and concerns about the psychological well-being of would-be suicides are genuine. Therefore, many states retain laws making it a crime to assist a suicide. Prevention of suicide is a legitimate beneficent concern where the would-be suicide is too mentally disabled to make an autonomous choice for death; criminal penalties against such persons are considered pointless. Whether there can ever be "rational suicide" is a different issue. Still another issue is whether preventing suicide is a legitimate societal concern in refusal of treatment cases. The courts have uniformly held that it is not.

Courts addressing this question have often disposed of it simply by reasoning that refusal of treatment is not suicide. There are two ways to make this argument. First, the courts reason that the patient does not wish to die but, rather, does not wish to live under the conditions of treatment—and therefore accepts death, but only as the outcome of his or her refusal of burdensome treatment. Jehovah's Witnesses do not refuse blood in order to die but in order to avoid damnation. Patients who refuse to stay on their respirators do not want to die; they want to end the discomfort of enforced artificial ventilation and know that they may not survive without it.

Second, courts argue that the cause of death is not an act by the patient, the physician, or anyone else, but rather the underlying disease. This argument is easiest to make when the refusing patient is terminally ill and the issue is thus merely postponement of death; but it also is applied to cases in which life support is withdrawn and death results from an underlying chronic disease, as when, for example, a patient withdraws from dialysis.

Although in many cases of terminal illness and severe impairment these arguments about intent and cause may seem appropriate and therefore may help us to support most patients' refusal of treatment, it is easy to find more troubling cases, in which this reasoning is less persuasive. The cases of Dax Cowart and Elizabeth Bouvia are excellent examples.

At the age of twenty-six, Dax suffered extremely serious full-thickness burns over 67 percent of his body as a result of an accidental explosion. He was left blinded, badly deformed, and seriously impaired, but survived. His continual refusals of burn treatment were not honored.

The treatment of severe burns to promote healing and prevent infection is agonizingly and unavoidably painful and lasts for many months. The pain of graft surgery and rehabilitation is also severe and long lasting. Dax asserts that he refused treatment in order to avoid that pain, with the expectation that he would then die from infection. He preferred death to pain, and perhaps it could be said that he did not wish or intend to die, but the line is very hard to draw.[7] If he had left the hospital, as he wished, and developed an infection, he would have died of an eminently treatable condition.

Elizabeth Bouvia's case is even more destructive of the fine lines courts have tried to draw. She is a young woman afflicted with severe cerebral palsy since birth, which has resulted in almost total paralysis, severe limb deformities, and increasingly extensive and painful arthritis. She needs constant care and has had difficulty obtaining support from either friends or the state. In 1983 she entered a California state hospital facility with the announced intention of starving to death and receiving palliative care in the process. A court determined that the hospital could discharge her rather than comply (Annas 1984; *Bouvia v. County of Riverside* 1983). But in 1985, when she entered another hospital in order to obtain care and pain relief for her arthritis, she was no longer able, because of her increasing pain and disability, to swallow enough food to sustain her. The hospital then, over her refusal, inserted a nasogastric tube in order to ensure the sufficiency of her nutritional intake.

This time, when she sued for the tube's removal, the appellate court agreed with her that she could refuse the treatment (*Bouvia v. Superior Court* 1986). The court's majority pointed out that she did not intend to starve; she was simply incapable of eating enough, did not wish to undergo the discomfort of the nasogastric tube, and accepted that her capacity to swallow would gradually decrease and that she would ultimately weaken and die. It was her underlying muscular incapacity that would cause her death, not the act of will represented by a hunger strike. One justice, however, in a separate opinion concurring with the majority's conclusion, failed to see these distinctions as real differences from the first case involving Ms. Bouvia, in which she simply did not make her own argument for death carefully enough to assuage the conscience of the court. This justice was prepared to assert that suicide is a right of all individuals and that it stems from autonomy as clearly as does refusal of treatment.

On the basis of cases like Dax Cowart and Elizabeth Bouvia, it seems evasive to attempt to argue that it is still appropriate to prevent suicide (for the individual's own good) but that suicide is never, or almost never, involved in treatment refusal. A more plausible posture might be to assert a moral interest in discouraging suicide but not a legal power to prohibit it, thus maintaining respect for the autonomy of individuals while still addressing their wishes and needs.

The cases of Dax Cowart and Elizabeth Bouvia received enormous attention, and many accounts and discussions of them can be found in professional and popular literature. Our fascination with them, and with others like them, stems from our uneasiness about such cases; we search for a "true" description of their circumstances that will explain which decision is the "right" one. For example, a prominent scholar, Robert Burt, has examined Dax's case and concluded that his refusal of treatment was not really autonomous and not really a refusal—that it stemmed from unmet needs for support from his mother and caregivers, and from other unresolved issues (Burt 1979). Burt's sensitive and probing psychological analysis quite naturally strikes a chord with those concerned lest "autonomy" become a catchword for oversimplifying a profoundly complex human situation; yet it is also easy to grasp at psychological explanations as a means of distrusting patients' choices.

Similar speculations proliferated about Elizabeth Bouvia's "true" reasons for her decision to stop eating; moreover, she became a focus for advocacy groups for the handicapped, who argued that judicial support of her refusal to be artificially fed would send the public message that life is not worth living for handicapped persons and that, therefore, those who choose to live with handicaps deserve no public assistance in so doing (Kane 1985). This argument would have placed her symbolic value, as a means of fostering certain views, above her own autonomous choice—which brings us to an examination of whether society has an interest in the preservation of life that can curtail autonomous treatment refusal.

Preservation of life is the term used in court decisions to describe a societal interest in the sanctity of life. It is not an interest that is set up directly to challenge individual autonomy, like the prevention of suicide. Instead, the argument goes, we need to promote social values that help to ensure respect for others and the well-working of society as a whole. Preservation of life accomplishes these goals by preventing patients from making medical choices that ultimately would devalue others' lives in our eyes and weaken the social fabric overall. This asserted interest is the counterpart of a general moral proposition that discouraging treatment refusal is part of promoting the proper valuation of human lives. Individuals' choices are not contravened for their own good but because of the negative message that would be sent to society if their choices were honored: the "slippery slope" of progressive contempt for weak, imperfect, or disfavored humans (*Bouvia v. County of Riverside* 1983).

Here also the courts have argued, in many refusal cases, that although the state's interest in preservation of life is real, it does not apply to the facts at hand. The first widely known expression of this position came in the celebrated *Quinlan* case, where Karen Quinlan's parents sought to remove her respiratory support in the full expectation that she would die very soon thereafter: "We think that the State's interest *contra* weakens and the individual's right to privacy grows as the degree of bodily invasion increases and the prognosis dims" (*In re Quinlan* 1976, 355 A.2d 647, 654).

During the 1960s and 1970s, many of the celebrated treatment refusal cases were cases like Karen Quinlan's was thought to be; if the patient was not terminal, death was nonetheless not very far away. Perhaps the archetypal situation might be something like the Joseph Saikewicz case (*Superintendent of Belchertown State School v. Saikewicz* 1977). Mr. Saikewicz was a profoundly retarded institution-alized adult, sixty-seven years old and diagnosed as having acute leukemia, which in his age group has a very dim prognosis. With vigorous chemotherapy, there was a 30-40 percent chance that he might experience a 2- to 13-month period of remission; cure was not possible. If Mr. Saikewicz had not been retarded, his choice to refuse chemotherapy would almost certainly have been honored by a court using the *Quinlan* balancing test. The prognosis is dim—certain death, albeit a small chance of a short postponement—and the invasiveness of chemotherapy is devastating. The prospect of a remission period might be enough to encourage many patients to try chemotherapy, but a contrary decision is certainly understandable, and many rational arguments might be offered in its support.

But what would the court that permitted the withdrawal of Karen Quinlan's respirator have decided had it known then that she would breathe on her own for many years (finally dying in 1985 from pneumonia that her family decided should not be treated)? Is ten years of significantly demented existence the kind of dim prognosis originally envisioned by the court? And is artificial nutrition and hydration "invasive"?

The preservation-of-life interest is important but not specific. It does not belong to identifiable individuals but is really a societal posture that seeks to forestall certain choices but not others. Courts have not had much difficulty with decisions that "merely hasten death," as the decisions in the *Quinlan* and *Saikewicz* cases were viewed as doing. In cases like those of Dax Cowart and Elizabeth Bouvia, many courts and caregivers have more difficulty with upholding decisions that cannot be said to "merely hasten death" and thus appear to be based on disvaluing the patient's life. Yet there are some lives that are genuinely unbearable in the eyes of those living them, and often courts and caregivers can identify with patients' decisions to end them. The risk to society is that we all will come to prefer the choice of death to that of giving support and help to persons who choose to live with their discomfort and pain. The risk seems remote, however, when we are face-to-face with patients' own choices. As the concurring justice in the second *Bouvia* decision (*Bouvia v. Superior Court* 1986) pointed out, refusing to permit a patient to refuse treatment because of the message that choice would send to others is—no matter how honorable that concern—to force the patient to endure a continued existence that the patient believes unendurable. Understood in this way, the preservation-of-life interest, important though it may be as a cautionary influence, appears cruel.

In cases like Elizabeth Bouvia's, where the patient's autonomous choice is clearly expressed, many courts have articulately shown themselves willing to support termination of treatment. The case of Mr. William Bartling (*Bartling v. Superior Court* 1984) is an example.

Mr. Bartling was hospitalized for multiple severe and chronic problems, including depression and emphysema. Routine diagnostic procedures were complicated by his poor health, and he was placed on a mechanical ventilator when a poorly healing biopsy incision resulted in a collapsed lung. He found the pain, discomfort, and degradation of the respirator and its attendant restrictions unbearable; but none of his afflictions were terminal, and he was considered likely to live another year.

After a lower court refused to permit removal of the ventilator, the appellate court phrased the central question as "whether the right of Mr. Bartling, as a competent adult, to refuse unwanted medical treatment is outweighed by . . . the preservation of life." And its answer was straightforward: "[I]f the right of the patient to self-determination as to his own medical treatment is to have any meaning at all, it must be paramount."

In many cases, however, the patient is not terminally ill, continued treatment is somewhat painful or burdensome, and in addition the patient cannot make a contemporaneous choice and has not written an advance directive memorializing a strong autonomous statement refusing treatment under such circumstances. Such cases are therefore complicated by several additional factors: (1) questions about the reliability of any evidence of the patient's preferences, (2) the possibility that treatment termination decisions in these cases may reflect a devaluing of the lives of the helpless handicapped and demented rather than a genuine attempt to honor their wishes, and (3) uncertainties about the meaning and role of the patient's "best interests" when the patient appears to have no real experience of his or her circumstances.

Nonetheless, patients' choices have been upheld under these circumstances as well. The case of Paul Brophy (*Brophy v. New England Sinai Hospital* 1986) is a good example. Mr. Brophy, a fire fighter, suffered a ruptured aortic aneurysm. After brain surgery he lapsed into a persistent vegetative state, able to breathe on his own but with no higher brain functions and virtually no chance of recovering any consciousness. He required extensive personal care and had to be fed liquid nutrition through a gastrostomy tube directly into his stomach. Although he apparently was conscious and communicative at times between the onset of his illness and surgery, he never specifically gave directions expressing his treatment wishes during that time. But as the Supreme Judicial Court of Massachusetts stated:

> About ten years ago, discussing Karen Ann Quinlan, Brophy stated to his wife, "I don't ever want to be on a life-support system. No way do I want to live like that; that is not living." He had a favorite saying: "When your ticket is punched, it is punched." Approximately five to six years ago, he helped to rescue from a burning truck a man who received extensive burns and who died a few months later. He tossed the commendation he received for bravery in the trash and said, "I should have been five minutes later. It would have been all over for him." He also said to his brother regarding that incident, "If I'm ever like that, just shoot me, pull the plug." About one week prior to his illness, in discussing a local teenager who had been put on a life support system he said, "No way, don't ever let that happen to me, no way." Within twelve hours after being transported to Goddard Hospital following the rupture of the aneurysm, he stated to one of his daughters, "If I can't sit up to kiss one of my beautiful daughters, I may as well be six feet under." (*Brophy v. New England Sinai Hospital* 1986, 497 N.E. 2d 626, 632 n.22).

The court viewed these statements as sufficient to conclude that Brophy would refuse continued gastrostomy tube feeding, even though he could potentially live for many years. Other courts might disagree or require more specific declarations; these are matters of interpretation and fairness, to be discussed in a later chapter. For our present purposes, it is most significant that the court applied the *Quinlan* balancing formula here, weighing the interest in preserving life against the burden to the patient, even though Mr. Brophy was not likely to die soon and could not be said to be in pain or currently experiencing the burdens of his treatment:

[W]e must recognize that the State's interest in life encompasses a broader interest than mere corporeal existence. In certain, thankfully rare, circumstances the burden of maintaining the corporeal existence degrades the very humanity it was meant to serve. . . .

The duty of the State to preserve life must encompass a recognition of an individual's right to avoid circumstances in which the individual himself would feel that efforts to sustain life demean or degrade his humanity. . . . While . . . continued use of the G-tube is not a highly invasive or intrusive procedure and may not subject him to pain or suffering, he is left helpless and in a condition which Brophy has indicated he would consider to be degrading and without human dignity. . . . Additionally, in our view, the maintenance of Brophy ["bathing, shaving, mouth care, grooming, caring for his bowels and bladder, changing his bed linens and clothing, turning him in bed to prevent bed sores and providing him with food and hydration through the G-tube"], for a period of several years, is intrusive treatment as a matter of law. (*Brophy v. New England Sinai Hospital* 1986, 497 N.E. 2d 626, 636).

Thus, the societal interest in preservation of life is unable to override meaningful refusals of treatment. Indeed, the U.S. Supreme Court so recognized in the *Cruzan* decision (*Cruzan v. Director* 1990). Cases like *Cruzan* and *Brophy*, along with the stories of Dax Cowart and Elizabeth Bouvia, have begun to alter our collective reasoning about the burdens of treatment and the quality of existence, so that even as we seem to lose some of our ability to distinguish between treatment refusal and the desire to die (*Cruzan v. Director* 1990, Scalia, J., concurring; Tribe 1988, 1365–68), we may be reaching consensus about nontreatment in many common cases (Angell 1994; Meisel 1992).

There remains, however, the state's fourth interest to consider. Should caregivers like Mr. Brophy's physician, who believed that clamping Mr. Brophy's G-tube was professionally unethical, be able to prevent it for this reason? This fourth interest, *preserving the integ-*

*rity of the medical profession*, is often sidestepped. The issue is raised when physicians, other caregivers, and hospitals object to a patient's refusing treatment and continuing to receive other care from them or when withdrawal of support is authorized by the court and someone has to actually pull the plug. It is a distillation of the problem that physicians face with all patients who fail or refuse to follow advice. What do you do with the rest of the patient's care? How do you as a caregiver understand your role, your freedom to give the best possible care? Facing a patient's treatment refusal is harder than the dilemma of how to treat the patient who will not quit smoking, however, because not only the physician's effectiveness but also the patient's whole life and freedom are at stake.

The courts get around this, essentially, by questioning whether good medical practice is always consistent with the prolongation of life. The *Quinlan* court first raised this issue with a historical discussion demonstrating that "physicians have always distinguished between curing the ill and comforting the dying" (*In re Quinlan* 1976). In addition to citing the Hippocratic Oath's reference to avoiding futile treatments, the court in *Quinlan* examined Roman Catholic theology to find additional support for the distinction between "ordinary" and "extraordinary" efforts to preserve life. The court viewed it as a proper medical judgment to determine the point at which preservation of life was futile; therefore there could be no categorical determination that refusal of treatment contravened a professional commitment to the best care. It then remained to determine, in each instance, whether the care refused was under the circumstances "ordinary" or "extraordinary"—whether the refusal was something no physician could condone or something the profession in general could support.

This analysis is easy in some factual settings—namely, where the patient is clearly terminal and the proposed treatment invasive and plainly futile, or where the caregivers in question agree with the patient's decision and are simply seeking protection for their actions, or where transfer to a willing physician is possible. It is unsatisfactory in others, however, and in general the ordinary/extraordinary distinction, though still influencing our thinking, is now viewed as outdated and not generally useful (Tribe 1988, 1364–65). When physicians oppose the patient's choice and no other caregivers stand ready to support it, when transfer is not possible, or when the patient's choice does not merely hasten death but chooses death over disability, this view of the physician's interest does not necessarily protect the patient. According to this view, the medical profession as a whole could decide to continue the treatment of a patient who has nowhere else to go and no effective way to refuse. But why should medicine have the definitive say in these matters?

Perhaps there are medical values that identify preservation of life and health as a good and condemn futile care, which is predicted to accomplish neither. But suppose the care being considered is usually but not always futile. It cannot be solely *medicine's* place both to assess the risk of futility and to decide when it is too great or too small. The values of the patient must also be considered and may be in some cases decisive. These are not simply medical questions, no matter how entangled with medicine they may be.[8]

If the integrity of the medical profession is a legitimate interest, it surely should ensure that physicians who choose not to participate in the care of persons refusing treatment should not be compelled to participate. Other health care professionals and institutional providers should similarly be empowered to withdraw from caring for such patients. Nonetheless, there are limits to the physician's power to disengage from a patient's care. All caregivers and institutions are obligated never to abandon a patient in need. In this context, the prohibition against abandonment effectively means that the patient should not be forced to endure treatment because no caregivers are willing to support nontreatment. New Jersey courts have held that an institution that failed to give a patient timely notice of its policy against cessation of treatment cannot force the patient to leave the institution (*In re Jobes* 1987; *In re Requena* 1986); presumably, then, the institution must permit the patient access to caregivers (from other institutions) who are willing to withdraw treatment. So long as there are some caregivers who will support a patient's choice and some who will not, the question whether there is a genuine issue of professional integrity involved in these cases will be obscured, just as the *Quinlan* court obscured it.

The patient's right to make contemporaneous treatment decisions that are likely to result in death is thus stronger than the four interests commonly arrayed against it. A last ground exists, however, upon which to oppose the decisions of patients. It does not interpose a new countervailing interest but instead challenges the validity of the patient's decision directly, by challenging the patient's ability to make it.

## DECISIONAL CAPACITY; OR,
## THE "COMPETENCE CONUNDRUM"

"Competence" is the term generally employed in health care to describe a patient's ability to make autonomous decisions about his or her treatment. A competent patient is one whose treatment decisions are considered valid and to be honored by caregivers. "Incompetence" describes the condition of patients who cannot make decisions about their care or cannot make decisions that carry sufficient validity to be honored. About this much there is general agreement. In fact, however, incompetence is properly a term applied only to persons *legally* determined to be incapable of autonomous decisionmaking. It has therefore been suggested that the term be limited to this use and that "capacity for autonomous decisionmaking" be used instead of "competence" where a more general term is wanted (Hastings Center 1987, 131–32). "Decisional capacity" is rapidly gaining ground over the common but imprecise "competence."

There is little or no agreement about how decisional capacity and its absence are recognized and determined, what kinds of decisionmaking skills are necessary for decisional capacity, and what skill levels are sufficient. To delve fully into this large, rich, and freewheeling debate is beyond the scope of this volume, but some acquaintance with the problem is clearly necessary (Annas and Glantz 1986; Appelbaum, Lidz, and Meisel 1987; Buchanan and Brock 1986, 1989; Culver and Gert 1982; Dworkin 1986; Faden and Beauchamp with King 1986; Lo 1990; Morreim 1993; President's Commission 1983).

In common language, "competence" is a term with two possible meanings. According to one of these, competence is the ability to do anything adequately: "He is a competent accountant"; "She is an incompetent orthopedic surgeon"; "Jane is competent at golf"; "Bill is incompetent behind the wheel." Thus, "competence" standing alone is contentless, but when an answer is supplied to the question "Competent at what?" we know in a general way how to decide what skills are necessary for a particular competence—that is, competence at a particular activity—and what level of skill is required.

The second common meaning of "competence" is more specific. It refers to our common understanding of incompetence as a mental state resulting in the inability to look after one's own life: "We had to commit Cousin Herbert because he'd become completely incompetent"; "The family is contesting Grandfather's will on the ground of incompetence." Although only one particular activity is referred to by this usage, it is usually left unspecified. And because this meaning refers to a mental state, it is often conflated with the even more specific issue of decisional capacity. It is easy to forget that the capacity for medical decision-making is more than just a generalized psychological status and that it must be associated with particular decision-making activity. How that activity is defined and measured when a patient's medical decision-making capacity is at issue is crucial.

"Making health care decisions" is the most general statement of the relevant activity; for advance directives, "making *prospective* health care decisions" is a better description. Whether it is necessary to go further and distinguish between different decisions or at least different categories of decisions (e.g., life-and-death choices versus decisions with less serious consequences) is still debated, even though most agree that because competence is task-specific, decisional capacity should be measured in terms of the particular decision(s) faced by the patient. Patients with limited mental capacity, who might be viewed as "generally incompetent," may still be capable of making certain decisions—just as a "generally competent" person may be incapable of making some choices (*Matter of Conroy* 1985; Hastings Center 1987, 132).

Assessing decisional capacity in the health care setting is a problem principally because there is no common understanding of what's "normal" under the circumstances of health care decision-making. When decision-making capacity in other areas is assessed, the inquiry is a little bit easier: We have at least some idea what it means to be able to manage one's business affairs, provide food, clothing, and shelter for oneself and one's family, or dispose of one's property by will. When it comes to health care decisions, however, it may be difficult to assess the appropriateness of a decision-making process in such an unfamiliar setting. Once we recognize that having decisional capacity does not necessarily mean following the doctor's advice, we have to have some way to evaluate "normal" decision-making under conditions of stress, pain, discomfort, invasion of privacy, pressures of various kinds, depression, separation from family and routine, helplessness, reduction of dignity, poor communication, and the assimilation of new information very much outside the patient's previous experience.

With such a catalogue of adverse conditions, it is not surprising that there should be a widespread temptation to underestimate the decision-making capacity of the ill and the institutionalized. It is easy to overlook the fact that a similar catalogue might be made for other kinds of decisions: What if a person writing a will did so while very near death or after an emotional dispute with an expected beneficiary? What if the young mother who just bought a new station wagon was distracted by her misbehaving children, pressured by her isolation and by her husband's complaints about her inefficiency, manipulated by the salesman's charming sleight of hand, handicapped by her poor grasp of mathematics, budgeting, and automotive engineering?

Thinking clearly about the capacity to make health care decisions requires the recognition that health care decisions do not need to be "better" decisions than other kinds of decisions about other matters. They need to be only as good as the decisions we will accept that are of comparable magnitude. Buying a car; buying a house; investing in the stock market; choosing a college major, a career, a spouse; having children; engaging in a potentially dangerous sport or recreation—all of these major life decisions may be of magnitude comparable to that of many of the health care decisions about which people are most concerned, while many other health care decisions are nearly trivial by comparison. Recognizing that health care decisions in general are like other decisions causes us to realize that there is in fact little agreement about how to measure the capacity of ordinary decision-makers in day-to-day life. We know that as a general principle, decision-making capacity is presumed and decision-makers are given a lot of leeway; but beyond that, what? Are there reasons for making some decisions, like buying a car or getting married, that are so bad we shouldn't allow some decisions to be made?

In general, society does three kinds of things to regulate decision-making. We institute some type of regulation of the transaction (e.g., truth in advertising; marriage blood tests) to reduce—usually minimally—some of the harmfulness of bad decision-making; we use information, education, and persuasion to improve decision-making; and we rely on psychiatric determinations of mental incapacity if we believe that the decision in question demonstrates a deeper problem. We do not usually intervene in decisions that are not about health care simply because we believe that they are not sufficiently well reasoned, have failed to appreciate certain information, are not mature enough, or have been affected by any of the adverse circumstances recited earlier. Yet we are tempted to intervene in health care decisions for all these reasons.

Many people wish to argue that health care decision-making is different from all other decision-making because of its life-and-death character. Not all health care decisions are life-and-death matters, however, and when stress and illness are present, they affect all decisions, not just health care choices.

Decisions to refuse treatment and decisions at the end of life are (usually but not always) more important, with more serious and irrevocable consequences, than many (but not all) other life choices. It has been argued that they must therefore be required to be "better" decisions before they are honored by others. This argument ignores the fact that in the case of advance directives the most important decisions are also the decisions most important for the decision-makers— decisions that implicate deeply held wishes and values, decisions about which people feel most strongly. To require a higher decisional standard because of the importance of the decision runs the risk of disenfranchising people from the choices most important to them, unless the strength of the wishes, values, and convictions underlying these choices is taken into account in evaluating the choices.

Medical choices seem different because many of them entail risks and/or certainties of very bad outcomes. It must be acknowledged that many ordinary life choices also contain significant risks and also that though many people would describe themselves as risk-averse, many others are forced by circumstances to choose between the proverbial "devil and the deep blue sea." Though hard decisions may be unprecedented in the life of a given patient, and therefore more difficult to make well, the very difficulty of end-of-life choices between certain death and the risks and burdens of continued treatment suggests that the decisional standard for such choices ought perhaps to be lower than the standard chosen for other decisions, where the better choice is clearer. This would more readily permit patients to make their own choices when there is no obviously "good" option available. At least, standards of capacity based solely on rational decision-making should not necessarily be dispositive in the hardest cases.

The argument that medical decisions are different really amounts to a declaration that some choices should not be permitted, for the patient's own good. When the patient is able directly to contest others' views of his or her own good, it is hard to maintain this position except by claiming that the patient lacks decisional capacity; but where the only evidence of that lack of capacity lies in this disagreement with caregivers and others, no valid grounds exist to support the claim.

Certainly we would like to be able to ensure that medical care decisions, and all decisions, are mature, well reasoned, adequately justified, sufficiently informed, and sufficiently appreciative of all relevant issues. Yet agreement is lacking about what constitutes sufficient maturity, appreciation, and reasoning and how they should be measured. It seems only sensible to do inside the health care context what we do outside that context: Set a minimal standard that is enforced by regulation of the setting or the provider (e.g., informed consent law); use psychiatric evaluation to uncover disorders that preclude "normal" life decision-making; and attempt, by means of information, discussion, and persuasion, to encourage the best possible decision-making process.

Advance directives clearly present a special problem in this regard. Like wills, they are put into effect only when their writers do not have the capacity to write them, and are not even available to be examined, questioned, informed, or persuaded. The retrospective evaluation of decisional capacity at the time the document was written is very different from a contemporaneous analysis, because the evidence available for consideration is likely to be quite limited.

As a result, in the case of wills, property law has developed a very commonsensical (and frequently litigated) definition of testamentary capacity: Did the testator know "the natural objects of his bounty," and did he understand the consequences of the distribution he chose? The capacity of the testator is examined by establishing the formal validity of the will document itself, by examining its terms, by interviewing the witnesses to it about the testator's apparent capacity and understanding, and by means of other relevant evidence extrinsic to the document—evidence that is more often from friends and relatives than from psychiatrists. Most wills are also discussed with, and reviewed by, attorneys at some point before, during, or shortly after their making. This affords the attorney an opportunity to assess the testator's capacity according to the cited definition as well as to improve the testator's decision-making.

Advance directives can provide similar assurances of capacity. Most directives are witnessed and notarized to conform with state law; a properly validated directive provides evidence that the writer was capable of appreciating the necessary formalities, and of course the witnesses may be called upon to give their impressions of the writer's state of mind. The terms of many state statutory directives are sketchy and may not in themselves offer much proof of capacity; but the makers of directives very often enlarge on the statutory forms, adding detail and specificity, enumerating decisions, or even starting from scratch, writing a document meant to express personal philosophy. Such emendations, while recommended for other reasons, are also useful in supporting the presumption of capacity.

The capacity problem with advance directives persists because it is possible to make a perfectly good directive without consulting with anyone—family or friends, doctor or lawyer. You do not need a lawyer, and you may not have friends or family or even a doctor at the moment. Everyone is presumed to have capacity until *proven* otherwise; thus, the lack of evidence of any such discussion and consultation cannot itself give rise to a determination of incapacity (and therefore of the invalidity of the directive). Writers of directives can help to ensure that their capacity is clearly apparent by having such consultations—which also have the very valuable result that their directives may be improved in content and expression, better understood by family and physician, and thus more likely to be obeyed. For those who have no regular physician when the directive is written, the best alternative is to bring up the directive during later encounters with caregivers. This opportunity to reaffirm the directive before others accomplishes all of the goals that can be achieved by discussing it when first written. Of course, there will still be instances when a directive has not been discussed with anyone. The question of implementing such directives is the subject of later discussion.

When the patient cannot directly contest others' determinations, as is the case when an advance directive is brought into play, the future factor does present a problem. Does its prospective character imply that there is anything special about the capacity to write an advance directive? In this respect, advance directives are not like wills, even though wills are also prospective decisions, for in a will you can only give away property you have to people who exist—you do not need to imagine what it would be like to have more money or to have to divide your estate among different children. Because prospective health care decision-making seems to labor under special handicaps of anticipation and imagination, it might be thought that making good advance directives requires a supercapacity.

A "bad" decision does not necessarily indicate decisional incapacity. Nor is it necessarily the case that a decision later rejected by its maker was incompetently made. The possibility that a different choice could have been made should not invalidate a directive by itself. Besides, we don't really know what *is* a bad decision about future treatment. None of us, not even physicians, can imagine the future well enough to know with certainty each time anyone else is doing so poorly at such imagining as to be judged incapable of doing it. We may be able to recognize some bad choices, and when we do, we must try to correct them. That is not the same as declaring someone incapable of choosing because we believe the choice was wrong. We should certainly ensure that writers of advance directives know that the future is uncertain and contains unknowns. Much more than that seems impossible to ask. (The future factor will be considered at greater length in chapter 3.)

Decisional capacity is a conundrum because it must be both described and detected and because the description and means of detection we choose are chosen, at least in part, according to our moral judgments about individual freedom and responsibility, about right choices and what it is to be human. "Competence" is a value-laden label that only pretends to scientific objectivity and attempts to deny the reciprocal relationships between patients and physicians, tests and standards, individuals and societies.

Clinicians should examine the tools and information they and their colleagues use to determine the decisional capacities of patients whose mentation has been questioned. A vast array of evidence and test instruments is regularly used by clinicians to make such judgments, and the relevance and weight of these data must always be carefully considered.[9] We presume all adults to be capable of free and responsible choices. The correct question to ask is whether there is any reason to suspect that a particular person is not choosing freely and responsibly. Then, what are these reasons? Can we eliminate these obstacles to free and responsible decision-making? This is the sort of inquiry that seems to me most fruitful. Some of the reasons for not deciding freely and responsibly may correspond with what we would currently call "incapacity," and others may not. Some of them may be remediable, and others may not. Capacity is no special hurdle in health care decision-making. If physicians and others act on the presumption that all advance directives can be freely and responsibly made, advance directives will be better supported by caregivers and thus will become better documents, more thoughtful and more often honored.

# 3

# The Future Factor: The Conceptual Foundations of Advance Directives

[O]n occasions of momentous choice we are in the position of carrying forward a pattern of self that is, in the nature of things, necessarily understood only with imperfection. Occasions of such choice are occasions of judgment and discernment, not occasions of algorithmic calculation. (Churchill 1989, 177)

Chapter 2 argued that patients' own contemporaneous health care choices should be honored so long as the patients who make them have sufficient decision-making capacity, even when those choices are viewed by caregivers and others as not in the patient's best interests.[1] The patient's autonomy thus serves as the foundation for contemporaneous treatment choices. Advance directives are not contemporaneous decisions, however. Whether they take the form of instruction directives, which list decisions about various interventions and various circumstances, or proxy directives, which give to a named individual the power to make decisions for the patient, or a combination of the two, all advance directives announce decisions that are to be carried out in the future, at a time when the patient does not have the capacity to discuss or change them. This chapter addresses two central concerns about the moral validity of this *prospective decision-making*.

First, do patients really have the capacity to make autonomous prospective decisions about future medical treatment despite the uncertainties and unknowns involved, including the likelihood that such decisions will take effect when they themselves are mentally and physically changed? Can the future be adequately anticipated? Some caregivers and scholars believe that patients' advance directives simply cannot be sufficiently informed about the future to be practically meaningful.

Second, even if such decision-making is possible given its uncertainties, are incapacitated patients so different from their former selves and so lacking in the attributes that characterized their former selves that it does not make sense to treat their former choices as binding or even relevant? Some caregivers and scholars believe that the interest and concerns of the writers of advance directives are so far different from the needs and interests they will have when they become severely incapacitated that it is wrong to view patients' autonomy as having any application once they are disabled. In a sense, they claim, such patients who wrote advance directives and have been incapacitated must have changed their minds about their wishes.

Both of these concerns raise important questions worthy of careful consideration, but neither is ultimately persuasive. They suggest, however, that our understanding of autonomy, and of who the patient is, needs a richer exploration in order to apprehend how autonomy and respect for persons serve as the foundations for advance directives. This exploration should enable clinicians to think more clearly about the nature of advance directives and how best to accomplish their purposes.

## APPRECIATING THE FUTURE FACTOR

Part of what distinguishes humans from other animals is our ability to live in a way that encompasses not only the present but also the past and the future. Many of us spend a good part of our lives planning for our own and others' futures. We are accustomed to making resolutions, promises, and agreements that we intend to have a binding effect on our future actions. Continuity of personal identity, of self, is thus in some practical sense both assumed by and necessary to human living.

In addition, we are accustomed to making resolutions, promises, and agreements to change ourselves and others in the future. We send our children to school to assist in their becoming good people and good citizens; we rehabilitate drug abusers and lawbreakers; we vow to change our type A behavior, to lose weight, to learn gardening, to study Eastern philosophy; we decide to become parents or to undertake the search for faith. Thus, we recognize change—sometimes great change—as falling within the continuity of an individual self. We look back and acknowledge how differently we viewed life when we were young, or before we were married, or while we were still in school. Nonetheless, we know that although in one sense we are no longer "the same person" as we were then, we are still the same person in some deeper sense.

Two principal questions arise for people's attempts to write advance directives expressing choices about future actions affecting themselves: First, have they sufficiently anticipated what may come to pass in the future? And second, what if they change their minds? Both these questions have great significance for advance directives. "Appropriate anticipation," though not part of the minimal standard of decisional capacity, is clearly desirable in decision-making. We would not decide, for example, that a person who does not know what he really wants to do as a career is therefore not able—and should not be permitted—to choose a job. Still, appropriate anticipation becomes a pressing concern as soon as one attempts to write an advance directive. There is enormous difficulty in specifying particular decisions for particular circumstances in advance, especially for patients who do not currently suffer from or anticipate a particular disability. There are many possible decisions, many potentially relevant circumstances, and many unknowns.

It is possible that the breadth of the problem accounts in part for the popularity of short, sweepingly general directives that make broad statements using vague terms. Many early model and statutory directives took this form, and some of this language persists in many advance directives today. General, exhortatory directives may contain no real instructions, and may not intend to; the writer may simply want caregivers to be aware of a general wish to avoid a prolonged dying. On the other hand, many patients may be unaware how difficult these broad directives can be to apply.

Advance directives of either the instruction type, which enumerates the writer's wishes in particular circumstances or about particular procedures, or the proxy type, which names a substituted decision-maker, require the writer to consider and decide about a vast array of possible conditions and events. When the writer prepares an instruction directive, these decisions appear in the body of the document itself. In a proxy directive, these decisions ordinarily must be discussed with the proxy holder even though they need not appear in the document. Both types of directives are extensively described and discussed in chapter 4.

Although it is difficult to anticipate all of the circumstances necessary for the best possible prospective decision-making, that does not mean that appropriate anticipation should be an additional requirement for assessing the ability to write an advance directive. The reason is simple: It is a requirement impossible to measure fairly. Like

other, similar requirements for decisional capacity that have been proposed but discarded—maturity, for example—it is hard to measure
such a standard and even harder to test for it, in light of the value
judgments it would impose and the variety of ways people make
decisions. All tests of decisional capacity run the risk of setting unre-
alistically high standards, standards that promote the values of the
person applying the test and that treat other ways of reasoning as
less valid. An anticipation component would increase this risk even
more and therefore would be undesirable unless we are prepared to
declare many people who wish to write directives incapable of making prospective decisions at all. Such determinations mean that the
power to decide for these people must be given to someone else.

For example, imagine two nursing home patients with similar
health histories: arthritis, diabetes, and one mild stroke. Grace Bow-
man has spent many hours thinking about her advance directive and
has written a document that exhaustively considers the possibilities if
she should have another stroke or experience any of the serious possible complications of her diabetes. She decides she does not want
mechanical ventilation, because she hates her memory of the experience of being intubated briefly after her stroke. In contrast, Robert
Fielding's advance directive is short and sweet: "No hospitalization."

How are we to judge these two patients' capacities to write their
directives in terms of their anticipation? Naturally, the best thing that
can happen is that their own caregivers will discuss their directives
with them as soon as they know of their existence. That way, it might
be noticed that Grace has not said anything about whether she might
agree to *temporary* ventilation if her life could be saved thereby or
whether she would agree to forms of respiratory support that are less
uncomfortable and burdensome, though perhaps less effective. Robert, on the other hand, might convince a clinician that his dislike of
hospitals is unshakable. In both cases, any factual misconceptions
that might form the basis for their decisions could be uncovered and
corrected.

Even when patients can talk with their physicians and their mental state, level of information, and understanding can be assessed,
how can anticipation be measured? Suppose Grace's health crisis,
when it comes, stems from a wholly different cause—a traffic accident on an outing. Must her directive be invalid because she did not
anticipate all possible health problems? Or suppose you ask Robert—
whose directive does in fact cover every medical crisis imaginable

(except those not requiring hospitalization)—what would happen if he changed his mind and he says, "But I won't! That makes no sense to me! I've never set foot in a hospital and I never will, and I'll *sure* never change my mind about *that*!" Should his directive later be treated as invalid because he has written off the possibility that he could change his views?

No! Both directives should stand as valid—but not because Grace and Robert should be penalized with the consequences of their decisions. The argument that would include appropriate anticipation as necessary to a valid directive would also devalue many patients' ways of making decisions, without necessarily helping to encourage better decisions. Moreover, the remedy is draconian. Some ways of tackling problems of the future factor do not require that the whole directive be discarded—and this can help to encourage better decisions.

## IMPROVING AWARENESS OF THE FUTURE FACTOR

Decision-making in circumstances of inherent uncertainty can be improved, but the uncertainty can never be eliminated. So long as patients understand that the uncertainty exists, they should be allowed to live or die with it if they so choose. But they can be encouraged (or even required) to do some things that will reduce caregivers' discomfort about that uncertainty and help others to extract the most guidance (imperfect though it may be) from their directives.

The potentially massive undertaking represented by writing an advance directive can be bounded in two standard, easy ways that directly address the practical aspects of the problems of anticipation and change of views. First, virtually all statutory advance directives contain clauses making them very easy to revoke at any time, in any intelligible manner, and regardless of whether the patient is otherwise decisionally capable at the time of revocation. Thus, anyone able to formulate a change of mind and express it in any way should be able to revoke a directive.[2] Even when a patient is no longer able to revoke the directive formally, by destroying it or defacing it, revocation can be effective in many ways. Any interested caregiver, family member, or friend may elicit the patient's response to the directive and thereby witness the revocation.

Second, the possibility of a change of mind can be considerably reduced if the authors of directives periodically reexamine, update, and reaffirm their advance directives. Though bearing superficial resemblance to the updating of a last will and testament, updating an advance directive serves additional and different purposes. It permits the authors of directives to keep up with increases in their knowledge of their own conditions and with advances in medical treatment, both of which may affect future choices as reflected in the directive. Moreover, periodic updating encourages regular assessment of one's own views and preferences as they may change with time and as a result of other changes, medical advances aside. Because we know that our views on many things may change, we would without question be remiss in failing to acknowledge the need for at least occasional reassessment of an advance directive.

## PERSONAL IDENTITY AND ADVANCE DIRECTIVES

The question of changing one's mind also has deeper ramifications. Regardless of the frequency with which we update directives, they still set out decisions, made at one time, that are intended to govern actions at another time, a time when revocation may well be impossible. If we do not make these decisions for ourselves, someone else will have to make them for us, without benefit of our guidance. Other examples of prospective decision-making—a last will and testament or a statement authorizing organ donation—are more readily accepted than advance directives. Why? Because they take effect only after death, and anticipated death or disability is separable from their subject matter. Advance directives, in contrast, are capable of hastening death, rather than simply altering its consequences. When patients are fully capable of making decisions, reasoning about their views, changing their minds, and understanding the relationship between their past and present choices, and yet are far from experiencing the circumstances under which the decision will actually be made, can they make valid decisions that if honored may result in death?

It is important to see that this question is very different from asking whether patients have the legal right to make medical choices resulting in death. That question has already been answered: Patients do have the right to refuse any medical treatment regardless of whether death will result.

But that question was discussed assuming the chooser was capable of decision-making at the time of the choice. The advance directives scenario seems different at first because it implies an enlargement of the circumstances under which we were initially willing to permit choices leading to death. We might be prepared to acknowledge that a competent person could decide to refuse a treatment that was painful or burdensome, or even to refuse treatment in order to end a life felt to be painful, limited, and degrading, but some of us might also feel that to prefer death to being permanently unconscious or severely demented is somehow wrongly devaluing life (Dresser 1986).

Two related types of argument are made in support of the position that patients should not be able to write advance directives, at least in certain kinds of cases. Both these arguments assert that decisionally capable persons do not have the power to make certain kinds of decisions that will take effect when they are no longer decisionally capable.

### The "Black Box"

This argument holds that no one should be permitted to make a decision about treatment under circumstances entirely beyond our experience. No matter how carefully writers of advance directives anticipate and imagine their future medical circumstances, it is impossible to experience a permanent coma, persistent vegetative state, or irreversible severe dementia—these states are a "black box" to us. If we try to imagine such a state, by making use of knowledge about apparently similar states like temporary coma and acute delirium or psychosis, we can only get to an approximation at best. Technical knowledge of brain functioning in different states is imperfect and cannot really provide understanding. Indeed, this argument goes, it is possible, and cannot be ruled out, that patients in these severely demented states experience an inner life to which we can have no access. How can we know that Karen Quinlan did not have some kind of ten-year-long vision? We cannot.

And therefore, the argument goes, we also cannot accept the decision of the decisionally capable person who purports knowingly to reject the possibility that severely demented life has value. It is not possible to reject something about which we are—inevitably—too ignorant.

The black box argument is currently empirically supported by our still great ignorance about the relationships among brain function, consciousness, and experience. The argument does not depend upon that ignorance, however, unless we agree that internal experience corresponding with minimal selfhood must be perceivable and demonstrable empirically. Our increasing technical knowledge is likely to squeeze the possibility that such patients partake of some intangible experience into a vanishingly small corner (Cranford 1991; Multi-Society Task Force on PVS 1994; Kinney et al. 1994). Many patients with dementia do experience their existence, however, and some scholars, most notably Rebecca Dresser, have made powerful arguments that their experiential world must take precedence in the decision-making process (Dresser 1994a; Dresser and Whitehouse 1994).

Another aspect of the black box argument does not rest on the unknown character of the severely demented patient's experience but proceeds to remove all arguments against continued existence for these patients. According to this reasoning, the kinds of arguments adduced for withholding or withdrawal of treatment have to do with physical pain, discomfort, and burden, and also with their psychic counterparts (e.g., concerns about dignity and degradation). This argument holds that given what we know about brain function, consciousness, and experience, we can tell when pain is a problem and we can then eliminate it. In the many cases in which physical pain is not a problem, because it is not perceived by the patient, there is no "merciful" reason to terminate treatment.

And as for psychic pain, the black box argument maintains that it is even less likely that patients in severely demented states can sense any loss of dignity or experience their existence as degraded. These psychic pains are felt only by conscious, decisionally capable persons who imagine themselves in such conditions; they cannot be a real thing, cannot matter, for unconscious and severely demented patients.[3]

By removing most of the justifications for treatment termination in unconscious and demented patients and leaving these patients with only existence alone or existence with the unknowable possibility of great value, the black box argument seems to seek to give life itself an overriding value by defining away the costs of preserving it. This amounts, in effect, to prohibiting nontreatment of permanently unconscious or severely demented patients.

### The "Stranger"

Picking up from where the black box left off, the "stranger" argument holds that what writers of directives count as significant reasons for treatment termination cannot be reasons in the experience of patients at the time a directive would be invoked. Therefore, the argument goes, those reasons (privacy, dignity, the risk of suffering, concern about being a burden to family, or a personal definition of what makes life worth living) cannot be the basis for advance directives. People who write directives are different people from their incapacitated selves, with different needs and interests, and it is not necessarily in the best interests of the incapacitated patient to be bound by the advance directive written by that patient when decisionally capable (Dresser 1986, 1994a; *Evans v. Bellevue Hospital* 1987). In effect, this argument holds that the decisionally capable patient who wrote the directive is a stranger to the permanently unconscious or severely demented patient for whom the directive is to be invoked.

Both of these arguments would disqualify patients from making their own choices about their future health care precisely *because* those choices involve important values. It is claimed that the values that influence patients to refuse treatment are incompatible with the needs and interests of persons who have lost the higher brain capacity to affirm those values. Thus, decisionally capable persons are no closer than strangers to the unconscious patients they will become. In fact, true strangers should make better decisions for decisionally incapable patients than the latter's own advance directives make. Someone who knows only the impaired patient will not be tempted to compare him or her with a functioning person or with prior wishes and will focus only on current needs (Dresser 1994a; Dresser and Robertson 1989).

These arguments thus replace advance directives with a strictly contemporaneous best interests assessment. Because the present interests of the incapacitated person—avoiding pain, experiencing pleasure, and recovering capacity (Dresser 1986; Dresser and Robertson 1989; Feinberg 1984)—simply do not include privacy, dignity, and the other concerns of the directive writer, incapacitated persons are not better off if these particular strangers, the former selves, control their care than they would be if any other strangers, such as caregivers, appointed guardians, or courts, were the decision-makers.

## THE CONTINUITY OF A LIFE

These arguments presume a radical discontinuity in the selfhood of patients in severely demented states. Essentially, these arguments hold that at least some incapacitated patients currently would disagree with the decisions in their advance directives but cannot say so.

Either the patient would be experiencing value from continued existence and therefore would not wish to die, or the patient's current
inability to experience value would make him or her indifferent to
dignity considerations as well as to most other justifications for preferring death. The arguments postulate two different "personhoods,"
with a disjunction occurring upon the onset of permanent serious
loss of mentation. Why should we accept such a break? Why cannot
decisionally capable persons seek to direct their future lives until
death, so long as they understand how radically their circumstances
may change?

There are strong practical arguments against postulating a point
beyond which an individual no longer has the right to control his or
her life. Most obvious is the difficulty of finding such a point. If permanent serious loss of mental capacity is to be the point of disjunction, there must be both an agreed-upon standard of irreversible
dementia that places the patient in this category and an agreed-upon
test for determining whether that standard has been met. Our current
scientific ignorance alone should be enough to make sufficient agreement impossible.

There are significant moral difficulties with picking such a point,
of course. How different is different, when the difference between
any two points is so clearly on a continuum (Rhoden 1990)? Perhaps
the point should be placed at the patient's loss of decisional capacity—that is, exactly where an advance directive should take effect.
But this could be a point where many patients, though profoundly
incapacitated, have memories, desires, values, and interests that link
them much more deeply with their former selves than persons in permanent coma or persistent vegetative state could be linked. Perhaps,
then, the point should be moved later, to a time of even further
diminished capacity, in which case we could have a paradoxical
result: Patients who are incapacitated but still responsive could have
their advance directives honored, but the profoundly demented
could not. But that seems the reverse of what should be, and presents
the troubling possibility that the "stranger" argument is more about
what decisions ought to be made than it is about how we should
regard the relationship between past and present selves.

There is the additional difficulty of persuading people—especially patients and their families—to see this discontinuity between
"selves" and act in accordance with it. For those who did not know
the patient before he or she became incapacitated—caregivers, for

example—this may seem less a problem than it does for family members and others who know more of the patient's history. And there are additional reasons to resist discontinuity between persons with decisional capacity and their permanently demented selves. The effect of such a discontinuity is to deny people the right to envision and treat their lives as wholes—to deny them autonomy in the Kantian sense while they are alive—and this is wrong. It is not the presence or absence of "value," "humanity," or "personhood" in permanently unconscious or severely demented patients that should determine whether their prior decisions should be valued. We already agree that decisionally capable individuals, who clearly have value, may decide to refuse treatment. Thus, we agree that competent individuals may determine their own value for themselves, even if the determination results in treatment refusal and death. How decisions should be made about demented patients who did not make prospective decisions while they had the capacity to do so is a vitally important issue, but it is not at all affected by the determination that patients who choose to direct their own lives until death should be permitted to do so.

Rebecca Dresser, an articulate proponent of the "stranger" argument, nonetheless has acknowledged that patients have some interest in having their choices applied to their future selves:

> Incompetent patients . . . fail to retain an interest in having their former treatment preferences honored. Competent patients, however, can have an independent interest in directing their future care . . . that can survive the alteration in an individual's interests or identity that accompanies the onset of incompetency and serious illness. Joel Feinberg has explained how persons can possess interests that survive their deaths. . . In Feinberg's view, the . . . thwarting of [a future-oriented] interest harms the person before death, even though the harm does not become obvious until later, when the person no longer exists.
>
> Similarly . . . honoring . . . past preferences demonstrates respect for patients in their former competent states. The past preferences principle . . . embodies a . . . choice to protect this interest of competent patients in controlling their future treatment, rather than a decision to protect any such interest incompetent patients possess in their incompetent states. (Dresser 1986, 393–94 [footnote omitted]; Feinberg 1984, 92)

Saying that the patient's interest in having an advance directive runs from the past to the present but not from the present to the past seems to be a distinction without a difference if the effect is the same. Dresser argues that the effect is not exactly the same, because the patient's interest in advance directives is not as strong as an interest in making contemporaneous decisions, but is more like the interest in organ donation or property distribution after death. Ronald Dworkin gives the patient's interest greater weight, however:

> A competent person's right to autonomy requires that his past decisions, about how he is to be treated if he becomes demented, be respected, even if they do not represent, and even if they contradict, the desires he has when we respect them, provided he did not change his mind while he was still in charge of his own life. . . . For competent people, concerned to give their lives the structure integrity demands, will naturally be concerned about how they are treated when demented. Someone anxious to insure that his life is not then prolonged by medicinal treatment is anxious exactly because he thinks the character of his whole life would be compromised if that life were prolonged in that way. (Dworkin 1986, 13)

Dworkin admits that his argument "has austere consequences" and that we may be unable to follow it in some cases, but he asks us to recognize that whatever good reasons we have for failing to honor past choices, we nonetheless violate the patient's autonomy in so failing. Loss of decisional capacity to many people means the complete devaluation of personal dignity, concern for family, control over one's life, and many of the other values and interests that we customarily consider significant in planning our lives and futures (Cantor 1993, 1990). Surely, many of us would feel injured and affronted now if we were told that, after we lose capacity, our choices for ourselves will have no meaning.[4]

Of course, there will be troubling cases, in which caregivers may find themselves reluctant to implement some directives. The patient whose directive refuses all treatment "if I become irreversibly incompetent" may not simply become unconscious. Instead he may have a drastically reduced IQ and impaired memory and spend his days sitting in a wheelchair—perhaps making sounds or performing stereotyped movements but still apparently extracting something from life that is positive to his current self (e.g., *Matter of Conroy* 1985; see also Cantor 1993; Dresser 1994; Dresser and Whitehouse 1994). These troubling cases suggest that there are times when the patient's autonomy must bow to the good-faith concerns of the community and its valuation of the patient's current needs and interests (Dresser 1994; Rhoden 1990). Such cases call for a sensitive balancing of autonomy and beneficence, with proper weight given both to the advance directive and to current circumstances. They should be a warning to doctors and patients to think carefully and to talk together when writing directives. But they should not be taken to invalidate directives.

To argue that advance directives lack value because incapacitated patients are not capable of finding value in their earlier expressed concerns for their own privacy and dignity is to claim that the interests of the incapacitated patient can be defined and given value only by someone other than that patient when decisionally capable. But there is little reason to suppose that anyone else will be better at doing that than the patient, especially if the patient considers carefully the questions involved. It is true that the particulars of the patient's condition are best appreciated by someone who is on the scene at the time (Buchanan and Brock 1986), but that person is not really any closer to being inside the patient's current experience than a well-informed patient was when writing the directive.

Most significantly, patients clearly have by far the best grasp of their own values. If the current interests of decisionally incapable patients are determinative of treatment, then the value placed by others on the patient's current state, rather than the value placed on that state by the patient in the past, is determinative. This disregard for the autonomous choices made by patients themselves is an injury to their autonomy even though they may be unaware of it.

Granted, there is no means of perfectly ascertaining what is best for decisionally incapable patients; but we accept decisionally capable patients' choices not because they are perfect but because they are *theirs*. Conscientiously made advance directives can reflect patients' decisions in this way without offending our sense of what is ours the way discontinuity arguments do. Patients who choose to direct their entire lives should indeed have the right to do so, in the sense that no propositions about selfhood should be able to interrupt the continuity of a life by invalidating prospective decisions about it. This is only the right to have one's life treated as a whole. Such a right can be exercised by means of many different kinds of health care decisions, and other interests may still prove able to override particular choices, but not by replacing the individual's valuation of his or her own life with some other valuation.

If advance directives carry less weight than contemporaneous choices, as some would have it, then they could be outweighed—by the present interests of the patient or even by family interests or those of society. How these interests are valued is critical.

For example, incapacitated patients have an interest in recovering capacity, if indeed that is a possibility. How the possibility of recovery should be valued then becomes a central concern. If the patient, when decisionally capable, expressed a desire to terminate treatment "unless I am substantially certain to regain my decisional capacity," or "after I have been in a persistent vegetative state for six months," or in some other way assigned a value to the possibility of recovery, there appears little if any justification for using anyone else's valuation of the possibility of recovery to determine whether the directive should be honored. But a less explicit directive might make it harder to determine what value to give to the chance of recovery, and then it might be necessary to use someone else's evaluation. Essentially, then, if advance directives do count for less than contemporaneous decisions, the reason is that they cannot always be made more precise by discussion at the time. If, however, a directive is always the basis for treatment choice and a guide for determining the best choices, the better guidance a directive offers, the more weighty it should be. This returns us to the practical questions of how directives should be used—and how they should be written if they are to be used well.

Patients have an interest in having their lives treated as continuous, but the real issue lies in what the continuity of a life implies about the degree of reflection that should be part of the writing of an advance directive. This is where a relationship arises between our prudential interest in writing directives that give good guidance to others about our future selves (Cantor 1990, 1993) and others' duties to honor our directives in good faith, insofar as they can be honored. Patients who wish their directives to take effect when they are permanently demented but still capable of having experiences must not fail to consider the implications of their choices, both for their future selves and for their caregivers. If it is right to consider the experiential reality of the demented patient in applying advance directives (Dresser 1994), then the same consideration is most important in writing advance directives.

## OTHERS' OBLIGATIONS REGARDING DIRECTIVES

Although others have duties to the persons who write directives, they may also feel obligations toward the often drastically changed and limited selves those persons become in the future, when their directives must be honored (e.g., Dresser 1994). Naturally, the duties involved may be different if their objects are different. Naturally also, the appropriate objects may be different for different duty holders. Does the physician have a duty to the former, decisionally capable person, the present, incapacitated person, or both? How about a spouse, or a sibling, or a child, or a court? To whom are their duties, if any, to be directed?

Honoring a directive essentially means agreeing to recognize the life continuity envisioned by its writer. This is not exactly the same as recognizing the past but not the present self; it is the more difficult task of giving the present self a continuity with its past, and it includes recognizing the decisionally capable patient's own valuation of incapacity and gaining some experience of the incapacitated patient.

The relationship of caregivers to the incapacitated patient with a directive is different from that of the patient's family and friends. The health professional–patient relationship gives rise to an obligation of service to the patient that is strongly grounded in the caregiver's role. This role is likely to be more clearly delineated and better defined than are the manifold obligations felt by the friends and family of the patient. Yet caregivers, like others, may represent a wide range of involvement with, and commitment to, the patient—they may have helped the patient to write the directive, or they may meet the patient and learn of the directive while the patient is still decisionally capable, or they may admit the patient to the emergency room and discover a living will card in the patient's wallet. Is there a way to talk about the caregiver's obligations that covers all these cases?

The relationship between health care professional and patient creates a duty in the caregiver to exercise his or her skill, knowledge, and judgment in the patient's best interest. As we saw in chapter 2, this duty includes the obligation to obtain the patient's informed consent before performing any procedures. Through informed consent, then, the caregiver's duty to act in the patient's best interest is shaped by the patient's choices and preferences. Similarly, when the patient's wishes are captured in a paper from the past and the caregiver is faced with an incapacitated patient, it is the duty to treat in accordance with the patient's informed choice that knits the patient's present and past into a single life.

When it comes to contemporaneous informed consent, the caregiver has no power to act against the decisionally capable patient's will, except in a few very narrowly drawn instances. Yet many caregivers may believe they have good reasons to avoid the daunting task of discovering and acting in accordance with the patient's choice in the case of advance directives. Let us evaluate the reasons a caregiver might offer for failing to implement a patient's advance directive.

## Time

Emergency circumstances can be a real barrier to the implementation of advance directives. The emergency room physician treating an accident victim is not really in a position to halt things immediately when a nurse, looking through the patient's wallet for people to contact, finds a living will card. Yet in a great many cases, lack of time is much less of an excuse than it is made to appear. Sometimes it may be very clear that an advance directive is valid, applicable to the current situation, and unequivocal. For example, suppose a person with a known, particular, progressive condition has written an advance directive refusing respiratory support, or dialysis, or some other treatment that the progression of this illness renders foreseeable. If there is time to ascertain that, there is time to implement it. If there is not time to avoid initiating treatment, there is always time to gather more information and withdraw treatment later.

One of the most important things about time is that spending some early always saves some later. Many caregivers, out of a reluctance to broach sensitive issues with patients and families, fail to begin discussion of patients' preferences, or to suggest that patients write advance directives, at times when there is more leisure to do so. Even when directives are discovered at the bedside, there is often enough time to read them reasonably carefully and discuss them with the patient's family and friends.

Quite a bit of information gathering takes place in the emergency room, whenever there is any time to do so; it is part of good health care. Most of what we need to know about an advance directive can be sought and obtained in a comparable amount of time, if it becomes similarly ingrained as a part of good care to seek it. The PSDA's requirement that health care institutions inquire about, and attend to, patients' advance directives can help develop such habits of good care as a matter of institutional policy; see chapter 4 for further discussion.

## Confusion

Uncertainty about the meaning and application of a directive is another reason given for not implementing it once it has been found and examined. As we shall see in chapter 4, directives take many forms, and some confusion is almost inevitable. Many directives are couched in terms that are reasonably clear but global and unexplained. This produces uncertainty about whether the particular decisions at issue are addressed by a directive's general pronouncements. Alternatively, directives that list many specific decisions may not provide many clues about how a decision not listed should be treated. Caregivers may also have concerns about the decisions of a named proxy when the basis for the proxy's decision-making is not made explicit in the directive. Finally, changes in state law may create ambiguities when patients add their own more liberal provisions to restrictively worded statutory directives.[5]

When there is any time available at all to talk with family, get a history, and the like, there is time to gather information that can at least begin to allay the confusion. Except in emergencies, caregivers always have opportunities both to ask patients whether they have written a directive and to resolve potential confusion about the application and scope of an advance directive. The caregivers who know of the document should discuss it with the patient in order to understand it as thoroughly as possible and to help clarify it if necessary. The patient's primary physician bears the additional responsibility of informing other caregivers about the document and its meaning, especially if the physician knows the patient well and has discussed the directive with him or her. Many times the primary physician will have helped to draft it.

Most of the confusion about a directive's application and scope can be readily resolved by discussion—with the patient if possible and, if not, with others. For example, sometimes, when patients' directives refuse a particular treatment or technology, the physician may be uncertain whether the patient meant also to refuse a trial of that treatment or temporary dependence on that technology. Discussion can easily clarify this. If doubt still remains after discussion, declining to honor the directive most certainly does not dispel that doubt. It is the physician's duty to make an effort in good faith to apply an advance directive to the decisions faced regarding the directive's author. A caregiver who feels unable to apply a directive to a decision because the directive seems ambiguous or unclear must take the directive elsewhere, outside the family and friends, for further scrutiny or action: to a new caregiver who feels able to act, to a hospital ethics committee, or to a court for interpretation.[6]

## Avoiding the Issues

Another reason that can keep caregivers from implementing directives is their fear of unpleasantness, which can arise from a number of sources: family infighting, publicity, the disapproval of institutional administration, and the spectre of the law.

The problem is undeniable; everyone tries to avoid unpleasantness, and health professionals one way or another face more of it than anybody else, even at the best of times. It is small wonder that all of us wish to avoid making the most painful circumstances even more painful. There is a powerful and hard-to-overcome impulse in health care to avoid asking certain questions and raising certain issues. Failing to raise those issues and ask those questions, however, can give rise to serious problems. When physicians do not know their patients' wishes, they have no guidance for the decisions that will need to be made. Especially in crises, this lack of knowledge can seriously complicate decision-making. In addition, when the physician knows a patient's wishes but does not have the patient's directive, it may be difficult to convince family members to abide by those wishes, or even to persuade a cautious institution that implementing those wishes is legally permissible. Discussion is therefore important because of the increased pain and difficulty that can be avoided by means of advance directives.

The desire to avoid difficult questions is an untenable reason for failing to implement advance directives. The informed consent doctrine establishes the honoring of the patient's wishes as both a moral and a legal imperative; living will laws convey support for caregivers who implement them in good faith; and the courts make it clear that careful documentation of the decision made and the reasons for it will, in the great majority of cases, protect caregivers from liability by offering explanations of their actions. Failing to implement a directive out of fear (whether fear of lawsuits or fear of upsetting families) or out of reluctance to complicate matters is a serious and unacceptable breach of duty. As time passes, more directives are honored, and talked-about cases become means of educating caregivers, institutions, and the public to view implementing directives as a familiar routine, avoidance of the issue will come to be recognized as less and less desirable.

## Questions of Capacity

Legal fears, though not sufficient to justify failing to honor directives, are nonetheless reason to proceed circumspectly in implementing them. One legal (and moral) concern that deserves attention is the eternally recurring problem of the patient's decisional capacity at the time of writing a directive.[7] Caregivers who know patients before they become obviously incapacitated are able to ascertain their capacity to write and to reaffirm advance directives for health care decision-making by talking with them then. But suppose a caregiver who was not able to do that has concerns about the directive. Is the possibility of the patient's incapacity when the directive was written a reason not to honor it?

The answer is no. As discussed in chapter 2, ordinary soundness of mind is something that everyone is capable of evaluating, and most health professionals are no more and no less expert in ascertaining it than anyone else. Advance directives usually demonstrate that the writer's mind is sound in this sense in two ways. The directive itself is intended to be a coherent statement that exhibits self-awareness, gives reasoning and argument, and states values and preferences, so that simply having thought about these decisions and written a directive is proof of soundness of mind. Many directives are not written by patients, however—they are merely adopted as is and signed. Still, witnesses are usually present, and they sign the document attesting to their belief that the writer is rational and serious about the directive. That is what the witnesses are there for; it is unnecessary for a caregiver to hold back from implementing a directive because he or she was not a witness.

Suppose the caregiver's concern is a little different—not merely for the patient's soundness of mind but for the patient's foresight and imagination. Suppose the directive provides for the refusal of any treatment that can save the patient's life but will result in severe intellectual impairment. Suppose further that the patient has suffered a massive stroke and needs surgery to reduce pressure on the brain but the location of the clot guarantees permanent brain injury nonetheless. And suppose finally that the caregiver believes that with proper foresight and understanding, the patient would not have decided to forgo treatment under these circumstances, because stroke victims have valuable abilities in addition to their considerable weaknesses. The caregiver reasons that ordinary witnesses cannot know whether the writer of a directive is deciding on the basis of accurate knowledge and appreciation of the situation but that experienced caregivers can.

The flaw in this well-meaning argument lies in the assumptions it makes about how patients should make decisions. The argument is correct in proposing that one who writes a directive should have good information and should carefully consider it. It does not follow, however, that a decision with which the caregiver disagrees is necessarily incompetently made. It is not fair for caregivers to discard directives made without their counsel because they suspect they were not made from what the caregiver judged to be the best possible knowledge.

But suppose that a heart disease patient's directive categorically states, "If I should become incapable of making my own health care choices, I wish to be allowed to die with dignity. Therefore, I refuse all cardiopulmonary resuscitation and all ventilatory assistance." The patient develops a severe pneumonia, is demented from fever and medication, and needs to be placed on a respirator temporarily to return her to the level of capacity, health, and function that preceded the infection. Her physician wonders whether, in writing her directive, this patient had thought about possibilities like this one; concerned that the directive does not reflect an informed choice, the physician decides not to honor it.

The same result—temporary use of the respirator to return the patient to relative health and decisional capacity—can be reached by *interpreting* the directive rather than rejecting it. As we shall see in chapter 4, most directives are intended to apply only when there is little or no possibility that the patient's decisional capacity can be restored by treatment. Yet it is so much a part of the basic idea of advance directives that it would be reasonable for any physician in this position to infer, in good faith, that a directive that does not explicitly contradict this limitation probably includes it. The best solution would be to read the patient's directive and discuss this very point while the patient is decisionally capable. The next best solution is to interpret this directive as applying only when the use of support would be permanent or when the patient's capacity and function cannot be restored, unless the directive explicitly states that the patient refuses even temporary support or that she refuses support regardless of whether she can be restored to "meaningful quality of life," or "a cognitive, sapient state." Family members and friends may, of course, also be asked whether they can shed light on how the patient intended this directive to be read.

The point here is simple but central: The caregiver who harbors a legitimate concern about the meaning of a directive, and therefore about the completeness of the information on which the patient based the directive, does not always have to discard the directive and start from scratch. Instead, whenever possible, the directive can be interpreted in good faith, so that all of the directive's contents are still available to help guide decisions.

No directives are made from perfect knowledge. Many are made from nearly perfect knowledge, with the close advice and counsel of another caregiver; and most are made from enough knowledge and consideration that they make sense when caregivers attempt in good faith to implement them. If a directive can be implemented and there is no reason to think it was not competently made, it is not fruitful to require further demonstrations. The clinician's interest in discussing a directive further with a still capable patient in order to improve the patient's deliberations does not extend to the power to discard directives that are clear enough to implement after the opportunity for improving them is past.

There are already many proofs of validity and patient capacity in most advance directives. To require more than the amount of knowledge, consideration, and safeguards sufficient to enable others to implement a directive[8] may really amount to something else. Caregivers who have a very high level of concern about the patient's information and deliberation may sincerely believe that any patient who considered the question carefully and properly would not refuse treatment. To these caregivers, it may seem that the only effective proof of autonomous decision-making would be a particular decision. Yet it is very clear that "making the right decision" is a wrong standard by which to judge decision-making capacity (Faden and Beauchamp with King 1986; Roth, Meisel, and Lidz 1977).

This brings us to the remaining reason caregivers give for refusing to honor directives. If concerns about decisional capacity are examined carefully, sometimes a more basic issue is unearthed.

## Dislike and Discomfort

The bottom line is that many caregivers are uneasy about the decisions that advance directives represent. Directives refusing care go against professional imperatives; they appear to disvalue the impaired lives that health care professionals strive to preserve; they can seem to represent immaturity and cowardice; and they may offend the religious and moral sensibilities of some. These concerns are real and call for sensitive exploration and discussion. But none of them can override the patient's moral claim of self-direction and decision-making freedom and responsibility.

The time to engage these issues is with the decisionally capable patient. Caregivers should discuss all of these issues with patients—should argue, persuade, and engage the patient in the important process of making, examining, and confirming choices. But the comatose patient with a new doctor should not suffer because the doctor could not talk with him or her a month ago. The caregiver must attempt to understand the directive with whatever help necessary; and a directive understandable enough to be implemented must be implemented. If the caregiver will not honor it, the patient must be transferred to the care of someone who will obey it. To fail to do so would be to abandon a patient in need of assistance. Caregivers can choose not to implement all or any directives so long as they give patients or their proxies ample notice and help them to make alternative arrangements.

With advance directives, decisions must sometimes be quickly made. It is possible that caregivers sometimes may have to act against their own wishes in order to avoid putting patients at the mercy of those wishes. Because the obligation to honor patients' wishes is so strong, caregivers with strong moral views may need to consider ways of making their views known to patients as early as possible and to establish pathways for arranging alternative caregivers who will implement directives.

## EMERGENCIES, OPPORTUNITIES, AND THE QUALITY OF LIFE

It is easy to exhort caregivers to honor directives and respect the choices they embody. Some directives will always be especially difficult to implement, however—for instance, directives that ask others to refrain from action in certain situations where the window of opportunity for action is small.[9] A patient's request for a do-not-resuscitate order—whether the patient faces surgery, with its ever-present risk of cardiorespiratory arrest, has a condition that makes an arrest a real possibility, or is simply hoping for a way to die—is really an advance directive. It will go into effect when the patient is experiencing cardiorespiratory arrest and thus is incapable of making a decision at that time.

When a decision about resuscitation is necessary, patients must either be resuscitated or not. It is not possible to take a little more time to decide, as may be the case when the decision is whether to continue dialysis or mechanical ventilation. When patients specifically refuse the institution of a particular procedure, caregivers may feel more pressured, and more inclined to refuse to honor directives that place them under that pressure.

Nonetheless, directives about events that call for quick action and decision by caregivers are just as valid as directives that allow for more leisurely deliberation. The circumstances under which advance directives are to take effect cannot be required to be serene and pristine. Moreover, the need for quick response to a directive need not preclude taking the time to make a thoughtful decision about implementing it and to have thoughtful conversation about it with the patient and others.

The DNR request is an example of a directive where the patient explicitly refuses intervention regardless of the possibility of a "good" outcome. Clearly, without such an explicit statement, the caregiver could not be expected to refrain from all resuscitations. But just as clearly, explicit directives to this effect must be considered thoughtfully, and caregivers do need to understand them in order to honor them.

Conversation about DNR orders is likely to address why the patient has decided to refuse resuscitation. In a thoughtful article in the *New England Journal of Medicine*, Tomlinson and Brody usefully divided "no-codes" into three categories: medically futile (i.e., probably unsuccessful) resuscitations; resuscitations that are undesirable because, if successful, they are likely to result in an unacceptable quality of life for the patient; and resuscitations that are undesirable because the patient's present quality of life is unacceptable (Tomlinson and Brody 1988). The latter two types of refusals are harder for caregivers to accept, because they are refusals of genuinely lifesaving or life-prolonging treatment.

Yet all that has been said so far in this volume supports the patient's right to say, "Doctor, I don't want you to save my life." Patients have that right, just as they have the right to sign out of the hospital against medical advice or to refuse to go in the first place. This may be difficult for caregivers to accept, but it is so.

The patient who refuses to accept the initiation of lifesaving or life-prolonging treatment thus may present a situation not unlike the Jehovah's Witness, who is willing to undergo surgery, but only "bloodless" surgery. The limitation placed by the patient on the physician's exercise of skill and judgment seems very great; but advance directives are, after all, essentially intended to guide and limit the physician's discretion in various ways. Time and opportunity should be made to discuss these limitations with the patient, and the physician is always free to refuse them so long as someone else is found who can accept them. But every physician has a responsibility to consider very seriously all advance directives, even these, and no physician may undertake the patient's care without the intent to honor them.

One especially controversial type of DNR order is the perioperative DNR order—that is, an advance directive intended to be implemented in the operating room as well as in other hospital and institutional settings (Cohen and Cohen 1991; Veatch 1993). Perioperative DNR orders pose unique ethical and practical problems for operating room personnel, whose extreme reluctance to withhold resuscitation in that setting frequently results in hospital policies requiring that DNR orders and other advance directives be suspended perioperatively. This reluctance has three principal causes: a perceived incompatibility between having a DNR order or other advance directive and wanting surgery; the difficulty of determining what interventions ought to be forgone in a setting where the need for maximal temporary support has been deliberately induced; and concerns about the cause of the patient's death after honoring a perioperative DNR order—concerns not only about civil or criminal liability but about operative mortality statistics, which are recorded and reported.

The first concern can be allayed by the recognition that many procedures to preserve or improve patients' functioning or comfort are compatible with the overall desire to withhold or abate treatment. This and the second concern require good communication between surgery-bound patients and all their caregivers so that patients' needs and desires can be understood and practical and realistic plans can be made to accommodate them perioperatively. The third concern requires an enlightened data-gathering policy at the institutional and state levels. If operative mortality statistics cannot take account of deaths caused by honoring DNR orders and other advance directives, policy makers and others using them could unfairly penalize a hospital seeking to maximize patients' autonomy.

One last category of advance directive deserves discussion here: the out-of-hospital DNR order. Out-of-hospital DNR orders were devised to help ensure that patients' advance directives are honored outside the hospital setting by health care personnel, such as emergency medical technicians and nurses, who lack the authority and training to exercise independent judgment regarding directives. These special DNR orders apply when a panicked relative calls the rescue squad for a patient under hospice care; when a patient is being transported by ambulance; and potentially in a variety of other public and private settings, such as schools or nursing homes (Veatch 1993). A distinctive and easily recognizable form is used; when adopted by statute at the state level, or at the county level by the medical director who issues standing orders to emergency personnel, that form—and that form alone—permits emergency personnel to refrain from acting when there is no attending physician on the scene to so order. Out-of-hospital DNR orders are useful and growing in popularity,[10] but the need to adhere strictly to a particular form can unacceptably limit their effectiveness. Patients outside the hospital setting should not rely on them alone but should endeavor to address potential problems of implementing their advance directives in other settings: with family members, hospice workers, nursing home staff and their attending physicians, or even in school or workplace. Clear and frank communication and planning may avoid many difficulties.

## REASONS OR JUSTIFICATIONS?

What of the patient's reasons for refusing treatment? An advance directive refusing a procedure may give a "good" reason (e.g., unacceptable quality of life after the procedure), a "poor" reason (e.g., unacceptable quality of life now), or no reason at all. How do any of these reasons matter?

The reasons patients have for making advance directives should occupy a limited place in the clinician's assessment of a directive. The right to refuse treatment does not depend on reasons. The patient's capacity to make decisions about medical care is often displayed through reasoning, but the standard used to measure that capacity is a minimal standard, and the right of the patient to make decisions for good, bad, or no reasons is well established so long as the patient is capable of reasoning.[11]

Yet throughout this book it has been emphasized that comprehensive explanation of the values underlying treatment choices is the best assurance the patient has of writing a directive that can be followed. How is that not the same as saying to the patient, "You must justify yourself to me or I cannot implement your wishes"? How is that different from requiring good reasons?

Though the difference is subtle, the clinician who understands it can elicit the patient's reasons while still avoiding the temptation to ask patients to justify their choices. Reasons help caregivers to know what the patient wants—what the choices are. When a patient writes a comprehensive directive, reasons and explanations of underlying values enable caregivers to apply the directive to situations that include decisions not precisely specified in the directive; explanations help caregivers determine what the patient would have done (Cantor 1990). In contrast, a directive that says nothing but, "I refuse resuscitation in the event of arrest during surgery," is clear enough on the question of cardiac arrest during surgery but no help on anything else. Inclusion in the directive of reasons for the patient's choice could suggest to a clinician that broader application is desired or that further discussion with the patient is needed. The patient who cites the risk of an unacceptable quality of life after resuscitation as the decisive factor in her choice has broadened the clinician's understanding of that choice in a way that may make it easier to follow it. Perhaps the patient is not yet fully informed about the magnitude of the risk and would choose differently if she were. Or perhaps her choice suggests that other procedures and treatments that incur similar risks should be discussed with her as well.

These uses of the patient's reasons help the clinician to answer the question "*How* can I know and do what this patient sees as best for her?" They are not intended to answer the question "*Why* should I do what this patient thinks is best?" Reasons are not meant to be justifications for the patient's choices; advance directives need not be justified to be implemented.

In his remarkable book, *The Silent World of Doctor and Patient*, Jay Katz discusses a patient of Dr. Mark Siegler, Mr. D. (Katz 1984, 156–60), who refuses diagnostic tests without explanation but is perceived by all concerned to be rational and autonomous in his refusal of these interventions. Without this additional diagnostic guidance, his condition worsens; he refuses to go on a respirator, suffers a respiratory arrest, and dies.

Katz gives an eloquent account of what he would have done differently if he had the opportunity to speak with Mr. D. about his refusals. He says he would tell Mr. D. that he could not honor Mr. D.'s wishes until he understood the basis for them, for lack of explanation might conceal serious misconceptions or grave disorders of thinking and feeling that would indicate an unsound decision. He would tell Mr. D., "[Y]ou must not hide behind silence" (Katz 1984, 159). In short, Katz claims the right to know why Mr. D.'s choice should be honored.

In a thoughtful rejoinder to Katz, Charles Baron points out that "the sort of doctor-patient conversation which Professor Katz offers us . . . is one in which the patient is made to feel that the doctor carries the ultimate authority. The doctor has merely conceded to the patient some portion of the decision-making authority subject to the condition that the patient pass some test by giving the 'right' answers concerning the reasons for refusing treatment" (Baron 1987, 39).

Baron argues that it is physicians' uncertainty, rather than patients' lack of decision-making capacity, that moves physicians to treat patients over their objections when they do not explain their refusals well enough. He suggests that caregivers "make clear that what they need is to be reassured by their patients that the patient's refusal to accept treatment is not the result of some failing in the doctor's handling of the case and its presentation. Patients thus realize that they are not . . . being put through some test by those in authority before they can get what they want. Rather, one human being [the physician] is asking another human being [the patient] to do the first . . . a favor. . . . Is it likely that any patient would refuse such a request?" (Baron 1987, 40).

Baron, who is not a physician, puts the matter of equality in the physician-patient relationship quite baldly by stating that the patient does the doctor a favor by explaining. Katz speaks like a physician, declaring that he could not let Mr. D. die because he did not understand his choice. Katz is right to assert as strongly as he does that continuing conversation between caregivers and patients almost always succeeds in establishing a mutual understanding. But when it comes right down to it, patients do not owe doctors explanations, and Baron is right.

This sensitive issue has special significance for advance directives, because they do not represent contemporaneous decisions. If explanations are required but not supplied by a document, there is no opportunity for further discussion: The document may be invalidated. On the other hand, if explanation is desirable but not mandatory, the document will be considered valid and applied insofar as is possible. Explanations will simply assist in its interpretation.

Baron suggests that no patients who understand why the caregiver wants to understand their choices would refuse to give an explanation. Naturally, then, a patient's refusal to explain could still suggest that the patient is being unreasonable in a way that calls his or her decision-making ability into question. The difficulty cannot be avoided: The patient can refuse the doctor's care without explanation, but the doctor must fear that the patient's refusal to explain is pathological. There is no way out of this. Yet caregivers can and should control their fears about the patient's decisional capacities. Clinicians who talk with patients about their choices and elicit reasons for them in order to increase their own understanding of their choices will rarely face a patient who will not explain.

Only if lack of explanation makes it excessively difficult to interpret and apply a directive in good faith should a clinician feel justified in not honoring it. Explanations are not owed but freely given, and understandings are shared.[12] The caregiver who feels that he or she cannot follow advance directives that do not sufficiently explain their choices must converse with their authors while that is still possible. If it is not, the caregiver must pass such directives on to others who will follow them, or to an ethics committee or other body that will attempt to interpret them.

## ADVANCE DIRECTIVES IN THE IDEAL WORLD

The conceptual foundations of advance directives are, first, autonomy and, second, community. Advance directives are documents that both preserve and foster autonomous individual choice. They preserve autonomy by their mere existence: They declare choice. They foster autonomous choice by requiring those who write advance directives to think about what they want and to explain that to others. Because the making of an advance directive requires a reasoned, articulable attention to one's own wishes, it can be said to foster autonomy by encouraging more thoughtful choices, in much the same way as the legal doctrine of informed consent has been said to promote rational decision-making (Capron 1974) because it requires that the patient hear—though not necessarily use—information and reasons about medical treatment choices.

In the law of informed consent, however, an informed decision need not display its reasoning in order to be valid. Yes or no will suffice (except insofar as the patient may need to be determined capable of reasoning). This is so because—in theory at least—the process of informing for decision has given the patient and the physician some opportunity to understand each other's goals. Advance directives do not have the same luxury of simply declaring themselves. There is often little connection between the reasoning process of the patient-writer and the involvement of the caregivers, friends, and family who must act to implement the directive—no exchange on which to build any assessment of the decisional process and no chance for the further exchange that may be necessary once the directive is implemented. Yet in many instances, the involvement required of those implementing a directive is profound. Thus, it is reasonable to require that advance directives explain themselves to the degree necessary to enable others to follow them. The problem lies in determining what minimal level of explanation is sufficient.

In treatment decision-making where the patient is currently decisionally capable—the run-of-the-mill informed consent case—direct exchange between caregiver and patient is essential, and continued exchange is possible. Moreover, in many instances, the patient is able to exercise the option of just shutting the relationship down and getting another doctor. In the case of advance directives, however, continuing exchange is unavailable, and the patient cannot leave the relationship. The patient has no other choices. To be fair, then, we should not substantively limit the validity of well-conceived advance directives by honoring them only when the patient is "ill enough" or by permitting them to express decisions about some treatments but not others. Nor should we set an excessively high standard of autonomy or decisional capacity that invalidates directives not containing indicia of a sophisticated, comprehensive examination of all possible future scenarios.

We should nonetheless be demanding of persons writing directives, but in a different way. We should make certain specific assumptions about the thinking of persons who write directives unless we have evidence that is clearly to the contrary. We should assume that writers of directives have used foresight and carefully considered the implications of their choices, and we should honor and interpret directives on that basis. We should not be tempted to second-guess the authors of directives, to argue that they could not really have anticipated what their circumstances would be like and that they might have changed their minds. We must instead assume that they were autonomous agents who considered these possibilities in reaching their decisions. To do otherwise would reduce many advance directives to frustrating ephemera impossible to obey, impossible not to second-guess. And concomitantly with this move to assume a high degree of moral agency in writers of directives, we must endeavor to make that assumption a reality. Advance directives are valid expressions of patients' medical treatment choices. As such, they should be presumed to reflect a high degree of commitment to the choices they express, resulting from thoughtful and circumspect consideration of relevant medical and nonmedical circumstances and future probabilities, including the possibility of the unexpected and the chance of a change of views. Thus, a directive should be followed unless genuine reason to doubt it appears from the document itself or from surrounding circumstances (*In re Westchester County Medical Center* [*O'Connor*] 1988). Doubts should immediately be discussed with the patient's family and friends and with other caregivers, or taken before an ethics committee or even a court.

But directives can only be implemented insofar as they instruct. Whenever a directive does not speak directly to the choice at hand, caregivers will have to treat it not as the embodiment of the patient's choice but as evidence of the patient's likely choice. Because the course of life is so unpredictable, many directives will be honored primarily or only in this special evidentiary sense. When a directive does not speak about the particular decision at hand, it must provide a basis for determining what the patient would have chosen, if it is to be useful as evidence.

Caregivers have, and whenever possible should exercise, the moral right to ask the patient for an accounting, either at the time the directive is made or when it is later presented and discussed. The caregiver may require the patient to articulate as fully as possible his or her choices, the basis for them, the priorities the patient has identified and their weights, preferences in specific situations, awareness of family feelings and views, awareness that unanticipated things might happen, and awareness that a change of mind might result at a time when it cannot be expressed. All of this information helps caregivers to understand the patient's wishes and apply them effectively to treatment decisions. The patient can then go on record—in the document itself or in discussion with physician or family—about issues of particular importance. In addition, the patient can designate a physician or another person as decision-maker,[13] to learn as much as possible about the patient's views and desires and to make choices when there is no direct guidance from the directive. The reason clinicians may require this from patients is not that patients must explain and justify themselves to satisfy their doctors but that both patient and doctor have a duty, whenever they have an opportunity, to make the patient's directive good guidance for others. The difference may be subtle, but it is fundamental.

*Patients have an obligation to make their advance directives good guidance for others.* The consequences of failing to do so are simple. You may not get what you want, because nobody is sure what that is— not because they have a technical excuse to fail to honor your directive, or because they do not like the idea of it, but because the endeavor to imagine what you would have said about X is not aided by what you said about Y. Patients who want their directives followed may have to be overwhelmingly thorough and clear: in writing, in conversation with their physicians, in conversation with friends and family or with persons designated as surrogate decision-makers. Simply put, as much as they may seek firm and direct control of their health care choices, patients with directives are patients in search of an advocate. And it is neither effective nor fair to call upon an advocate who is unprepared and ill-armed for the role. The directive acts as the advocate's ammunition. Or less dramatically, the directive enables the caregiver to know the patient's interests, without which knowledge the caregiver cannot follow them.

This view grounds advance directives in autonomy while acknowledging that discussing, interpreting, and applying them takes place in a community. Such a view encourages sophistication and foresight in the writing of directives, without requiring it—without imposing criteria for validity that would be likely to invalidate many carefully and deliberately executed directives. This view also holds patients to what they say in their directives, thereby both encouraging them to take directives very seriously and reducing the concern that whatever they direct will be second-guessed or ignored. It encourages physicians to discuss their patients' directives with them extensively so that directives can give the best possible guidance. Finally, it provides physicians with a plan of action to deal with what is currently the most common advance directive scenario: a new admission, an unknown and unconscious patient, with a directive.

That plan is this: If the directive meets state validity criteria (see chapter 4) or appears otherwise to have been thoughtfully conceived, prepare to honor it insofar as you can confidently apply it to the problems at hand. Consult with the patient's own physician, family, and/or friends for information that sheds light on the directive, whether it is information that could overcome your presumption that the directive is valid or information that will provide additional guidance about the patient's thinking and preferences for any decisions the directive cannot entirely answer. If questions become unanswerable or the answers become contradictory, consult your institutional ethics committee or some equivalent; if necessary, seek a court's interpretation.

The caregiver must presume that a coherent set of values and opinions underlies every directive.[14] To look for that underlying meaning makes it easier to recognize it, and to expect it means that the caregiver is not required to make it up if the patient did not put it there. In this way, the patient's autonomy is protected and encouraged, but its exercise is also directed by patients' obligations to facilitate the work of the moral communities who must act on their behalf.

# 4

# Advance Directives: Current Forms, Legal Fears, Moral Goals

Legislation has many advantages, not the least of which is clarification of the law on a particular subject. But it is a serious error to assume either that in the absence of legislation there is no law, or that legislation will solve the myriad of personal and emotional factors that control the way both physicians and non-physicians deal with difficult issues. (Annas 1988, 366)

## THE PSDA AND BEYOND

After the U.S. Supreme Court issued its decision in the *Cruzan* case, much changed suddenly for advance directives in the fifty states and the District of Columbia. Caregivers, researchers, and scholars in health care are still sorting out these changes and tracking changes yet to come. The *Cruzan* decision approved as constitutional a state advance directive scheme that acknowledged only the patient's own choices, expressed while the patient had decisional capacity. Missouri did not even recognize the validity of a substituted judgment standard to determine what the patient would want; the state only considered what patients actually said to be sufficient.[1] In a concurring opinion, Justice Sandra Day O'Connor endorsed proxy directives as constitutional and necessary to effectuate patients' wishes. Health law scholars hurried to correct misconceptions about the Court's opinion and to endorse Justice O'Connor's concurrence, explaining that Missouri's scheme was deemed by the Court permissible but not required and noting that most states' advance directive statutes, and many state constitutions, were more liberal in their provisions (Annas et al. 1990).

Soon after the *Cruzan* decision, two things happened: State legislatures rushed to pass proxy statutes to supplement their living will laws, and the Patient Self-Determination Act (PSDA) (1990) was passed to require health care institutions to give patients information about advance directives in their states. The PSDA went into effect in late 1991. It applies to health care institutions that receive funds through either Medicare or Medicaid. In addition, the national accreditation agency for health care institutions, the Joint Commission on Accreditation of Healthcare Organizations (JCAHO), has implemented standards to help institutions comply with the law and regulations (Health Care Financing Administration 1992; JCAHO 1994).

The PSDA has a very straightforward purpose: to increase public knowledge about, and use of, advance directives as one of the means for making health care decisions. Its language is simple, requiring health care institutions (hospitals, nursing homes, home health agencies, HMOs, and hospice programs) to have written policies and procedures:

1. to provide their patients or clients information about (a) their "rights under State law (whether statutory or as recognized by the courts of the State) to make decisions concerning . . . medical care, including the right to accept or refuse medical or surgical treatment and the right to formulate advance directives" and (b) the policies the institution has in place to implement those rights (this information is to be given to patients and clients at the time of admission to the facility or at the time they become clients of the program);

2. to document in the medical record whether each patient has executed an advance directive;

3. "not to condition the provision of care or otherwise discriminate against an individual based on whether or not the individual has executed an advance directive";

4. to ensure that the institution complies with state law on advance directives; and

5. to provide staff and community education on issues concerning advance directives.

The PSDA defines advance directives as written documents recognized under state law (either by statute or by the state courts). It explains that the nondiscrimination clause does not require the provision of care in conflict with an advance directive. And it also permits states to pass and apply "conscience clause" legislation permitting individuals and institutions to refrain from implementing advance directives.[2]

As discussed in chapter 2, discussion about advance directives is related to, and derived from, the informed consent requirement. Morally and legally, informed consent is part of the relationship between patient and physician, and the duty to obtain informed consent rests with the physician. Why, then, should an information-giving requirement concerning advance directives be applied not to physicians but to health care institutions? The answer is deceptively simple: The requirement was applied where it could be enforced. Before and since the passage of the PSDA, debate has flourished over the best place and time to initiate discussion about advance directives. Most agree that the outpatient setting is the best place and time for such discussion; some believe that discussion of advance directives works best when specific serious health concerns can frame the issues for the patient; but nobody has argued that hospital admission is even a distant second-best setting. What Congress hoped for was an administratively easy way to improve education and discussion about health care decision-making and advance directives. What Congress may have achieved instead is bureaucratization of the issues (Sabatino 1993; Mezey and Latimer 1993; Wolf et al. 1991).

Because of the PSDA, everyone admitted to hospitals and other health care institutions is given information about the advance directive laws in his or her state. As a result of this requirement, more than a few states have moved to expand and clarify their laws (Teno et al. 1994a). Even so, for persons who do not have an advance directive, the PSDA as it is implemented by most health care institutions may not do much to encourage or facilitate their executing one. Many institutions, reluctant to give the appearance of proselytizing about advance directives, do little to initiate discussion with new patients who do not have them. Many of the hospital personnel whose job it is to answer questions and help patients to execute advance directives (usually nurses, social workers, hospital chaplains, or patient relations officers) have insufficient training about, and understanding of, the documents and the issues. And so far, few institutions have done enough to link these hospital requirements with the medical team's independent duties to learn their patients' wishes, to discuss the issues with their patients, and to ensure that their patients' wishes are noted in the chart, known to the entire team, and acted on appropriately (Danis et al. 1991; Gianelli 1993). Thus, even patients who come into health care institutions with their advance directives must continue to pursue their wishes with diligence lest bureaucratic safeguards prove inadequate protection for their autonomy.

A second significant problem with the PSDA is its apparent tendency to reinforce misconceptions about what counts as a valid advance directive. Health care institutions, and their attorneys and risk managers, can be rigid and limited in their understanding of what is "legal." Such rigidity has always been a problem for advance directives (Meisel 1989; Weir 1994). As discussed in some detail later in this chapter, the suggested directive forms provided in state statutes have never been intended to be the only legal form to use; they are merely "pre-approved," and variations are legally acceptable within certain broad limits. However, administrative and legal caution has too often resulted in concern that a different-looking directive is not acceptable. This concern may have grown close to a conviction in some institutions, now that the PSDA has focused attention in every state on the statutory forms and no others. For this reason, persons whose choices and preferences are not encompassed by the standard form for their state—and even those who have supplemented their directives with personal statements, values histories, and other documents that clarify and expand upon state forms—should be prepared to explain and justify their directives when they become patients, just in case.[3]

What, then, is an advance directive, really? This chapter turns to an examination of directives as legal documents: the types, their varieties, and their goals.

## WHAT CAN A DOCUMENT DO?

Advance directives take two basic forms. Commonly used names for these forms are "instruction" directives and "proxy" directives: directives that give caregivers instructions about the patient's choices, and directives that name a proxy to make choices on the patient's behalf and convey them to caregivers (President's Commission 1982, 156–66). Many directives combine these forms in various ways. In this chapter, we examine the characteristics of these two types of directives and some of the statutory directives that display these characteristics in order to familiarize caregivers with the many forms directives take and to assist them in interpreting and honoring directives of whatever form.

No attempt is made here to generate a new model directive or to promote any of the existing models. Nor is any attempt to present a comprehensive discussion of state law—it changes too fast in this area for any such discussion to be valuable. An appendix containing the citations to all state living will and health care proxy statutes as of September 1995 is, however, included for reference purposes.

This book does not avoid a statutory catalogue merely for reasons of convenience. Instead, it reflects the understanding that state laws can assist patients in refusing treatment but do not create their right to do so. Therefore, one of this chapter's goals is to get away from the idea that there is a best way to write a directive, and move toward the idea that advance directives, in whatever form, are valid so long as they are based on thoughtful consideration and give clear guidance to those who are to honor them.

A crucial question, then, is what constitutes "clear guidance" in an advance directive. All directives need to answer, in some way, certain questions for caregivers and others who are to implement them. Many different kinds of answers to these questions may be acceptable. Therefore, model directives, with their single set of possible answers, are invariably too narrow to recommend as best for all patients.

Some refusal of treatment decisions may be recognized as generally acceptable in any properly executed directive, such as any of the state statutory living wills. Other, more controversial decisions (e.g., refusing treatment for a potentially reversible life-threatening condition) are likely to be acceptable only if they have been explained satisfactorily to someone who can implement the directive (e.g., the patient's physician), to someone who can explain it in turn to the one who will implement it (e.g., a named proxy), or in extensive commentary in the directive itself (e.g., Cantor 1990). Thus, some directives can only provide clear guidance if patients, caregivers, family, and friends can discuss things beforehand and if someone can be available at the right time. The directive that adds a request to call the patient's personal physician for verification is most likely to be honored for this reason. The directive that is most likely to be honored when no one who knows the patient well is available will be one that is less bold in its choices, unless it can explain itself persuasively and in detail.

The questions directives must answer include the following:

When does the directive take effect? (Must the patient be decisionally incapacitated only, or also terminally ill?) To which health care decisions would it apply? (To all decisions, to life-and-death decisions, to decisions about certain interventions only? Which interventions?)

What decisions should be made, or who should make those decisions, or both? (Is treatment refused? On what basis? Is a philosophical statement included, or just a "laundry list"? Can other decisions be discovered from these general rules, or are only the explicitly mentioned choices intended? Has a proxy been named? On what basis should such a proxy decide?)

A second, different set of concerns must be answered by the directive as well: Is the patient serious? Is he or she sufficiently informed? Has he or she been thoughtful? Is there any reason to suspect lack of decisional capacity? These questions, too, are best answered by persons with knowledge of the patient. But in order to serve patients' choices fairly, advance directives themselves must be able to answer them when no other advocate is available.

## ADVANCE DIRECTIVES AS LEGAL DOCUMENTS

Many people—caregivers and patients included—regard advance directives in a kind of narrow, legalistic way. They treat them as orders from patients to doctors, orders that are binding only if they conform strictly to what a law has said they should say and how a law has said they should say it. As a result, patients often prepare, and are advised to prepare, advance directives that bristle with notary seals and witness signatures and with clauses that match word for word the terms of all the living will statutes in all the states in which they are most likely to fall ill. More important, physicians and hospital administrators often look for these things in the directives they encounter and, if they are not all there, refuse to honor the directive because it is "not legal."

Without a deeper understanding of advance directives, it is hardly surprising that caregivers should have a high degree of concern both for preserving the lives of their patients who have written directives and for their own potential liability for not doing just that. Yet in this light, advance directives appear as documents that must be obeyed if they are airtight and cannot be obeyed if they are not.

Should caregivers want directives to be "airtight"? And what should be done if they are not? It is important to recognize that there are two different kinds of legal concerns that caregivers may have about advance directives.

## "NONCONFORMING" DIRECTIVES

The first concern is that a directive is not valid if it does not match the suggested document given in state law. This view is contradicted by the language of the great majority of state advance directive laws, which commonly begin with a statement like, "This statute provides an optional and nonexclusive procedure by which patients can exercise their rights." Thus, most state laws explicitly acknowledge that other versions of advance directives—other written forms and even evidence of oral statements—may also provide patients with the means of exercising their rights.[4] Therefore, directives that do not conform precisely to the form prescribed by state law may well be valid and cannot be dismissed out of hand because they are "nonconforming."

There are two general ways in which a directive can fail to match state law. First, it may fail to fulfill all of the state's indicia of reliability—witness statements, notary seals, physician certifications, and the like. This *formal* nonconformity might be minor (e.g., one witness rather than two) or it might be major (e.g., the entire document is a barely legible handwritten sentence in pencil on a sheet of notebook paper with no signature). With assistance from the patient's family and, if necessary, from the institution's administrative and legal representatives, the caregiver must decide whether such nonconforming directives contain enough other indicia of reliability—that is, whether it is clear from the directive itself that the patient understood the import of the directive, believed it important, and took it seriously.

Such seriousness of purpose can be shown by the patient's having added language to the directive that explains the reasons for it, adds lists of procedures and treatments or conditions covered, or names a proxy decision-maker. Seriousness of purpose can be shown if the document has been periodically reaffirmed by initial and date. It can also be shown by extrinsic evidence, such as affirmation by family members or notes in the medical record indicating that the patient discussed the directive with other caregivers. The key to evaluating directives that do not conform formally to state statutes is to remember that the patient must somehow show seriousness about the directive. A directive that only lacks one witness is likely to show sufficient seriousness in some way, while one that is substantially nonconforming in this formal sense is highly likely to fail reasonable scrutiny.

The second way in which a directive can fail to conform to state law is more difficult to evaluate, because it represents a *substantive* nonconformance—for example, directives intended to apply when the patient is neither terminally ill nor in a persistent vegetative state (as in less than severe dementia), directives refusing treatment for temporary or reversible conditions, or directives seeking to refuse treatment during pregnancy when the state statute attempts to preclude such refusals. A few states have written directives purporting both to narrow the broad common-law right to refuse treatment and to challenge the proposition that all treatment refusals are constitutionally protected. More commonly, however, people just assume that advance directive statutes create the right to make advance treatment decisions and that therefore the right to refuse treatments is bounded precisely by the statutory document.

The rights upon which treatment refusal are based are of two types: American common (court-made) law supporting the rights of informed consent and refusal of treatment, and an American constitutional right, sometimes labeled the right to privacy in intimate personal and medical decision-making and more recently left unspecified (*In re A.C.* 1990) or denominated a liberty interest in freedom from bodily intrusion (*Cruzan v. Director* 1990).[5] All states acknowledge the common law basis for advance directives. Thus, advance directives will be treated as evidence of the patient's wishes even in states without advance directive statutes, and "nonconforming" directives, in all states except those few attempting explicitly to narrow the common law, will also always constitute evidence of the patient's wishes.

The constitutional right that forms the basis for advance directives has been imperfectly articulated in case law. As discussed in chapter 2, most treatment refusal cases have, without much analysis, viewed the common-law and constitutional rights of refusal as essentially coextensive. In 1988, a federal district court in Rhode Island became the first federal court to hold that the right of privacy encompasses the right to refuse medical treatment, including artificial nutrition and hydration (*Gray v. Romeo* 1988). At the same time, in a highly controversial and much-criticized opinion, the Missouri Supreme

Court came to the opposite conclusion (*Cruzan v. Harmon* 1988). Early in 1990 the District of Columbia Court of Appeals firmly acknowledged, without further specifying its nature or origins, a constitutional right of bodily integrity "to accept or refuse medical treatment" and suggested that U.S. Supreme Court precedent assumed the existence of such a right (*In re A.C.* 1990). Then, at the end of its 1990 term, the Supreme Court, in deciding the case from the Missouri Supreme Court (*Cruzan v. Director* 1990), asserted that a decisionally capable patient has "a constitutionally protected liberty interest in refusing unwanted medical treatment" (497 U.S. at 278), and assumed that this constitutionally protected right would encompass the refusal of "lifesaving hydration and nutrition" (497 U.S. at 279). The Court named as the source of this right not a generalized right of privacy but a "Fourteenth Amendment liberty interest" (497 U.S. at 279 n.7).

If there were no constitutional basis but only a common-law basis for advance directives, then states would be free to pass statutes that greatly changed the common law. The many statutes that establish "optional and nonexclusive procedures" for advance directives are specifically saying that they do not intend to change the common law. Instead, states with such statutes will recognize any directive that accords with common law; they simply offer one suggested form for directives. A few states have statutes purporting to prohibit patients from writing certain kinds of directives. In the past, a number of statutes attempted to preclude patients from refusing artificial nutrition and hydration. The *Cruzan* decision reversed that trend, but a number of states still attempt to preclude pregnant women from refusing treatment.[6]

In order to narrow the common law in this area, where it is deeply rooted and of long standing, states must be explicit in their intent and persuasive in their reasoning and must not exceed the limitations posed by the Constitution. Moreover, no state can hope to preclude purely private decision-making by patients, their families, and their physicians without applying criminal sanctions. Caregivers should remember that no criminal charges have been successfully brought against anyone for honoring patients' or families' requests for withdrawal of treatment,[7] nor has civil liability successfully attached.[8] Caregivers implementing written advance directives, even those not conforming precisely to state law, are very unlikely to be at risk, even after *Cruzan* has given the states the ability to require directives to be "clear and convincing." Indeed, greater risk may lie in the failure to honor directives (see chapter 6).

In the *Cruzan* decision, the U.S. Supreme Court did not directly address the constitutionality of Missouri's "living will" statute. Instead, it found a constitutional right to refuse medical treatment, while allowing the Missouri *courts* to require that a decisionally incapable patient's desire to refuse artificial nutrition and hydration be shown by "clear and convincing evidence." The Missouri Supreme Court had found that Nancy Cruzan's parents did not meet that standard with evidence about her general character and about several conversations she had with friends and family members.[9] Written directives of the types advocated by this book, including health care powers of attorney and thoughtfully composed nonconforming directives, would certainly meet such a standard. Moreover, informal evidence about the patient will always be available to assist physicians (and, if necessary, courts) in interpreting existing directives.

Even Missouri does not require that all decisions to implement advance directives be reviewed by a court (*Cruzan v. Director* 1990, 497 U.S. at 314–15, n.15, Brennan, J., dissenting). Caregivers need not fear that judicial bottlenecks will preclude the implementation of patients' directives (Coordinating Council 1993). Most important of all, this decision allows, but hardly requires, other states to follow Missouri's lead. Essentially, the *Cruzan* decision requires states to recognize nonconforming directives and permits them to test the validity of such directives by a relatively stringent subjective standard. Only three states have embraced this "clear and convincing evidence" standard. The rest of the states whose courts have ruled in treatment refusal cases have emphasized common law and constitutional commitments to flexibility and individual freedom and have recognized standards of substituted judgment and best interests (see the discussion of these standards in chapter 5).

There are still not many cases on advance directives or even on treatment refusal; thus, it is hard to say that there are many settled issues in the field, though a consensus is developing (Meisel 1992). The Supreme Court's ruling in *Cruzan* left many issues unresolved. But the clear majority of states and state courts that have dealt with treatment refusal view advance directives as capable of having many valid forms and containing many different valid choices (Legal Advisors Committee 1983). The *Cruzan* decision did not change this (Annas 1990; Annas et al. 1990; Weir and Gostin 1990). Physicians and their institutions should understand that they need not await definitive judicial pronouncements in their states before acting in good conscience to implement nonconforming directives (Coordinating Council 1993). If that were so, no law could ever be interpreted or challenged.[10]

## IMPLEMENTING DIRECTIVES

A second type of legal concern about advance directives is the fear of "guessing wrong," the concern that after a directive is implemented, someone will claim it should not have been. (Caregivers should also fear that a decision *not* to implement a directive could be challenged in court, unless their concerns about implementing it are well founded and clearly articulated. Failing to implement a directive has thus far been viewed both as legally less consequential and morally less problematic, though this is changing, as we will see in chapter 6.)

The fear of guessing wrong, or, more properly, *second*-guessing wrong, about advance directives tends to lead to conservatism in their interpretation; the result may be effective invalidation of directives that do not closely match state statutory forms. In addition, however, caregivers may feel that even the statutory form does not help them to know whether patients really knew what they were doing, so that they may be reluctant to implement directives any time the family indicates disagreement with a directive. These concerns are not illegitimate but can easily grow far out of proportion to the real issues behind them and the real risks to caregivers from implementing directives.

The central point is this: Advance directives—like any product of law or policy—have to exhibit a balance between the interests of the patients writing them and the interests of those who are to honor them, between fairness and faithfulness to moral goals on the one hand and clarity, certainty, and convenience on the other. An advance directive serves as *evidence* of the patient's choice—good evidence or poor evidence, depending on what it is able to say about the decision at hand.[11] Because every directive will be judged legally—if it *is* judged—on its own merits and the actions of caregivers will similarly be judged individually, the outcomes of such judgments (or even whether judgment will occur) cannot be predicted. This prospect of individual judgment by the courts carries with it both an obligation of individual judgment, by every caregiver, of every directive and a promise that a caregiver's good-faith, conscientious judgment about a directive, when explained in court and supported by the record, will very probably be protected from liability. This is as firm a promise of legal support as can be given for any activity that has not been granted immunity from prosecution. Good-faith decisions, carefully made and fully explained, may be challenged and tested but will rarely be found wanting.

One of the reasons people incorrectly believe that advance directives must agree with statutes before they may be implemented is that all advance directive statutes contain a provision stating that good-faith obedience to a directive conforming to the statute shall not be grounds for civil or criminal liability. These provisions lead caregivers and their institutions to conclude that good-faith obedience to directives *not* conforming to their state statutes will be grounds for liability.

There are several reasons this is not true. First, the liability protection given to physicians who honor statutory directives is very limited.[12] It does not preclude suit but instead provides the physician with a very good defense, all but guaranteeing that unless evidence other than the directive itself is introduced, the case will be disposed of at an early stage and the physician will win. Any evidence that the physician did not act in good faith or that the directive was not valid could eliminate even the limited protection offered by the "right" kind of directive. For example, a patient's family could claim that the patient was tricked into signing the directive or that the physician knew the patient was mentally incompetent at the time of signing.

The liability protection offered by statutory directives is thus more like "preapproval" than real legal insulation. Statutory directives are assumed to be trustworthy and reliable, but this presumption may be overcome by evidence to the contrary, and then the matter is reopened and the physician's protection gone. At this point, the physician must prove that he or she was right to implement the directive. To do so, the physician may simply show (1) that the patient's wishes were discussed and recorded in the chart, along with the physician's impressions of the patient's decisional capacity and understanding of the meaning and implications of the choices expressed; or (2) that the directive was discussed with the patient's friends and family, who verified that it appeared consistent with views the patient had expressed to them when he or she still had capacity; or (3) that the directive itself expressed clear wishes, appeared to be based on good information and written to express personal values, could be reasonably applied to the decision at hand, and gave no indications for suspicion that it ought not to be implemented.

Even a physician who honored the "wrong" kind of directive, or no written directive at all, is nonetheless very likely to win any lawsuit challenging end-of-life decisions for a patient—and preclude the filing of most such lawsuits—by following the same good standard practice of knowing the patient and family, thoroughly documenting all discussions about treatment choices, and giving compassionate and responsible care. These things are enough to protect the physician when it comes to advance directives, as with all aspects of caregiving. Because this kind of discussion and documentation is good medical practice and the physician should be doing it whether or not an advance directive is involved, the written directive itself is, at best, confirmatory of this other, equally good or better evidence of the patient's wishes and the doctor's actions.

Sometimes directives that follow statutory models can make it harder for physicians to discover and do what their patients really want. Such directives often give poor evidence of what the writer wanted. Statutory models are all-purpose, least common denominator, compromise directives (President's Commission 1983). They contain only what *everyone* is prepared to agree is inoffensive and are usually very generally worded, leaving little opportunity for writers to make known strong particular preferences of any kind. The treatment decisions faced by a patient's family and physicians do not always fall squarely and clearly within the vague, narrow bounds of such directives; a caregiver who has only such a directive to rely upon is likely to find it of little help for many decisions.

It is paradoxical that these statutory directives provide some legal protection even though the decisions protected by such statutes are more likely to be poorly guided than if there were a fuller directive. Many caregivers will be more comfortable, legally and morally, if they supplement the contents of a bare statutory directive with additional evidence of the patient's wishes. A caregiver who wishes to be sure of acting responsibly will interview family and friends and do whatever else is necessary to increase his or her knowledge of the patient and the patient's wishes. The patient who writes a thoughtful and thorough advance directive can convey that same evidence to caregivers more efficiently, fully, and accurately. Most bare statutory directives, however, are not extensive enough to do that without modification.

Some caregivers may feel that a "legal" statutory directive gives them permission to seek real evidence of the patient's wishes on this sensitive subject and that therefore they are best off with such a directive in hand—giving them the maximum legal protection, slight though it is—and nothing else in writing. Even when there is no directive, however, physicians are still bound to seek evidence of the patient's wishes for all medical treatment decisions and to honor the patient's wishes if the evidence of them seems sufficient. Since written statements from the patients themselves will always be better evidence, in every respect, than the same statements repeated to caregivers by others, there is no ground for preferring a "legal" directive if a more detailed version is available or could be written.

## LEGAL, MORAL, BOTH, OR NEITHER?

Before the PSDA, many advance directive advocacy groups, whose target audiences are patients and families, recommended that writers of directives complete the directive prescribed by their state of residence and attach supplementary documents that set forth their treatment choices with more accuracy and detail. This can be somewhat problematic advice, however, when the statutory directive is narrowly drawn but the patient wishes to refuse treatment under broader circumstances—for example, if the statutory directive is limited to terminal illness or PVS (as most are) but the patient wishes also to refuse treatment in the case of severe chronic illness and dementia. Patients writing these double-barreled directives must be aware of the confusion that could ensue when the clinician tries to reconcile the directive's two parts, and should state specifically and clearly that their supplementary, nonstatutory directives are intended to have priority. If no such statement is included, clinicians should be sure to clarify these patients' wishes whenever possible. Many advance directives now contain priority statements. (See discussion in "Combining the Forms" below.)

A Florida decision illustrates the problem of the double-barreled directive well. Estelle Browning was an eighty-eight-year-old nursing home resident in a persistent vegetative state, maintained by means of a nasogastric tube for several years since a stroke despite an advance directive executed in accordance with Florida law, because the Florida statutory directive authorized termination of treatment only when death was "imminent." Ms. Browning had supplemented

her directive with strong, clear verbal statements and discussions
with the witnesses to her directive, her named guardian, and her physician. She had much experience visiting incapacitated friends and
believed that artificial support, including artificial feeding, was an
intolerable indignity. Nonetheless, because of the limiting language
in her statutory directive, the medical director of the nursing home in
which she resided ordered the institution of artificial feeding and
antibiotics over the objection of her treating physicians.

The court concluded that Ms. Browning's directive could not
serve as the basis for withdrawal of the tube, but held that her guardian could assert the right to make the withdrawal decision, based on
her constitutional right of privacy. Thus, the temptation to prepare a
statutory directive but reach a private understanding with family,
friends, and caregivers about what really should happen can give rise
to problems when not all parties agree. In this case, the difficulty
probably stemmed from liability fears on the part of the institution. If
Ms. Browning had put her full wishes in writing as a supplement to
the statutory directive, it might at least have been a little easier for
her guardian and her physician to assert her interests in the face of
the nursing home's concerns, and perhaps it would even have been
possible to stay out of the judicial forum entirely, which the Florida
Supreme Court acknowledged to be preferable (*In re Guardianship of
Browning* 1990).

On the other hand, clinicians should not *require* patients to write
these double-barreled directives in order to gain the liability limitation of the statutory directive. The concern—legal, moral, and even
professional—of physicians, friends, and family is their ability to
determine what the patient wanted or would have wanted. The usefulness of a directive depends only upon whether it provides sufficient evidence of this. Caregivers should require good evidence, that
is, enough evidence on which to act, in whatever form it appears. The
patient's own self-conscious writing is best. If a directive fails to
match a statute because it gives more detail than the law requires, the
failure is very unlikely to matter. There is no airtight directive and
there cannot be. The only guarantees that can be had by physicians
and other caregivers are substantive, rather than formal: Rely on
directives that guide you well; and help your patients to write them
that way.

Clinicians who recognize the importance of viewing patients'
directives as legitimate guidance rather than legal orders will also see

that a viewpoint that encourages patients to write directives and express their wishes is not precisely compatible with many institutions' legal and policy perspectives on termination of treatment. Focusing on patients' choices bypasses, for those patients who express choices, a network of treatment policies, patient protocols, and legal procedures reflecting the legitimate but sometimes shortsighted goal of limiting institutional liability. It is within this institutional context that the pressure for directives to be "legal" has mounted.

For example, it is often not caregivers but their institutions that are reluctant to accede to patients' wishes to withhold or withdraw treatment. Hospitals may fear criminal prosecution for the removal of a feeding tube even though all of the patient's family and caregivers seek the tube's removal. Nursing homes may establish policies requiring transfer of patients to a hospital whenever treatment is necessary, thus requiring families to obtain court orders to enforce advance directives refusing hospitalization and life-sustaining treatment.

Although institutional concerns in this area are understandable, it is nonetheless burdensome to families to seek court endorsement of all advance directives. Institutions need to be shown that, regardless of the perceived risks of honoring patients' treatment refusals, a written document supporting the withholding or withdrawal of treatment makes successful prosecution even less likely. (See chapter 6 for further discussion of this issue.) Even though there might be no case law on advance directives or treatment refusal in a particular state, this absence of precedent does not signal the necessity of prior court approval for implementing a directive. Instead, caregivers and institutions should feel able to guide the courts by example, making thoughtful good-faith choices based on directives. More and more courts are coming to recognize that end-of-life decisions are private ones, to be made privately unless there is significant reason to doubt their validity. This is especially true when an advance directive evidences the patient's prior reflection about the decision that must be made.

Avoiding the consequences of an unnecessarily conservative institutional perspective is not necessarily difficult but requires interested clinicians to do more than simply request that the hospital administration or the hospital attorney develop a clear policy on advance directives. A more effective approach would probably be for clinicians to draft a statement explaining their viewpoint and asking for discussion about how institutional policy can best reflect the real value and purpose of directives, respect patients' choices, and support clinicians' conscientious efforts to honor those choices without unduly compromising the institution's concerns. In this way, advance directive policy can be developed, like other institutional policies, as part of the institution's attempt to support the delivery of good medical care (Special Supplement 1994).

The remainder of this chapter is devoted to helping clinicians develop a sense of how to strike the necessary balance between fairness and certainty both in helping patients to write directives and in examining and interpreting directives after patients have lost decisional capacity. It will also help patients write directives that are flexible and clear.

## STATUTORY ADVANCE DIRECTIVES

This chapter's discussion of instruction directives and proxy directives is intended to illustrate some problems balancing fairness and certainty, and to suggest possible solutions. This is not a comprehensive inventory of law on the subject. Many such inventories exist, published in legal and medical literature and by patient advocacy groups or included in books about writing advance directives (e.g., Choice in Dying 1994, 1994a; Meisel 1989). The intention here is to provide enough of an overview to help health care providers make the best use of the schemes provided by the laws of their states, and gain the deeper understanding that promotes flexibility in using advance directives.

Most patients now base their directives on state statutory forms. (They are encouraged to do so by advocacy groups and by the PSDA.) In order to know what a statutory directive means, it is necessary to examine the whole of each statutory scheme—not just the model directive itself but also definitions, penalty clauses, and all of the other provisions meant to help specify how the directive should be read and where the limits of its interpretation should lie.

Advance directive statutes, whether they are called state natural death acts, medical treatment decision acts, death with dignity statutes, or whatever else, for the most part share a common set of features. It cannot be overemphasized that most advance directive statutes themselves acknowledge that directives may be less than carbon copies of the model and still enjoy full statutory protection and that in their purpose statements, many statutes explicitly acknowledge that treatments may be refused by means other than directives (e.g., oral statements to family, friends, or caregivers, as in most of the court decisions on treatment refusal). In addition, most statutes contain (1) one or more model directives; (2) purpose declarations, which recognize the patient's right to make treatment decisions; (3) definitions of key terms like "life-sustaining procedure" or "terminal illness," which help to specify the decision-making limits given by the model directive; (4) specifications about how the directive should be witnessed and solemnized; (5) liability protection for persons honoring a valid-appearing directive in good faith; and (6) provision for revocation of the directive (which is usually made very easy). Most statutes also provide that (7) an attending physician's refusal to honor a validly executed directive or to transfer the patient into the care of a physician who will honor it shall be considered "unprofessional conduct." Many set out procedures for effecting transfer. And most also provide that termination of treatment according to a valid directive can neither be considered suicide nor required as a condition of insurance.

Other features of advance directives are found in many statutes but are not universal. Many statutes contain reciprocity clauses, for example, explaining the circumstances under which out-of-state directives will be honored.[13] Many specify which type of directive—instruction directive or proxy appointment—takes priority in case there is conflict between them. Many statutes continue to use problematic, difficult-to-define terms, and the variety in terminology across the states is daunting.

In addition, state statutes generally restrict the scope of advance directives in several characteristic ways. First, virtually all require directives' authors to be adults, thus appearing to preclude minors from making their own prospective decisions about end-of-life treatment.[14] A number of state statutory directives address artificial nutrition and hydration separately from other treatments, requiring that it be specifically refused in an instruction directive or that a health care agent be specifically empowered to refuse it in a proxy designation; otherwise it will always be provided. Many state statutes also suspend advance directives during pregnancy, or at least after viability, thus unconstitutionally limiting a pregnant woman's right to refuse treatment.[15]

State advance directive statutes also characteristically limit who may witness advance directives, excluding relatives or anyone who potentially has a financial interest in the course of the patient's treatment. Relatives and others who stand to inherit from the patient are not precluded from serving as proxies; to do so would prevent too many patients from naming those who are closest to them and know them best. In almost all states, however, patients are precluded by statute from naming their attending physician as proxy. The intent is to separate the health care proxy from the provider's interest in either collecting more fees for more treatments or saving money by providing fewer interventions and allowing the patient to die sooner; sometimes the effect is to require a patient's personal physician to choose between supervising treatment and providing information and decisions for a patient with whom a long-standing relationship exists.

Before examining specific statutory model advance directives, it is helpful to understand something about the two types of advance directives and their characteristics.

## INSTRUCTION DIRECTIVES: LIVING WILLS

Instruction directives, popularly known in the United States as living wills (Kutner 1969), are probably the most familiar of advance directives. The name "living will" conveys the solemnity of the document, gives it a legal flavor, and suggests something about its format: a list of instructions akin to a testamentary disposition of assets. But "living will" is a misleading term as well (Francis 1989); it suggests that advance directives are only legal documents, and it too often consigns them to the company of other legal documents in the safe-deposit box, rendering them undiscoverable, and therefore useless, when they are needed.

### The Testamentary Model

Instruction directives are based on a "testamentary" model, which is to say that in their form and scope, they resemble a last will and testament. The model contains the following elements: a statement by the writer affirming the seriousness of the declaration ("I, being of sound mind . . ."); a list of instructions, which can be detailed and specific, brief and general, or anything in between; and usually the signatures of disinterested witnesses and some official acknowledging stamp or seal.

### Scope

Instruction directives become effective only when (1) the writer is no longer capable of making medical care decisions, (2) the writer is in a condition covered by the directive, and (3) a decision covered by the directive is called for. It is immaterial which of these conditions triggers inquiry into the others, but the determinations must be made or reconfirmed as close together as possible to ensure that both other conditions exist. Directives usually say very little about the first condition, relying instead upon our hazy but somehow commonly held notion of "competence," or decisional capacity.[16] The determination is more difficult when the patient is impaired or demented but not entirely unresponsive (e.g., patients with mental illness, stroke victims, etc.), so that "decisions" are indeed offered but appear ambiguous or untrustworthy. When an advance directive exists and the patient's ability to make a critical decision is in question, the directive can help guide the physician's assessment of the patient's decision-making capacity, if used to elicit the patient's current choices and reasoning.

The key component of an instruction directive is the decisions it covers. As we have already seen, an advance directive may apply to any and all health care decisions the writer wants it to apply to, from life-and-death decisions to less consequential personal preferences. To establish which decisions are covered, instruction directives generally consider two parameters: "When I am in X condition, I want/do not want Y treatment." (For example: "When I am terminally ill, I do not want to be placed on a respirator." "When I am permanently unconscious, I wish to be given food and water by whatever method necessary." "If I should have another stroke and later contract pneumonia, I do not wish to be treated with antibiotics.")

There is no inherent limitation upon the range of conditions that can bring a directive to bear. Of course, because people want directives in order to preserve the choices they believe important, directives will most typically be applied to life-and-death choices, circumstances of grave illness or debility, and strong personal preferences. Most directives, then, will concern terminal illness, permanent unconsciousness, and major interventions like respiratory support and resuscitation. But amputations and other major surgery, dialysis, cancer therapies, and artificial nutrition and hydration have all been the subjects of treatment refusals and have become important subjects for advance directives as well. In short, the range of conditions and decisions about which an advance directive may be written is not inherently limited, except that it applies to medical treatments and procedures when the patient is not able to make a choice.

Another way of delineating which decisions are covered by a directive is to specify what treatment should be withheld "if there is no reasonable possibility of recovery" or "if I cannot return to a cognitive, sapient state." This kind of statement in an instruction directive helps to make clear what is important to the patient and what underlies the patient's mention of specific treatments and specific circumstances. It also inevitably introduces highly subjective and value-laden terms, which some caregivers consider insufficiently clear and thus inappropriate. It is vital to recognize that subjectivity is absolutely appropriate in an advance directive; only genuine ambiguity[17] represents a problem of interpretation.

Most statutory living wills (and even some model directives) by their own terms limit their applicability much more than does the law of treatment refusal. They usually apply only when the patient is terminally ill or in a persistent vegetative state, both because living wills are meant to be effective after the patient has lost decisional capacity and because living will statutes contain only what is viewed as generally agreed upon and not too controversial. Living will statutes cannot limit patients' constitutional right to refuse treatments even when they are not terminally ill. The limitations contained in standard statutory instruction directives, however, do address the most common treatment refusal scenarios, while avoiding many difficult and controversial cases and minimizing problems of interpretation.

## Weaknesses

The potentially great scope of advance directives generates a problem: How can the authors of directives best address all the decisions and conditions they wish to address in their directives?

The laundry list approach that is characteristic of instruction directives has an obvious weakness. It is rarely possible to construct a specific and inclusive list of conditions and decisions to cover every contingency. If the author of a directive has a single overwhelming preoccupation, it may indeed be possible to isolate the condition(s) and decision(s) applicable to it. But many writers of directives will begin with a short list and, finding that it rapidly expands as they consider small alterations in circumstances, wonder whether these changes affect their choices and whether specificity about them is necessary.

Anticipation of every contingency is impossible. There will always arise circumstances and decisions not directly addressed by a directive. The problem is what to do when the directive does not address the circumstances at hand. A good directive can give clues to help others reconstruct the author's preferences. This means, in turn, that caregivers must attempt to look for such clues. For example, on the one hand, a situation similar to one addressed in the directive should perhaps be treated the same way, but on the other, since it was not named, perhaps the author did not perceive it as similar. If in a deliberately narrow directive the author felt strongly only about the situations named, what sort of standard should be used to make other, presumably less important, decisions that were not addressed?[18]

The testamentary model comes to the rescue here. The last will and testament is traditionally viewed not just as a laundry list disposing of assets but as a kind of life statement, expressing the deceased's philosophy, style of life, attachments, ties to friends and family, and the like. It is relatively common and very easy to write a will that is an explicitly personal statement, conveying the deceased's views and explaining bequests in light of these views.

Similarly, instruction directives can, should, and often do contain some form of general personal statement that serves to help explain and reinforce the decisions listed (see, e.g., Cantor 1990). Such statements may be brief and sweeping or very detailed, and they may stand almost alone in the directive or accompany an extensive laundry list of do's and don'ts.

## Strengths

It is easy to appreciate the problem of how to convey treatment choices in the form of an instruction directive: Just try to write one yourself. The ambiguities of interpretation that attend position statements are matched by the difficulties of making lists that are relevant and manageable in size. Yet the combination of position statements and lists of preferences and choices can paint powerful, clear, and compelling portraits of patients and their treatment decisions. Despite the near certainty that instruction directives will not be easy to apply to all the situations that will arise, their great strength is that they actually put choices on paper. Well-written instruction directives exist as evidence of, and guides to, patients' wishes. In general, their usefulness increases with their detail. They may be endlessly argued over, but they are accessible to all concerned with the patient's care, and what they say cannot be hidden.

## State Variations on the Living Will

Living will laws now exist in all but three states.[19] They are regularly reconsidered by the legislatures of all states, and frequently amended. Statutory living-will-type advance directives, also called instruction directives, almost always deal only with the refusal of treatment, although there are a few exceptions. Living will laws came into existence for several reasons. First, they provided state legislatures with the opportunity to declare sympathy with the "death with dignity" movement. These statutes thus provide a measure of support for those who promote patients' rights and encourage caregivers to recognize treatment refusals. In many states, living will laws were passed before state appellate courts had ever issued an opinion in a treatment refusal case. The existence of such a statute has often influenced courts to give support to nonconforming directives. The presence of a statute also causes more people to write advanced directives, conforming or not, since they are perceived as approved by the state.

Second, such statutes are often sought by the medical profession. Physicians with concerns about liability and a lack of confidence in the legal process naturally seek as much protection as they can for what they perceive as risky choices. These statutes really offer little more protection than the courts would provide without them, but they are down on the books in black and white, which helps to reduce the clinician's uncertainty and increase institutional acceptance of directives.

Third, living will statutes spell out the decisions with which a legislature is willing to acknowledge agreement: a sort of least common denominator of treatment refusal. Most of these statutes declare themselves to establish an "optional, nonexclusive procedure." The message that this conveys from the legislature to health professionals and the public is, "We are sure about these provisions, so we will specify them; others may be all right too, but we will not automatically approve them."

It is important to establish that common agreement, for the reasons given above; yet it has a serious risk, as was already noted. Too often, statutory living wills are perceived as going as far as the law will allow; variations on the statutory form are viewed as unreasonable and suspicious. Thus, the appropriateness of treatment refusal ends up being measured by a legislative majority standard— what most people would feel right about doing. This majoritarian approach, though very easy to fall into and something of a natural mistake, is a mistake nonetheless.

There are many different varieties of statutory instruction directive schemes; the variations among statutes are both major and minor. There is no efficient way to talk about all of the current instruction directive statutes, and interested clinicians must simply read the complete statutes in their states in order to understand them.

## Summary

Instruction directives can take a variety of forms, with small but potentially significant variations appearing in uncountable profusion. Slavish devotion to statutory form is not necessary in order for a patient to write an instruction directive that can be implemented with a minimum of uncertainty. A caregiver who seeks honestly to evaluate the meaning and validity of such a directive will probably not be placed at legal risk in the great majority of cases.

Directives must provide evidence of their own validity. Solemn witnessing statements and notary seals are important but not indispensable indicators of validity. In an original directive that does not conform precisely to a statutory model, a statement acknowledging the importance of the decisions stated, specifically accepting their consequences, and listing both the date of writing and reaffirmation dates is likely to be viewed as providing comparable evidence of due execution. To the extent that witness statements provide external evidence of the patient's mental state, such evidence could also be provided later by patients' physicians and attorneys.

The caregiver faced with helping a patient write an instruction directive, discussing an already written directive with a patient, or interpreting a directive with the help of the patient's family, friends, personal physician, and history needs both to feel confident about taking action in response to the directive and to be flexible in assessing the degree of imagination and forethought the patient needs to exhibit in the directive in order to inspire that confidence. The writer's mental capacity is always presumed and should need no special consideration unless some reason appears to question it. The best directive to look for is one that contains a general statement of beliefs and preferences as well as specific instructions (in short, a directive of more substance than many current statutory directives) and carries the same or similarly powerful assurances of solemnity, without necessarily carrying their restrictions. These directives should be implemented so long as there are indications of the seriousness and thoughtfulness of the document and it is clear from the directive that the patient intended and understood the consequences of its application.

## PROXY DIRECTIVES: DURABLE POWERS OF ATTORNEY FOR HEALTH CARE

Proxy decision making in health care is hardly new. It takes place every time a patient is incapable of choice but a decision must be made; it is simply one way of describing the health care decision-making process under those circumstances. But there are two significant variables in this process: Who acts as proxy? And by what criteria does the proxy decide (e.g., Emanuel 1993; Emanuel and Emanuel 1992; Juengst and Weil 1989; Special Supplement 1994)? Proxy directives, which name the patient's choice of person to act as decision-maker and specifically grant decisional authority to that person, eliminate the difficulty of finding the right person—a difficulty that can be substantial when there is disagreement not only about who of several is the right person but also about the standards by which the "rightness" of the choice should be judged. The U.S. Supreme Court's decision in the *Cruzan* case (*Cruzan v. Director* 1990, O'Connor, J., concurring) effectively moved proxy directives into a position of prominence as a means of effecting patients' constitutional right to refuse treatment.

It is generally agreed that when the patient's decision is unavailable, whoever decides must use what has been labeled the "substituted judgment" standard (*In re Quinlan* 1976; *Superintendent of Belchertown State School v. Saikewicz* 1977), that is, must attempt to determine what the patient would have wanted. If enough direct evidence of the patient's preferences is not available, then the patient's general character, values, past choices, and so forth are examined, along with the caregiver's medical advice, to determine what decision the patient would have viewed as being in his or her best interests (*Matter of Conroy* 1985). This standard expresses the recognition that in making medical decisions, most individuals determine what they believe to be in their best interests by weighing medical advice along with their own values and many other nonmedical factors.

When a patient names a proxy decision-maker, the proxy's decision-making method should be discussed by the proxy and the patient. Because the proxy is deciding in the patient's place, it is understood, unless otherwise specified, that substituted judgment is intended (see chapter 5). Sometimes a proxy statute will specify a decision-making standard or standards. If the patient so directed, however, a proxy could conceivably use any of many different decisional strategies, ranging from doing whatever the doctor says to refusing everything to making decisions based on finances or even to flipping a coin. Of course, unusual standards of decision must be carefully explained and justified in the directive in order to survive a good-faith scrutiny by caregivers or courts.

Most of the time, courts that approve the appointment of proxy decision-makers specify a decisional standard like the following, from a decision of the Florida Court of Appeals: "The surrogate decisionmaker's function is to make the decision which clear and convincing evidence establishes that the patient, if competent, would make" (*In re Guardianship of Browning* 1989). But it is often difficult to distinguish decisions based on substituted judgment from decisions based on best interests considerations when the decision-maker is a family member or friend, and proxies themselves may not be able to specify their decision-making process neatly (see the discussion in chapter 5). It should be acknowledged that friends and family acting as proxies may well be imprecise in their decisional standards, and that may be perfectly appropriate, since the named proxy is the patient's own choice. It is quite likely that some patients who name their spouses as proxies expect the spouse not to determine what the patient would have wanted but to choose, based on their relationship, what the spouse thinks is best for the patient—which is a different standard.

Proxy directives provide a neat and immediate solution to the instruction directive's central flaw, the impossibility of specifying a decision in advance on every conceivable occurrence. If an instruction directive fails to cover a particular set of circumstances, the language and outlook of the directive will be used as evidence by physician, family, and friends in the attempt to construct a consistent decision for the circumstances at hand. The addition—or substitution—of a proxy directive simplifies that construction process by handing it over to one designated individual.

## The Agency Law Model

Proxy decision-making is a common concept in law, used primarily for business convenience. Most of us are familiar with the concept of voting by proxy at shareholders' meetings and with the general idea that one person can act as the agent of another for business transactions and other activities. Insurance agents, real-estate agents, and the like are persons who act on behalf of, and in the name of, a "principal"—the insurance company or the homeowner. Agents have the power to do anything in the ordinary course of business in the principal's interest and to "bind" the principal to the consequences of any such action. In short, the agent has the power to act as the principal.

This very great power is overseen and controlled by the principal in two ways: by limiting the scope of the agency granted and by the power to terminate the agency relationship. Most agency relationships are clearly circumscribed in scope and given for a short, often self-limiting term: proxy voting during the annual meeting, representation by a real-estate agent until my house is sold, managing property while I am away, etc. Moreover, the relationship between principal and agent is basically contractual and can be terminated by either party in appropriate contractual fashion. From this it follows that the authority of an agent to act for his principal terminates when the principal is no longer able to act, or to scrutinize the agent's actions, or to revoke the power. Therefore, ordinary agency terminates upon the death or incapacity of the principal.

Although terminating agency upon the principal's incapacity is consistent with most common uses of agency law, there are many other valid transactions that are made impossible by that restriction. In an attempt to strike a balance between the desire to facilitate transactions that would otherwise be impossible and the risks of permitting agents to act when they cannot be closely watched by the principal, the durable power of attorney was created. "Power of attorney" is a general term for the grant of agency power, since an attorney is an agent for the principal in legal matters. "Durable" denotes a power that survives—or, very often, does not take effect until—the incapacity of the principal.

When patients name someone to make health care decisions on their behalf should they become incapacitated, they are essentially giving to the chosen decision-maker a durable power of attorney for health care decision-making. Before *Cruzan*, few states had health care proxy statutes; instead, patient advocacy groups suggested that persons wishing to name a decision-maker use the statutory durable power of attorney, available in some form in every state, in order to add formality and legality to the grant of authority.

All states have durable power of attorney statutes; most of these are based on, or very similar to, the Uniform Durable Power of Attorney Act (1982), which defines the power this way:

### Section 1. [Definition]

A durable power of attorney is a power of attorney by which a principal designates another his attorney in fact in writing and the writing contains the words "This power of attorney shall not be affected by subsequent disability or incapacity of the principal," or "This power of attorney shall become effective upon the disability or incapacity of the principal," or similar words showing the intent of the principal that the authority conferred shall be exercisable notwithstanding the principal's subsequent disability or incapacity.

### Section 2. [Durable Power of Attorney Not Affected by Disability or Incapacity]

All acts done by an attorney in fact pursuant to a durable power of attorney during any period of disability or incapacity of the principal have the same effect and inure to the benefit of and bind the principal and his successors in interest as if the principal were competent and not disabled.

Both ordinary and durable powers of attorney as treated in these statutes deal primarily with the principal's property and financial concerns; thus, statutes generally require that a document granting a durable power be registered with the local registry of deeds, that the agent make periodic accountings before an officer of the court, and other such provisions that seem far removed from the content of health care decision-making.

Although everyone recognized that formally naming an individual to make one's health care decisions was a good idea, it was also clear that using a standard durable power of attorney to do it could be an uncertain proposition. It was not clear whether statutes providing for this grant of a standard, all-purpose durable power contemplated grants of medical decision-making power, which are much more intimate than most grants of authority to make business decisions and require an utterly different expertise. Even before *Cruzan*, a rapidly growing number of state legislatures was addressing this uncertainty by adding provisions for appointment of a proxy to their living will laws or providing a separate "durable power of attorney for health care" statute. In response to this trend, the 1989 amendments to the Uniform Rights of the Terminally Ill Act included a health care proxy clause in its model instruction directive.[20]

## The Scope of Proxy Directives

Obviously, the purposes for which a durable power of attorney is granted must be enumerated. It is necessary to say, in or accompanying a proxy directive, that the grant includes, or is limited to, the power to make health care decisions.

The scope of special durable powers of attorney designed specifically to address health care decisions might logically be broad, covering all health care decisions when the principal is incompetent. Such a proxy directive would operate like the appointment of a guardian for an incompetent patient.[21] With so broad a grant of guardianship, the agent, or attorney-in-fact, would be consulted on every decision, just as the patient would have been.

Informally, of course, family and friends fill precisely this role all the time; often it is only when refusal of lifesaving or life-prolonging treatment is contemplated that formally recognizing a proxy decision-maker is seen as necessary. Such decisions are not ordinary for patients, and therefore end-of-life decisions may need more and different knowledge of the patient than do routine authorizations of treatment. It may even appear that for a variety of reasons, the person who routinely authorizes treatment for an incompetent patient is not the right person to make a decision to terminate care.

It would be wrong for caregivers to read a grant of authority to make health care decisions so narrowly as to preclude a proxy from making these most important decisions. Most patients do want their named proxies to make these decisions, even if they have failed to say so explicitly, since the central purpose for writing an advance directive is to have those very important decisions made according to one's own wishes.

It is preferable to avoid giving proxies partial decisional authority, good for some health care choices but not others. The proxy's involvement should be what the patient's would have been. It makes sense for the patient to identify a proxy for all health care decisions, including refusal of treatment; this is the way most health care proxy statutes are now drafted.

## Strengths of Proxy Directives

There are two great advantages to proxy directives, particularly from the caregiver's point of view. First, there is no need for the caregiver (with or without the help of the hospital legal department) to puzzle out the import of an instruction directive that does not precisely apply to the decision at hand. The proxy directive provides not decisions but a decision-maker, and it is that individual's job to make and justify decisions in light of the patient's preferences and values. The availability of a proxy can ease the uncertainties and burdens of these decisions for caregivers.

Second, the appointment of a decision-maker means that decisions can be made concurrently rather than prospectively, by someone who can see the situation and discuss it with the physician instead of having to imagine and anticipate it. Thus, someone other than the physician is involved *at the time of decision*. This helps ease the concerns of those who hesitate to credit decisions made by patients when they are far removed from experiencing the disease and disability about which they are deciding by directive (Buchanan and Brock 1986). The proxy does not directly experience the patient's condition, but neither does anyone else—not even the caregiver. The proxy does, however, know the patient well and can engage in contemporaneous discussion with caregivers, thus providing them with a better opportunity to respond to the patient's desires in light of the patient's condition than is offered by most instruction directives.

Some patients may prefer naming a proxy to completing an instruction directive because proxies can exercise decision-making flexibility of a particular kind on their behalf. When patients are highly concerned not only about their end-of-life treatment but also about the needs and values of the people they will leave behind, naming a proxy can better help to ensure consideration of these matters than trying to encompass them in an instruction directive. Who is named as proxy and how the proxy is prepared for decision-making are especially significant here.

## Weaknesses of Proxy Directives

What is gained by not having to specify instructions in an advance directive is an advantage only in the writing of the document itself. The process of choosing and informing a proxy can be subject to the same challenges as writing an instruction directive. It is difficult to anticipate everything you should anticipate and to explain everything you must explain to give meaning to your choices, regardless of whether you are putting it on paper or talking with someone chosen as your proxy.

In order for a proxy to represent the patient's wishes in health care decision-making, the proxy must know as much as possible, both about the patient's specific instructions and desires and about

the personal values, preferences, past experiences, and current circumstances that form the basis for them. In some instances, the process of informing a chosen proxy may be minimal. For example, a
patient who generally follows his physician's recommendations
could name a proxy with the direction that the physician's recommendations be followed. Or a patient might name a spouse or child and
say, "Do what you think best," relying on good knowledge of the
proxy's own views and on the proxy's acquaintance with the
patient's views. These designations are based on the patient's knowledge of the decision-making patterns of the proxy or the attending
physician. In other cases, patients must do more to establish the
proxy's decision-making patterns by giving the proxy information
about themselves and their own decision-making preferences.

For many writers of advance directives, the naming and education of a proxy may be particularly difficult. Many writers of directives have strongly held views that they cannot be certain are shared
by family and friends. Family members who would not hesitate to
refuse treatment for themselves are often nonetheless reluctant to
refuse it for a loved one. As treatment refusal is an emotional and
highly controversial issue, there are certain to be many families
divided about it. Patients who cannot be sure that proxies share their
views cannot be sure that even a proxy who is trying hard to do what
the patient wants will either know what the patient's choice would
have been in a given set of circumstances or, knowing it, be able to
advocate effectively for it. This is unsettling for the patient and burdensome for the proxy. Asking a loved one to act as your advocate
under difficult circumstances such as these is a lot to ask, even
though the burden is even greater on patients who cannot get proxies
to honor their choices.

The case of Brenda Hewitt is a thought-provoking example of
this complex problem. Although Brenda Hewitt's story, described by
her common-law husband, Dr. Engelbert Schucking (1985), in the *Vil-
lage Voice* and later in the journal *Law, Medicine, and Health Care*, is
important for many reasons, one of its most moving and tragic
aspects was Dr. Schucking's loving inability to comply with Brenda's
wishes at a crucial point.

Brenda Hewitt was a diabetic with many attendant chronic problems. She was wheelchair-bound, a home dialysis patient, and in constant severe pain. She had drawn up many legal documents and
statements expressing her intention to refuse treatment and even to

refuse hospitalization if complications of her chronic illnesses arose. Dr. Schucking held her durable power of attorney and had promised to do as she wished. But when she became semiconscious, apparently as a result of a blood infection, and refused hospitalization, saying, "I want to die at home," her physician, though he also knew her wishes, refused to prescribe antibiotics unless Ms. Hewitt was hospitalized.

Dr. Schucking reluctantly agreed to take her to a hospital. Though in his account of her death he goes on to describe a horrible hospital experience, Dr. Schucking fixes his own guilt upon that decision: "I shall regret that yes till I die. . . . I knew what I was doing was wrong. I had betrayed her" (Schucking 1985, 268). Later he describes Ms. Hewitt's proxy directive in this way: "What it said, in effect, was: 'I am all yours; *you* decide how much I shall suffer; *you* judge what will be done to me. Let me live if you want me to, let me die if you think it is time'" (Schucking 1985, 268).

If a proxy directive has this meaning, then its weaknesses are clear. There are many independent individuals who do not wish to be "all" anybody's; they would like to be more certain that their own choices are implemented. And even patients who feel confident about their proxy's ability to support their choices may understandably be reluctant to impose upon a loved one the burden of advocacy, which may be emotionally overwhelming—and, for many reasons, simply too much to ask of the person who knows you best.

And, finally, there may be no one to do it. More and more adults in American society find themselves in comparative isolation after social mobility and death have diminished family connections. Even people who live socially involved lives may lack friends and family close enough to agree to take on a proxy's responsibility. Many of those who feel most strongly about their health care choices may be in this position. Of course, if there is no one to designate, a proxy directive cannot even exist.

Proxy directives do not automatically accomplish the same goals as instruction directives; that is, they do not simply present patients' prior choices, unless we know that patients have made decisions or discussed their values and preferences with their proxies when still decisionally capable. It could therefore be argued that the authority of proxies ought to be limited to the decisions available in proxy statutes unless a proxy can produce evidence (such as a letter of instruction) to show that an unusual choice accords with the patient's wishes. It could also be argued, however, that placing undue restrictions upon the authority of proxies compromises the most important advantage of proxy directives—their flexibility—and introduces too many opportunities to challenge the proxy's authority (Annas 1991). Some states attempt to address this issue by designating in their statutes which form—the instruction directive or the proxy directive— has priority in case of conflicts between them; but these states do not all agree about which takes precedence.

## COMBINING THE FORMS

The strengths and weaknesses of the two prevalent models of advance directive—instruction directives and proxy directives— should now be easy to see. Those weaknesses and strengths tend to complement each other; thus, some combination of the two models may be the best choice for clarity and certainty. A directive that contains a statement of values and preferences, specific instructions, a proxy designation, and a statement indicating the basis for the choice of proxy (e.g., "I have discussed my wishes extensively with so-and-so and name her as my attorney-in-fact in the full expectation that she will act in accordance with them") has many advantages. (See, e.g., Emanuel and Emanuel's Medical Directive, [1989, 1990], set out in chapter 1.)

Such a combined directive gives specific instructions and a statement of values that will enable caregivers to make decisions immediately if there is a delay in involving the proxy or the proxy is no longer available. The proxy designation makes it easier to assign authority for decisions falling within the cracks of the directive's specific instructions. The directive itself contains information about the patient's values and preferences; this helps to support the credibility of both the proxy and the specific instructions and helps to establish the patient's seriousness and thoughtfulness about the directive. In addition, these features ensure that the proxy knows at least something about the patient's wishes, though it is far better for the patient to discuss the designation extensively with the proxy as well. Finally, the proxy is a live and articulate person whose reasoning may be scrutinized by caregivers and who is available for discussion of the patient's options. The proxy thus is an important source of ratification of the validity not only of the directive but of the decisions made for the patient through the directive.

Whether one type of directive or the other is better, and how the two might best be combined and prioritized, used to be a subject of considerable debate. Now, however, nearly all states have statutes providing models for both types of directive, and many of them offer a single statutory form combining the two.

## A PATIENT PROXY OFFICE?

Despite the increasing use of proxy directives, however, a person who has no one to designate in a proxy directive is unable to take maximal advantage of the advance directives modeled in many state statutes. Courts often appoint guardians (sometimes including caregivers) to act on behalf of incompetent patients who have neither directives nor relatives to act as proxies. A guardian who is appointed sooner, through a proxy directive, could learn much more from conversations with the patient, so that better decisions could be made.

Since the 1960s and 1970s, many proposals have been made for the establishment of patient advocates in hospitals and other institutions. The roles of such advocates are described in a variety of ways (Kayser-Jones and Kapp 1989), but one advocacy role that has not been much discussed is that of proxy decision-maker. Though, obviously, this would be only a partial solution to the problem, patient advocates could be made available within a hospital, nursing home, retirement community, and so forth so that everyone coming into the institution capable of writing an advance directive could have conversations with an advocate and ultimately name the advocate as a proxy. Then the advocate would be called upon to make decisions for that person as necessary, based on any instruction directive written by the patient and on the conversations they have had about the patient's wishes and rationale for them.

Of course, it is difficult for strangers to gain much knowledge of a patient within a short time. Nonetheless, the neutral, official, advocacy function of these proxies should increase the likelihood that express wishes will be obeyed and implied wishes discerned. An institution-based advocate would have to be credible within the institution but supported independently of it. There must be no risk that the advocate's proxy decisions would reflect the institution's interests rather than the patient's. The size of the case load that such an advocate could handle is not clear. Moreover, taking a newly institutionalized patient through this process might take a great deal of time. It might not always be possible to equip the advocate for decisions before incapacitating illness strikes the patient. But it is a partial answer.

## A SAMPLE OF STATES

The following state statutory directives have been chosen as examples to help illustrate the complexity and variety in current state laws. Only the directives themselves are included here; readers should remember that it is vital to be familiar with the entire statute for a particular state in order to understand all that is contained in its model directive. For each state both the instruction directive and the proxy directive are given, whether they come from the same statute or are set out in two different statutes.

Readers will note that in some instances the two documents are parallel but in others they are quite different. One of the reasons for these inconsistencies is that after *Cruzan* many states with restrictive instruction directive statutes loosened the restrictions not by amending the instruction directive statute but by enacting a more liberal proxy directive statute. The resulting inconsistencies can prove extremely confusing to patients and caregivers alike. (Worst of all, some states appear to permit proxies to make decisions that patients themselves cannot make by directive—making it imperative to remember that directives can be modified and still be "legal," that is, in accord with the common law, with the Constitution, and even with the terms of most statutes.)

Statutory directives from six states (in alphabetical order) will be examined in turn.

### *Arizona*
(Arizona Living Wills and Health Care Directives Act 1994)

The following form is offered as a sample only and does not prevent a person from using other language or another form:

### 1. Health Care Power of Attorney

I, _____, as a principal, designate _____ as my agent for all matters relating to my health care, including, without limitation, full power to give or refuse consent to all medical, surgical, hospital and related health care. This power of attorney is effective on my inability to make or communicate health care decisions. All of my agent's actions under this power during any period when I am unable to make or communicate health care decisions or when there is uncertainty whether I am dead or alive have the same effect on my heirs, devisees and personal representatives as if I were alive, competent and acting for myself.

If my agent is unwilling or unable to serve or continue to serve, I hereby appoint _____ as my agent.

I have _____ I have not _____ completed and attached a living will for purposes of providing specific direction to my agent in situations that may occur during any period when I am unable to make or communicate health care decisions or after my death. My agent is directed to implement those choices I have initialed in the living will.

I have _____ I have not _____ completed a prehospital medical directive pursuant to section 36–3251, Arizona Revised Statutes.

This health care directive is made under section 36–3221, Arizona Revised Statutes, and continues in effect for all who may rely on it except those to whom I have given notice of its revocation.

_____
Signature of principal

Witness: _____     Date: _____

_____     Time: _____

Address: _____     _____
                                      Address of agent
_____

Witness: _____     _____

_____     Telephone of agent

Address: _____     _____

_____

(**NOTE:** This document may be notarized instead of being witnessed.)


## 2. Autopsy
(Under Arizona law an autopsy may be required)

If you wish to do so, reflect your desires below:

_____ 1. I <u>do not</u> consent to an autopsy.

_____ 2. I <u>consent</u> to an autopsy.

_____ 3. My agent <u>may</u> give consent to <u>or refuse</u> an autopsy.

### 3. Organ Donation
(Optional)

(Under Arizona law, you may make a gift of all or part of your body to a bank or storage facility or a hospital, physician or medical or dental school for transplantation, therapy, medical or dental evaluation or research or for the advancement of medical or dental science. You may also authorize your agent to do so or a member of your family may make a gift unless you give them notice that you do not want a gift made. In the space below you may make a gift yourself or state that you do not want to make a gift. If you do not complete this section, your agent will have the authority to make a gift of a part of your body pursuant to law.)

If any of the statements below reflects your desire, initial on the line next to that statement. You do not have to initial any of the statements.

If you do not check any of the statements, your agent and your family will have the authority to make a gift of all or part of your body under Arizona law.

_____ I do not want to make an organ or tissue donation and I do not want my agent or family to do so.

_____ I have already signed a written agreement or donor card regarding organ and tissue donation with the following individual or institution: _____

_____ Pursuant to Arizona law, I hereby give, effective on my death:

[ ] any needed organ or parts.

[ ] the following part or organs listed:

_____

_____

_____

for (check one):

[ ] any legally authorized purpose.

[ ] transplant or therapeutic purposes only.

### 4. Physician Affidavit
(Optional)

(Before initialing any choices above you may wish to ask questions of your physician regarding a particular treatment alternative. If you do speak with your doctor it is a good idea to ask your physician to complete this affidavit and keep a copy for his file.)

I, Dr. _____ have reviewed this guidance document and have discussed with _____ any questions regarding the probable medical consequences of the treatment choices provided above. This discussion with the principal occurred on _____.

(date)

I have agreed to comply with the provisions of this directive.

_____

Signature of physician

## ARTICLE 4. PREHOSPITAL MEDICAL CARE DIRECTIVES

### 36.3251. <u>Prehospital medical care directives: form; effect; definition</u>

A prehospital medical care directive shall be printed on an orange background and may be used in either letter or wallet size. The directive shall be in the following form:

**Prehospital Medical Care Directive**
(side one)

In the event of cardiac or respiratory arrest, I refuse any resuscitation measures including cardiac compression, endotracheal intubation and other advanced airway management, artificial ventilation, defibrillation, administration of advanced cardiac life support drugs and related emergency medical procedures.

Paient:_____ Date: _____

(signature or mark)

Attach recent photograph here
or provide all of the following
information below:

Date of birth _____ Sex _____
Eye color _____ Hair color _____ Race _____
Hospice program (if any) _____
Name and telephone number of patient's physician

(side two)

I have explained this form and its consequences to the signer and obtained assurance that the signer understands that death may result from any refused care checked above.

_____ Date: _____
(Licensed health care provider)

I was present when this was signed (or marked). The patient then appeared to be of sound mind and free from duress.

_____ Date: _____
(Witness)

C. A person who has a valid prehospital medical care directive pursuant to this section may wear an identifying bracelet on either the wrist or the ankle. The bracelet shall be substantially similar to identification bracelets worn in hospitals. The bracelet shall be on an orange background and state the following in bold type:

**Do Not Resuscitate**

**Patient:** _____
**Patient's physician:** _____

＊　＊　＊

The following form is offered as a sample only and does not prevent a person from using other language or another form:

### Living Will

(Some general statements concerning your health care options are outlined below. If you agree with one of the statements, you should <u>initial</u> that statement. <u>Read all of these statements carefully before you initial your selection</u>. You can also write your own statement concerning life-sustaining treatment and other matters relating to your health care. You may initial any combination of paragraphs 1, 2, 3 and 4, but if you initial paragraph 5 the others should <u>not</u> be initialed.)

_____ 1. If I have a terminal condition I <u>do not</u> want my life to be prolonged and I <u>do not</u> want life-sustaining treatment, beyond comfort care, that would serve <u>only</u> to artificially delay the moment of my death.

_____ 2. If I am in a terminal condition or an irreversible coma or a persistent vegetative state that my doctors reasonably feel to be irreversible or incurable, I <u>do</u> want the medical treatment necessary to provide care that would keep me comfortable, but I <u>do not</u> want the following:

_____ (a) cardiopulmonary resuscitation, for example, the use of drugs, electric shock and artificial breathing.

_____ (b) artificially administered food and fluids.

_____ (c) to be taken to a hospital if at all avoidable.

_____ 3. Notwithstanding my other directions, if I am known to be pregnant, I do not want life-sustaining treatment withheld or withdrawn if it is possible that the embryo/fetus will develop to the point of live birth with the continued application of life-sustaining treatment.

_____ 4. Notwithstanding my other directions I <u>do</u> want the use of all medical care necessary to treat my condition until my doctors reasonably conclude that my condition is terminal or is irreversible and incurable or I am in a persistent vegetative state.

_____ 5. I <u>want</u> my life to be prolonged to the greatest extent possible.

<u>Other or additional statements of desires</u>

I have _____ I have not _____ attached additional special provisions or limitations to this document to be honored in the absence of my being able to give health care directions.

**Points of Interest and Analysis.** Arizona's statutory directives are part of a comprehensive scheme that provides for everything in the same piece of legislation. This scheme reflects a wholesale modification of an early model living will statute. It includes both types of advance directive, autopsy and organ donation forms, and a prehospital directive, all reproduced above; it also includes a provision for surrogate decision-making in the absence of a directive. The model forms are described as samples only, except for the prehospital directive, which needs to be standardized in order to enable emergency personnel to honor it.

The Arizona statute does not define terms like "terminal condition"; however, such terms appear only in the living will—which is, really, the only place where the patient is expressing a set of choices and desires that need to be related to condition, treatment, and outcome to be comprehensible. Neither the health care power of attorney nor (atypically) the prehospital directive places any limitations on when certain decisions can be made.

Note that the health care power of attorney form explains the relationship between the agent's authority and the choices indicated in a living will. The statute also contains a clear statement of the decision-making standards for surrogates, both health care agents and those given statutory authority in the absence of a directive. The surrogate is to do what the patient said in the living will; if there is insufficient information therein, the surrogate is to decide on the basis of the patient's values; if there is still insufficient information, the surrogate is to make decisions according to a good-faith belief about the patient's best interests.

This degree of clarity about surrogate decision-making standards is admirable, and is somewhat rare in the statutes. The relationship between a living will and a proxy appointed by the patient is a newly prominent problem, since so many statutory schemes have been amended to offer both options and so many patients exercise both. The Arizona scheme contains one striking exception, however; if there is no directive, a surrogate is prohibited from making any decisions about artificial nutrition and hydration—either choosing it or refusing it. This seems designed to encourage patients to execute directives, not to encourage them to think about artificial nutrition and hydration in particular, since it is possible to execute a bare proxy designation that in itself contains no information whatsoever about what the patient wants. Moreover, it leaves unclear who has the authority to make artificial nutrition and hydration decisions if no one connected with the patient can do so. Indeed, it suggests that the effect of this provision is to make artificial nutrition and hydration mandatory in the absence of a directive, since it is arguably a medical decision to initiate it but there are few medical indications for its removal. And certainly, at least for patients without directives whose friends and family can make good-faith assertions that withholding or withdrawing artificial nutrition and hydration accords with the patient's wishes or values or is in the patient's best interest, such a limitation seems constitutionally problematic at best.

George Annas has persuasively argued that including unrelated matters like autopsy and organ donation preferences in advance directive forms can confuse or alarm patients and that, in general, it detracts from the purpose of advance directives (Annas 1991, 1993). He is right, and such addenda to advance directives should be contained in separate forms. Nevertheless, the Arizona forms for these options afford patients admirably clear explanations of what will happen if they make designations and if they do not—information that is not made explicit often enough to the public at large.

Another interesting characteristic of the Arizona form is the optional "physician affidavit." It appears intended to encourage physician-patient discussion about end-of-life decision-making, but it has the additional benefit of reassuring other physicians that a directive they had no hand in preparing was thoughtfully made. So long as its optional nature is clear (that is, so long as the lack of this affidavit does not cause providers to assume that a directive was not thought about), this is a useful addendum, regardless of whether it is signed by the physician. I expect that it is rarely signed by the physician, and it is not clear what force a signature (or lack of one) would have, as the statute itself requires health care providers to comply with directives or transfer the patient to a willing provider.

The living will form contains several provisions worth noting. First, there is an optional clause permitting (but not requiring) provision of life-sustaining treatment during pregnancy if continuing the pregnancy to live birth is possible thereby. Most statutes with pregnancy clauses mandatorily suspend directives during pregnancy, with no explicit consideration of the likelihood that live birth could result. Second, statement #4 seems unnecessary and confusing. What could failure to initial it mean? Finally, there is a place where patients can indicate whether they have attached additional statements to the standard directive. This provision calls attention to such addenda and further legitimizes patients' altering or adding to the standard choices provided in the standard form.

The Arizona statute provides protection from liability for good-faith adherence to directives, and a scheme for courts to address questions about directives. There are witnessing and notarization provisions and a standard discussion of the effects of directives on insurance. Ethics committees are given a role in some decision-making, and a reciprocity clause recognizes all directives valid by Arizona standards or the standards of the state of preparation. Throughout, Arizona's comprehensive statutory scheme sets a high standard for clarity and practicality in advance directives.

## Maine
(Maine Uniform Health-care Decisions Act 1995)

Until June 30, 1995, Maine's advance directive statutory scheme was based on the Uniform Rights of the Terminally Ill Act (URTIA). It included two brief forms, to take effect when the writer was no longer able to make or communicate health care decisions and had "an incurable and irreversible condition that, without the administration of life-sustaining treatment, will . . . cause . . . death within a relatively short time." The first form directed the attending physician "to withhold or withdraw . . . treatment that only prolongs the process of dying and is not necessary for . . . comfort or to alleviate pain." The second appointed a health care agent to make decisions on the writer's behalf regarding withholding or withdrawal of such treatment. Each included a special box and note pertaining to artificial nutrition and hydration, which explained that according to Maine law, artificial nutrition and hydration was not a life-sustaining treatment that could be withheld or withdrawn unless the box was signed.

After URTIA was superseded in 1993 by the Uniform Health-care Decisions Act, it was inevitable that Maine's statute would change as well. Maine's comprehensive statutory form is now identical to that contained in the new Uniform Act, which is set out in Chapter 1, pages 23–29. The remainder of the new statute is equally elaborate and detailed, designed to fill gaps and solve problems in current advance directives practice.

*Points of interest and analysis.* This statement introduces the statutory model form:

> The following form may, but need not be, used to create an advance health-care directive. The other sections of this Part govern the effect of this or any other writing used to create an advance health-care directive. An individual may complete or modify all or any part of the following form.

By means of this language, writers of directives are told the effect of a nonconforming directive: Changes in the statutory form are acceptable, but other portions of the statute, which specify what has to be witnessed, how revocation takes place, and so forth, will apply to any writing. This is valuable guidance, underscoring the importance of understanding the entire statutory scheme rather than just knowing the model form.

The statutory definitions section contains a definition of "capacity" that includes the elements of informed consent:

"Capacity" means the ability to have a basic understanding of the diagnosed condition and to understand the significant benefits, risks and alternatives to the proposed health care and the consequences of forgoing the proposed treatment, the ability to make and communicate a health care decision and the ability to understand the consequences of designating an agent or surrogate to make health-care decisions.

Also included is a definition of "life-sustaining treatment" which demonstrates that Maine no longer considers artificial nutrition and hydration a special category of treatment:

"Life-sustaining treatment" means any medical procedure or intervention that, when administered to a person without capacity and in either a terminal condition or a persistent vegetative state, will serve only to prolong the process of dying. "Life-sustaining treatment" may include artificially administered nutrition and hydration, which is the provision of nutrients and liquids through the use of tubes, intravenous procedures or similar medical interventions.

The statute also explicitly acknowledges the authority of emancipated minors to make advance directives, and recognizes the validity of oral instruction directives. Powers of attorney for health care must be in writing and witnessed to be valid, and may only be revoked in writing or by personal communication to the supervising health care provider. By contrast, instruction directives and any other parts of directives other than the designation of a health care agent may be revoked "in any manner that communicates an intent to revoke," the standard found in most statutes. The power to revoke is in all situations explicitly limited to individuals with capacity; incompetent revocation is not contemplated.

Maine's statute also sets forth decisionmaking standards for both health care agents and surrogates authorized by statute in the absence of a directive. The agent or surrogate is to use the patient's instructions, if any, and other known wishes, or, if necessary, to make a best interests determination, including consideration of the patient's personal values. The statue also specifies that health care decisions made by agents or surrogates are effective without judicial approval—a point that seems obvious but could help to forestall some litigation. Interestingly, health care agents must have "capacity," but capacity is not mentioned in connection with surrogates.

The surrogate decisionmaking section contains a longer than usual ranked priority list, starting with the standard spouse, adult children, or parents, but going on to adult siblings, grandchildren, nieces or nephews, aunts or uncles, other adult relatives familiar with the patient's personal values and reasonably available, or "an adult who has exhibited special concern for the patient," is familiar with the patient's personal values, and is reasonably available. Patients who have no advance directive or health care agent may disqualify certain people from acting their surrogate by so informing their supervising health care provider, in writing or in person.

A member of one of the specified classes who assumes the authority to act as surrogate must notify all family members in the specified classes "who can be readily contacted." Since more than one class member or members of more than one class could step forward as decisionmaker, the scheme to handle disagreements is elaborate. If there is disagreement within a class, the supervising health care provider may choose either to comply with the decision of the majority who have communicated their views, or to refer the class members to a neutral third party for dispute resolution or to a court. If there is a dispute between classes, the supervising provider may either comply with the decision of the class with priority or make the same referrals. But: "If the class is evenly divided concerning the health-care decision and the supervising health-care provider is so informed, that class and all individuals having lower priority are disqualified from making the decision." This unusual caveat appears to render impossible any health care decisionmaking outside of a courtroom in many instances of family disagreement, and its intended scope is unclear.

Health care providers have a number of obligations under the statute. Many relate to communication and record notation about decisions, decisionmakers, and changes in capacity. Providers are also obligated to comply with the decisions of agents and surrogates, with instruction directives, and with reasonable interpretations of instruction directives made by agents. They do not have affirmative obligations to uncover information about the decisions of patients, agents, or surrogates, including discrepancies between patients' previously expressed wishes and the choices of agents or surrogates. However, both providers and institutions may refuse to comply with any instruction or decision that "appears not to be in compliance with this Act."

In a very comprehensive conscience clause, of the variety that is becoming more common but remains untested, providers may invoke "reasons of conscience" for declining to comply with a directive or decision, and institutions may decline to comply if a directive or decision "is contrary to the policy of the institution that is expressly based on reasons of conscience and if the policy was timely communicated to the patient" or to the authorized decisionmaker. Providers and institutions may also refuse to provide "medically ineffective health care or health care contrary to generally accepted health-care standards applicable to the health-care provider or institution." All refusals require providers and institutions to promptly inform the patient or authorized decisionmaker, provide continuing care until a transfer is effected or a court issues a final order about the decision in question, and make all reasonable efforts to assist in transfer to another willing provider or institution.

Maine's take on the new Uniform Act is admirable; its new advance directive scheme is far broader and more flexible than what it replaces. Nonetheless, the Uniform Act's determination to address every problem that has arisen in the interpretation and implementation of end-of-life decisions will inevitably give rise to almost as many new ones. A pragmatic approach to advance directives should not stumble too much over the kind of confusion that arises from the inherent ambiguity of language and the many ways in which small modifications can amplify that ambiguity. The more patients, proxies, and caregivers talk together about what patients want and what directives mean, the less documentary exegesis is needed.

## *Maryland*
### (Maryland Health Care Decision Act 1994)

### Form I
### Living Will
#### (Optional Form)

If I am not able to make an informed decision regarding my health care, I direct my health care providers to follow my instructions as set forth below. (Initial those statements you wish to be included in the document and cross through those statements which do not apply.)

a. If my death from a terminal condition is imminent and even life-sustaining procedures are used there is no reasonable expectation of my recovery—

_____ I direct that my life not be extended by life-sustaining procedures, including the administration of nutrition and hydration artificially.

_____ I direct that my life not be extended by life-sustaining procedures, except that, if I am unable to take food by mouth, I wish to receive nutrition and hydration artificially.

_____ I direct that, even in a terminal condition, I be given all available medical treatment in accordance with accepted health care standards.

b. If I am in a persistent vegetative state, that is if I am not conscious and am not aware of my environment nor able to interact with others, and there is no reasonable expectation of my recovery within a medically appropriate period—

_____ I direct that my life not be extended by life-sustaining procedures, including the administration of nutrition and hydration artificially.

_____ I direct that my life not be extended by life-sustaining procedures, except that if I am unable to take food by mouth, I wish to receive nutrition and hydration artificially.

_____ I direct that I be given all available medical treatment in accordance with accepted health care standards.

c. If I am pregnant my agent shall follow these specific instructions:

_____

_____

_____

By signing below, I indicate that I am emotionally and mentally competent to make this living will and that I understand its purpose and effect.

_____

(Date)       (Signature of Declarant)

The declarant signed or acknowledged signing this living will in my presence and based upon my personal observation the declarant appears to be a competent individual.

---

(Witness)                          (Witness)
(Signature of Two Witnesses)

**Form II**
**Advance Directive**
**Part A**
**Appointment of Health Care Agent**
(Optional Form)

(Cross through if you do not want to appoint a health care agent to make health care decisions for you. If you do want to appoint an agent, cross through any items in the form that you do not want to apply.)

(1) I, _____, residing at _____

_____

appoint the following individual as my agent to make health care decisions for me _____

_____

(Full Name, Address, and Telephone Number)

Optional: if this agent is unavailable or is unable or unwilling to act as my agent, then I appoint the following person to act in this capacity

_____

_____

(Full Name, Address, and Telephone Number)

(2)  My agent has full power and authority to make health care decisions for me, including the power to:

a.  request, receive, and review any information, oral or written, regarding my physical or mental health, including, but not limited to, medical and hospital records, and consent to disclosure of this information;

b.  employ and discharge my health care providers;

c.  authorize my admission to or discharge from (including transfer to another facility) any hospital, hospice, nursing home, adult home, or other medical care facility; and

d.  consent to the provision, withholding, or withdrawal of health care, including, in appropriate circumstances, life-sustaining procedures.

(3) The authority of my agent is subject to the following provisions and limitations: _____

_____

(4) My agent's authority becomes operative (initial the option that applies):

_____ When my attending physician and a second physician determine that I am incapable of making an informed decision regarding my health care; or

_____ When this document is signed.

(5) My agent is to make health care decisions for me based on the health care instructions I give in this document and on my wishes as otherwise known to my agent. If my wishes are unknown or unclear, my agent is to make health care decisions for me in accordance with my best interest, to be determined by my agent after considering the benefits, burdens, and risks that might result from a given treatment or course of treatment, or from the withholding or withdrawal of a treatment or course of treatment.

(6) My agent shall not be liable for the costs of care based solely on this authorization.

By signing below, I indicate that I am emotionally and mentally competent to make this appointment of a health care agent and that I understand its purpose and effect.

_____     _____

(Date)          (Signature of Declarant)

The declarant signed or acknowledged signing this appointment of a health care agent in my presence and based upon my personal observation appears to be a competent individual.

_____     _____

(Witness)                              (Witness)

(Signature of Two Witnesses)

**Part B**
**Advance Medical Directive**
**Health Care Instructions**
(Optional Form)

(Cross through if you do not want to complete this portion of the form. If you do want to complete this portion of the form, initial those statements you want to be included in the document and cross through those statements that do not apply.)

If I am incapable of making an informed decision regarding my health care, I direct my health care providers to follow my instructions as set forth below. (Initial all those that apply.)

(1) If my death from a terminal condition is imminent and even if life-sustaining procedures are used there is no reasonable expectation of my recovery—

_____I direct that my life not be extended by life-sustaining procedures, including the administration of nutrition and hydration artificially.

_____I direct that my life not be extended by life-sustaining procedures, except that if I am unable to take food by mouth, I wish to receive nutrition and hydration artificially.

(2) If I am in a persistent vegetative state, that is, if I am not conscious and am not aware of my environment or able to interact with others, and there is no reasonable expectation of my recovery—

_____I direct that my life not be extended by life-sustaining procedures, including the administration of nutrition and hydration artificially.

_____I direct that my life not be extended by life-sustaining procedures, except that if I am unable to take food by mouth, I wish to receive nutrition and hydration artificially.

(3) If I have an end-stage condition, that is a condition caused by injury, disease, or illness, as a result of which I have suffered severe and permanent deterioration indicated by incompetency and complete physical dependency and for which, to a reasonable degree of medical certainty, treatment of the irreversible condition would be medically ineffective—

_____I direct that my life not be extended by life-sustaining procedures, including the administration of nutrition and hydration artificially.

_____I direct that my life not be extended by life-sustaining procedures, except that if I am unable to take food by mouth, I wish to receive nutrition and hydration artificially.

_____I direct that no matter what my condition, medication not be given to me to relieve pain and suffering, if it would shorten my remaining life.

_____I direct that no matter what my condition, I be given all available medical treatment in accordance with accepted health care standards.

(4) If I am pregnant, my decision concerning life-sustaining procedures shall be modified as follows:

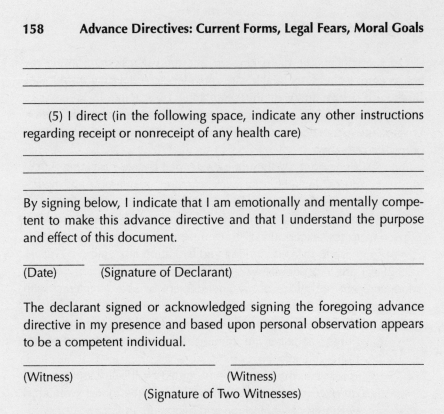

_____

_____

_____

(5) I direct (in the following space, indicate any other instructions regarding receipt or nonreceipt of any health care)

_____

_____

_____

By signing below, I indicate that I am emotionally and mentally competent to make this advance directive and that I understand the purpose and effect of this document.

_____     _____

(Date)          (Signature of Declarant)

The declarant signed or acknowledged signing the foregoing advance directive in my presence and based upon personal observation appears to be a competent individual.

_____     _____

(Witness)                        (Witness)

(Signature of Two Witnesses)

*Points of interest and analysis.* Maryland's statutory advance directive scheme is also new and comprehensive. In addition to containing several different types of optional model forms, the Maryland statute includes provisions for prehospital DNR orders and for decision-making by surrogates in the absence of an advance directive; a provision detailing the circumstances under which patients may be treated in the absence of consent; and a detailed plan for patient transfer when a provider refuses to comply with a directive. Most interestingly, the statute also contains provisions establishing that providers need not render medically ineffective treatment and setting up procedures for settling disputes about the delivery of treatment asserted to be ineffective. These provisions are also reflected in the language of the model forms, which provide patients with the option of requesting maximal treatment "in accordance with accepted health care standards." (Compare this language with that of the comparable option in the Arizona living will form, "I want my life prolonged to the greatest extent possible.")

The Maryland statute offers two different model forms, stating that they may be adopted in whole or in part or may be combined, and that different forms may be used. (Oral directives are also explicitly recognized and are stated to have the same effect as a written directive if they are made in the presence of the attending physician and one witness and recorded in the patient's medical record.) The two forms are rather confusingly named: The instruction directive is appropriately labeled a "living will;" but the health care proxy designation is called an "advance directive," presumably because it has two parts, one the proxy appointment and the other a list of instructions for the proxy.

Both the living will and the advance directive instruction list utilize a clear and simple model: I want no life-sustaining treatment, I want nothing but artificial nutrition and hydration, or I want everything. The two forms, however, do not have completely parallel structures, which could produce some confusion. Nor are they substantively parallel. Rather, the health care proxy is given the authority to withhold or withdraw treatment, if the patient so directs, when the patient has an "end-stage condition," whereas the living will form contains provisions addressing only terminal conditions and PVS. Thus, it appears that proxies have authority to refuse treatment in a wider range of circumstances than do patients themselves. This significant lack of substantive parallelism is not explained and presents another circumstance in which patients with a high degree of concern would do well to add a clause covering end-stage conditions to their living will forms.

The Maryland statute contains standard treatments of revocation, the effect of directives on insurance and liability questions, reciprocity, and the like. This scheme covers at least as much ground as Arizona's and Maine's. There is even a provision declaring that providing patients with model advance directive forms and helping them complete them is not the unauthorized practice of law!

### New Hampshire
(New Hampshire Living Wills Act 1992;
New Hampshire Durable Power of Attorney for Health Care 1991)

A person of sound mind who is 18 years of age or older may execute at any time a document commonly known as a living will, directing that no life-sustaining procedures be used to prolong his life when he is in a terminal condition or permanently unconscious. The document shall only be effective if the person is permanently incapable of participating in decisions about his care, and it may be, but need not be, in form and substance substantially as follows:

## DECLARATION

Declaration made this _____ day of _____ (month, year). I, _____, being of sound mind, willfully and voluntarily make known my desire that my dying shall not be artificially prolonged under the circumstances set forth below, do hereby declare:

If at any time I should have an incurable injury, disease, or illness certified to be a terminal condition or a permanently unconscious condition by 2 physicians who have personally examined me, one of whom shall be my attending physician, and the physicians have determined that my death will occur whether or not life-sustaining procedures are utilized or that I will remain in a permanently unconscious condition and where the application of life-sustaining procedures would serve only to artificially prolong the dying process, I direct that such procedures be withheld or withdrawn, and that I be permitted to die naturally with only the administration of medication, sustenance, or the performance of any medical procedure deemed necessary to provide me with comfort care. I realize that situations could arise in which the only way to allow me to die would be to discontinue artificial nutrition and hydration. In carrying out any instruction I have given under this section, I authorize that artificial nutrition and hydration not be started or, if started, be discontinued. (yes) (no) (Circle your choice and initial beneath it. If you do not choose "yes", artificial nutrition and hydration will be provided and will not be removed.)

In the absence of my ability to give directions regarding the use of such life-sustaining procedures, it is my intention that this declaration shall be honored by my family and physicians as the final expression of my right to refuse medical or surgical treatment and accept the consequences of such refusal.

I understand the full import of this declaration, and I am emotionally and mentally competent to make this declaration.

_____
Signed

State of _____
_____ County

We, the following witnesses, being duly sworn each declare to the notary public or justice of the peace or other official signing below as follows:

1.  The declarant signed the instrument as a free and voluntary act for the purposes expressed, or expressly directed another to sign for him.
2.  Each witness signed at the request of the declarant, in his presence, and in the presence of the other witness.
3.  To the best of my knowledge, at the time of the signing the declarant was at least 18 years of age, and was of sane mind and under no constraint or undue influence.

_____ Witness
_____ Witness

The affidavit shall be made before a notary public or justice of the peace or other official authorized to administer oaths in the place of execution, who shall not also serve as a witness, and who shall complete and sign a certificate in content and form substantially as follows:

Sworn to and signed before me by _____, declarant
_____ and _____, witnesses
on _____

_____
Signature

Official Capacity

The disclosure statement which must accompany a durable power of attorney for health care shall be in substantially the following form:

### INFORMATION CONCERNING THE DURABLE
### POWER OF ATTORNEY FOR HEALTH CARE

THIS IS AN IMPORTANT LEGAL DOCUMENT. BEFORE SIGNING THIS DOCUMENT YOU SHOULD KNOW THESE IMPORTANT FACTS:

Except to the extent you state otherwise, this document gives the person you name as your agent the authority to make any and all health care decisions for you when you are no longer capable of making them yourself. "Health care" means any treatment, service or procedure to maintain, diagnose or treat your physical or mental condition. Your agent, therefore, can have the power to make a broad range of health care decisions for you. Your agent may consent, refuse to consent, or withdraw consent to medical treatment and may make decisions about withdrawing or withholding life-sustaining treatment. Your agent cannot consent or direct any of the following: commitment to a state institution, sterilization, or termination of treatment if you are pregnant and if the withdrawal of that treatment is deemed likely to terminate the pregnancy unless the failure to withhold the treatment will be physically harmful to you or prolong severe pain which cannot be alleviated by medication.

You may state in this document any treatment you do not desire, except as stated above, or treatment you want to be sure you receive. Your agent's authority will begin when your doctor certifies that you lack the capacity to make health care decisions. If for moral or religious reasons you do not wish to be treated by a doctor or examined by a doctor for the certification that you lack capacity, you must say so in the document and name a person to be able to certify your lack of capacity. That person may not be your agent or alternate agent or any person ineligible to be your agent. You may attach additional pages if you need more space to complete your statement.

If you want to give your agent authority to withhold or withdraw the artificial providing of nutrition and fluids, your document must say so. Otherwise, your agent will not be able to direct that. Under no conditions will your agent be able to direct the withholding of food and drink for you to eat and drink normally.

Your agent will be obligated to follow your instructions when making decisions on your behalf. Unless you state otherwise, your agent will have the same authority to make decisions about your health care as you would have had if made consistent with state law.

It is important that you discuss this document with your physician or other health care providers before you sign it to make sure that you understand the nature and range of decisions which may be made on your behalf. If you do not have a physician, you should talk with someone else who is knowledgeable about these issues and can answer your questions. You do not need a lawyer's assistance to complete this document, but if there is anything in this document that you do not understand, you should ask a lawyer to explain it to you.

The person you appoint as agent should be someone you know and trust and must be at least 18 years old. If you appoint your health or residential care provider (e.g. your physician, or an employee of a home health agency, hospital, nursing home, or residential care home, other than a relative), that person will have to choose between acting as your agent or as your health or residential care provider; the law does not permit a person to do both at the same time.

You should inform the person you appoint that you want him or her to be your health care agent. You should discuss this document with your agent and your physician and give each a signed copy. You should indicate on the document itself the people and institutions who will have signed copies. Your agent will not be liable for health care decisions made in good faith on your behalf.

Even after you have signed this document, you have the right to make health care decisions for yourself so long as you are able to do so, and treatment cannot be given to you or stopped over your objection. You have the right to revoke the authority granted to your agent by informing him or her or your health care provider orally or in writing.

This document may not be changed or modified. If you want to make changes in the document you must make an entirely new one.

You should consider designating an alternate agent in the event that your agent is unwilling, unable, unavailable, or ineligible to act as your agent. Any alternate agent you designate will have the same authority to make health care decisions for you.

THIS POWER OF ATTORNEY WILL NOT BE VALID UNLESS IT IS SIGNED IN THE PRESENCE OF TWO (2) OR MORE QUALIFIED WITNESSES WHO MUST BOTH BE PRESENT WHEN YOU SIGN AND ACKNOWLEDGE YOUR SIGNATURE. THE FOLLOWING PERSONS MAY NOT ACT AS WITNESSES:

— the person you have designated as your agent;

— your spouse;

— your lawful heirs or beneficiaries named in your will or a deed; ONLY ONE OF THE TWO WITNESSES MAY BE YOUR HEALTH OR RESIDENTIAL CARE PROVIDER OR ONE OF THEIR EMPLOYEES.

**137–J:15 Durable Power of Attorney; Form.** The durable power of attorney shall be in substantially the following form.

## DURABLE POWER OF ATTORNEY FOR HEALTH CARE

I, _____, hereby appoint _____
of _____ as my agent to make any and all
health care decisions for me, except to the extent I state otherwise in
this document or as prohibited by law. This durable power of attorney
for health care shall take effect in the event I become unable to make
my own health care decisions.

STATEMENT OF DESIRES, SPECIAL PROVISIONS, AND LIMITATIONS
REGARDING HEALTH CARE DECISIONS.

For your convenience in expressing your wishes, some general
statements concerning the withholding or removal of life-sustaining
treatment are set forth below. (Life-sustaining treatment is defined as
procedures without which a person would die, such as but not limited
to the following: cardiopulmonary resuscitation, mechanical respiration, kidney dialysis or the use of other external mechanical and techno-
logical devices, drugs to maintain blood pressure, blood transfusions,
and antibiotics.) There is also a section which allows you to set forth
specific directions for these or other matters. If you wish you may indicate your agreement or disagreement with any of the following statements and give your agent power to act in those specific circumstances.

1. If I become permanently incompetent to make health care decisions, and if I am also suffering from a terminal illness, I authorize my agent to direct that life-sustaining treatment be
   discontinued. (YES) (NO) (Circle your choice and initial beneath
   it.)
2. Whether terminally ill or not, if I become permanently unconscious I authorize my agent to direct that life-sustaining treatment be discontinued. (YES) (NO) (Circle your choice and initial
   beneath it.)
3. I realize that situations could arise in which the only way to
   allow me to die would be to discontinue artificial feeding (artificial nutrition and hydration). In carrying out any instructions I
   have given above in #1 or #2 or any instructions I may write in
   #4 below, I authorize my agent to direct that (circle your choice
   of (a) or (b) and initial beside it):
   (a) artificial nutrition and hydration not to be started or, if
       started, be discontinued,

– or –

   (b) although all other forms of life-sustaining treatment be withdrawn, artificial nutrition and hydration continue to be
given to me.

   (If you fail to complete item 3, your agent will not have the
power to direct the withdrawal of artificial nutrition and
hydration.)

4. Here you may include any specific desires or limitations you
deem appropriate, such as when or what life-sustaining treatment you would want used or withheld, or instructions about
refusing any specific types of treatment that are inconsistent with
your religious beliefs or unacceptable to you for any other reason. You may leave this question blank if you desire.

_____

_____

_____

_____

(attach additional pages as necessary)

In the event the person I appoint above is unable, unwilling or
unavailable, or ineligible to act as my health care agent, I hereby
appoint _____ of _____ as
alternate agent.

I hereby acknowledge that I have been provided with a disclosure
statement explaining the effect of this document. I have read and understand the information contained in the disclosure statement.

The original of this document will be kept at _____
and the following persons and institutions will have signed copies:

_____

_____

_____

In witness whereof, I have hereunto signed my name this _____ day of
_____, 19___

_____

Signature

I declare that the principal appears to be of sound mind and free
from duress at the time the durable power of attorney for health care is
signed and that the principal has affirmed that he or she is aware of the
nature of the document and is signing it freely and voluntarily.

Witness: _____ Address: _____

Witness: _____ Address: _____


STATE OF NEW HAMPSHIRE
COUNTY OF

The foregoing instrument was acknowledged before me this _____ day
of _____, 19___, by _____


_____
Notary Public/Justice of the Peace

My Commission Expires:


***Points of Interest and Analysis.*** Unlike the foregoing statutes,
New Hampshire's advance directive scheme has two separate statutory parts: the living will statute, first enacted in 1985, and a newer
health care power of attorney statute. This is a rather common statutory pattern, which holds great potential for discrepancies between
the two statutory types of advance directives.

New Hampshire's living will form originally addressed only
terminal conditions, but the statute was later amended to include permanent unconsciousness; the result is a somewhat confusing combination of an extremely conservative standard ("death will occur whether
or not life sustaining procedures are utilized") with a decidedly
broader one ("the application of life-sustaining procedures would
serve only to artificially prolong the dying process"). An examination
of the statutory definitions not contained in the model document
clears up the confusion (or does it?): Life-sustaining treatment is
defined as treatment that serves only to artificially postpone the
moment of death—a third use of language that doesn't quite match
either standard in the model document but officially explains them
both. ("Sustenance" is defined to mean "natural" eating and drinking,
*not* artificial nutrition and hydration.)

Formally, the durable power of attorney looks quite different. No
mention is made of sustenance, however defined. There is yet
another definition of life-sustaining treatment: "Procedures without
which a person would die." But the options offered for patients to
agree or disagree with are the same in both statutes. The lack of paral-

lelism may thus be more apparent than real. Interestingly, however, the living will statute states that a document may, but need not be, substantially in the form of the model—whereas the durable power of attorney for health care *shall* be substantially like the statutory model and *must* be accompanied by an elaborate disclosure statement (actually a very useful addendum).

One other aspect of New Hampshire's scheme is worth examining on the issue of parallelism between types of advance directive: the treatment of pregnancy. No mention is made of pregnancy in the model living will declaration. Instead the statute contains an exceptions clause, which states in part: "Nothing in this chapter shall be construed to condone, authorize, or approve the withholding of life-sustaining procedures from or to permit any affirmative or deliberate act or omission to end the life of a pregnant woman by an attending physician when such physician has knowledge of the woman's pregnant condition." Although this may sound like no one is permitted to refuse treatment while pregnant, in fact it merely helps to make clear that the statute creates no presumption supporting treatment refusal in pregnancy and that whatever rights pregnant women might have are to be determined legislatively or judicially apart from the statute.

The durable power of attorney statute does much the same thing in a rather different way. Again, the document itself makes no mention of pregnancy, but the disclosure statement lists things the agent cannot consent to, including "termination of treatment if you are pregnant and if the withdrawal of treatment is deemed likely to terminate the pregnancy" unless continued treatment will be harmful or painful. Elsewhere, it is stated that nothing in the statute gives the agent authority to "consent to withholding life-sustaining treatment from a pregnant patient unless, to a reasonable degree of medical certainty, as certified on the patient's chart by the attending physician and an obstetrician who has examined the patient, such treatment or procedures will not maintain the patient in such a way as to permit the continuing development and live birth of the unborn child" or will cause harm or pain to the patient.

The difference in the durable power of attorney statute is the explicit recognition that there is no point in precluding agents from consenting to withdrawal of treatment that is unlikely to succeed in preserving a pregnancy. Thus, this statute clearly conveys a limited authority to refuse treatment on behalf of pregnant patients—something that is not clearly stated in the living will statute but makes obvious medical sense. Whether an agent may legally refuse treatment that can preserve a pregnancy, however, falls outside the purview of both the living will statute and the durable power of attorney statute.

Finally to be noted is the way New Hampshire deals with potential conflicts between a living will and a durable power of attorney: The newer statute, the durable power of attorney for health care, takes precedence.

### *North Carolina*
### (Right to Natural Death Act 1992;
### Health Care Powers of Attorney Act 1993)

Use of this form in the creation of a health care power of attorney is lawful and is authorized pursuant to North Carolina law. However, use of this form is an optional and nonexclusive method for creating a health care power of attorney and North Carolina law does not bar the use of any other or different form of power of attorney for health care that meets the statutory requirements.

1.  Designation of health care agent.
    I, _____, being of sound mind, hereby appoint
    Name:_____
    Home Address:_____
    Home Telephone Number _____ Work Telephone Number _____
    as my health care attorney-in-fact (herein referred to as my "health care agent") to act for me and in my name (in any way I could act in person) to make health care decisions for me as authorized in this document.
    If the person named as my health care agent is not reasonably available or is unable or unwilling to act as my agent, then I appoint the following persons (each to act alone and successively, in the order named), to serve in that capacity: (Optional)
    A. Name:_____
    Home Address:_____
    Home Telephone Number_____ Work Telephone Number_____
    B. Name: _____
    Home Address:_____
    Home Telephone Number _____ Work Telephone Number _____
    Each successor health care agent designated shall be vested with the same power and duties as if originally named as my health care agent.

2. Effectiveness of appointment.

(Notice: This health care power of attorney may be revoked by you at any time in any manner by which you are able to communicate your intent to revoke to your health care agent and your attending physician.)

Absent revocation, the authority granted in this document shall become effective when and if the physician or physicians designated below determine that I lack sufficient understanding or capacity to make or communicate decisions relating to my health care and will continue in effect during my incapacity, until my death. This determination shall be made by the following physician or physicians (You may include here a designation of your choice, including your attending physician, or any other physician. You may also name two or more physicians, if desired, both of whom must make this determination before the authority granted to the health care agent becomes effective.):

_____

_____

_____

3. General statement of authority granted.

Except as indicated in section 4 below, I hereby grant to my health care agent named above full power and authority to make health care decisions on my behalf, including, but not limited to, the following:

A. To request, review, and receive any information, verbal or written, regarding my physical or mental health, including, but not limited to, medical and hospital records, and to consent to the disclosure of this information;

B. To employ or discharge my health care providers;

C. To consent to and authorize my admission to and discharge from a hospital, nursing or convalescent home, or other institution;

D. To give consent for, to withdraw consent for, or to withhold consent for, X ray, anesthesia, medication, surgery, and all other diagnostic treatment procedures ordered by or under the authorization of a licensed physician, dentist, or podiatrist. This authorization specifically includes the power to consent to measures for relief of pain.

E. To authorize the withholding or withdrawal of life-sustaining procedures when and if my physician determines that I am terminally ill, permanently in a coma, suffer severe dementia, or am in a persistent vegetative state. Life-sustaining procedures are those forms of medical care that only serve to artificially prolong the dying process and many include mechanical ventilation, dialysis, antibiotics, artificial nutrition and hydration, and other forms of medical treatment which sustain, restore or supplant vital bodily functions. Life-sustaining procedures do not include care necessary to provide comfort or alleviate pain.

I DESIRE THAT MY LIFE NOT BE PROLONGED BY LIFE-SUSTAINING PROCEDURES IF I AM TERMINALLY ILL, PERMANENTLY IN A COMA, SUFFER SEVERE DEMENTIA, OR AM IN A PERSISTENT VEGETATIVE STATE.

F.  To exercise any right I may have to make a disposition of any part or all of my body for medical purposes, to donate my organs, to authorize an autopsy, and to direct the disposition of my remains.

G.  To take any lawful actions that may be necessary to carry out these decisions, including the granting of releases of liability to medical providers.

4.  Special provisions and limitations.

(Notice: The above grant of power is intended to be as broad as possible so that your health care agent will have authority to make any decisions you could make to obtain or terminate any type of health care. If you wish to limit the scope of your health care agent's powers, you may do so in this section.)

In exercising the authority to make health care decisions on my behalf, the authority of my health care agent is subject to the following special provisions and limitations (Here you may include any specific limitations you deem appropriate such as: your own definition of when life-sustaining treatment should be withheld or discontinued, or instructions to refuse any specific types of treatment that are inconsistent with your religious beliefs, or unacceptable to you for any other reason.):

_____

_____

_____

5.  Guardianship provision.

If it becomes necessary for a court to appoint a guardian of my person, I nominate my health care agent acting under this document to be the guardian of my person, to serve without bond or security.

6. Reliance of third parties on health care agent.
    A. No person who relies in good faith upon the authority of or any representations by my health care agent shall be liable to me, my estate, my heirs, successors, assigns, or personal representatives, for actions or omissions by my health care agent.
    B. The powers conferred on my health care agent by this document may be exercised by my health care agent alone, and my health care agent's signature or act under the authority granted in this document may be accepted by persons as fully authorized by me and with the same force and effect as if I were personally present, competent, and acting on my own behalf. All acts performed in good faith by my health care agent pursuant to this power of attorney are done with my consent and shall have the same validity and effect as if I were present and exercised the powers myself, and shall inure to the benefit of and bind me, my estate, my heirs, successors, assigns, and personal representatives. The authority of my health care agent pursuant to this power of attorney shall be superior to and binding upon my family, relatives, friends, and others.
7. Miscellaneous provisions.
    A. I revoke any prior health care power of attorney.
    B. My health care agent shall be entitled to sign, execute, deliver, and acknowledge any contract or other document that may be necessary, desirable, convenient, or proper in order to exercise and carry out any of the powers described in this document and to incur reasonable costs on my behalf incident to the exercise of these powers; provided, however, that except as shall be necessary in order to exercise the powers described in this document relating to my health care, my health care agent shall not have any authority over my property or financial affairs.
    C. My health care agent and my health care agent's estate, heirs, successors, and assigns are hereby released and forever discharged by me, my estate, my heirs, successors, and assigns and personal representatives from all liability and from all claims or demands of all kinds arising out of the acts or omissions of my health care agent pursuant to this document, except for willful misconduct or gross negligence.
    D. No act or omission of my health care agent, or of any other person, institution, or facility acting in good faith in reliance on

the authority of my health care agent pursuant to this health care power of attorney shall be considered suicide, nor the cause of my death for any civil or criminal purposes, nor shall it be considered unprofessional conduct or as lack of professional competence. Any person, institution, or facility against whom criminal or civil liability is asserted because of conduct authorized by this health care power of attorney may interpose this document as a defense.

8.  Signature of principal.

By signing here, I indicate that I am mentally alert and competent, fully informed as to the contents of this document, and understand the full import of this grant of powers to my health care agent.

_____    _____
Signature of Principal             Date

9.  Signatures of Witnesses.

I hereby state that the Principal _____, being of sound mind, signed the foregoing health care power of attorney in my presence, and that I am not related to the principal by blood or marriage, and I would not be entitled to any portion of the estate of the principal under any existing will or codicil of the principal or as an heir under the Intestate Succession Act, if the principal dies on this date without a will. I also state that I am not the principal's attending physician, nor an employee of the principal's attending physician, nor an employee of the health facility in which the principal is a patient, nor an employee of a nursing home or any group care home where the principal resides. I further state that I do not have any claim against the principal.

Witness: _____    Date: _____
Witness: _____    Date: _____


STATE OF NORTH CAROLINA
COUNTY OF _____


## CERTIFICATE


I, _____ a Notary Public for _____
County, North Carolina, hereby certify that _____

appeared before me and swore to me and to the witnesses in my presence that this instrument is a health care power of attorney, and that he/she willingly and voluntarily made and executed it as his/her free act and deed for the purposes expressed in it.

I further certify that _____ and _____, witnesses, appeared before me and swore that they witnessed _____ sign the attached health care power of attorney, believing him/her to be of sound mind; and also swore that at the time they witnessed the signing (i) they were not related within the third degree to him/her or his/her spouse, and (ii) they did not know nor have a reasonable expectation that they would be entitled to any portion of his/her estate upon his/her death under any will or codicil thereto then existing or under the Intestate Succession Act as it provided at that time, and (iii) they were not a physician attending him/her, nor an employee of an attending physician, nor an employee of a health facility in which he/she was a patient, nor an employee of a nursing home or any group-care home in which he/she resided, and (iv) they did not have a claim against him/her. I further certify that I am satisfied as to the genuineness and due execution of the instrument.

This the _____ day of _____, 19 ___

_____
Notary Public

My Commission Expires:

_____

(A copy of this form should be given to your health care agent and any alternate named in this power of attorney, and to your physician and family members.)

### 'Declaration Of A Desire For A Natural Death'

I, _____, being of sound mind, desire that, as specified below, my life not be prolonged by extraordinary means or by artificial nutrition or hydration if my condition is determined to be terminal and incurable or if I am diagnosed as being in a persistent vegetative state. I am aware and understand that this writing authorizes a physician to withhold or discontinue extraordinary means or artificial nutrition or hydration, in accordance with my specifications set forth below:

(Initial any of the following, as desired):

— If my condition is determined to be terminal and incurable, I authorize the following:
  — My physician may withhold or discontinue extraordinary means only.
  — In addition to withholding or discontinuing extraordinary means if such means are necessary, my physician may withhold or discontinue either artificial nutrition or hydration, or both.
— If my physician determines that I am in a persistent vegetative state, I authorize the following:
  — My physician may withhold or discontinue extraordinary means only.
  — In addition to withholding or discontinuing extraordinary means if such means are necessary, my physician may withhold or discontinue either artificial nutrition or hydration, or both.

This the _____ day of _____
                         Signature _____

    I hereby state that the declarant, _____,
being of sound mind signed the above declaration in my presence and that I am not related to the declarant by blood or marriage and that I do not know or have a reasonable expectation that I would be entitled to any portion of the estate of the declarant under any existing will or codicil of the declarant or as an heir under the Intestate Succession Act if the declarant dies on this date without a will. I also state that I am not the declarant's attending physician, or an employee of a health facility in which the declarant is a patient or an employee of a nursing home or any group-care home where the declarant resides. I further state that I do not now have any claim against the declarant.

                         Witness _____
                         Witness _____

The clerk or the assistant clerk, or a notary public may, upon proper proof, certify the declaration as follows:

## 'Certificate'

I, _____, Clerk (Assistant Clerk) of Superior Court or Notary Public (circle one as appropriate) for _____ County hereby certify that _____, the declarant, appeared before me and swore to me and to the witnesses in my presence that this instrument is his Declaration Of A Desire For A Natural Death, and that he had willingly and voluntarily made and executed it as his free act and deed for the purposes expressed in it.

I further certify that _____ and _____, witnesses, appeared before me and swore that they witnessed _____, declarant, sign the attached declaration, believing him to be of sound mind; and also swore that at the time they witnessed the declaration (i) they were not related within the third degree to the declarant or to the declarant's spouse, and (ii) they did not know nor have a reasonable expectation that they would be entitled to any portion of the estate of the declarant upon the declarant's death under any will of the declarant or codicil thereto then existing or under the Intestate Succession Act as it provides at that time, and (iii) they were not a physician attending the declarant or an employee of an attending physician, or an employee of a health facility in which the declarant was a patient or an employee of a nursing home or any group-care home in which the declarant resided, and (iv) they did not have a claim against the declarant. I further certify that I am satisfied as to the genuineness and due execution of the declaration.

This the _____ day of _____

                Clerk (Assistant Clerk) of Superior Court or
                Notary Public (circle one as appropriate) for
                the County of _____

***Points of Interest and Analysis.*** Like New Hampshire, North Carolina has two different statutory model forms, rather than a single comprehensive statutory scheme. Moreover, the model instruction directive, Declaration of a Desire for a Natural Death, is an old-style instruction directive, originally drafted to address terminal illness, that has been amended to include persistent vegetative state and to explicitly authorize refusal of artificial nutrition and hydration, whereas the health care power of attorney statute is new.

The instruction directive statute includes an elaborate preamble:

The General Assembly recognizes as a matter of public policy that an individual's rights include the right to a peaceful and natural death and that a patient or his representative has the fundamental right to control the decisions relating to the rendering of his own medical care, including the decision to have extraordinary means withheld or withdrawn in instances of a terminal condition. This Article is to establish an optional and nonexclusive procedure by which a patient or his representative may exercise these rights. . . . Nothing in this Article shall impair or supersede any legal right or legal responsibility which any person may have to effect the withholding or withdrawal of life-sustaining procedures in any lawful manner.

The statute prefaces the model directive with a set of requirements and procedures for withholding or withdrawing treatment and then states: "The following form is specifically determined to meet the requirements above."

The model directive's operative statutory term, "extraordinary means," is archaic but is defined the same way that "life-sustaining treatment," "life-prolonging procedures," and other such more meaningful terms are defined by other states. "Terminal" is deliberately not defined, and it has been interpreted broadly. North Carolina also has one of the earliest statutes enumerating surrogate decision-makers when there is no directive.

The newness of the health care power of attorney statute gives rise to discrepancies both characteristic and unusual. The general purpose clause contains language that is very similar to that preceding the living will statute, but that reflects its "younger" status:

The General Assembly recognizes as a matter of public policy the fundamental right of an individual to control the decisions relating to his or her medical care, and that this right may be exercised on behalf of the individual by an agent chosen by the individual. The purpose of this Article is to establish an additional, nonexclusive method for an individual to exercise his or her right to give, withhold, or withdraw consent to medical treatment when the individual lacks sufficient understanding or capacity to make or communicate health care decisions.

A recent amendment then states the intention that the instruction directive scheme and the health care power of attorney be consistent, but gives an instruction directive priority in case of conflict.

The proxy statute gives the agent authority to refuse treatment when the patient suffers from "severe dementia"—an undefined term that appears to give the health care agent (and the patient who has one) broader decision-making authority than the patient has under an instruction directive (or a surrogate has in the absence of a directive). Fortunately, this lack of formal consistency is mitigated by the statutes' clear recognition that alterations to the model form are permissible; thus, patients who do not name agents should be able to make and enforce comparable choices to limit treatment in their Declarations.[22] A more unusual discrepancy arises in the revocation clauses, however. The living will statute provides for revocation by the declarant "in any manner by which he is able to communicate his intent to revoke, without regard to his mental or physical condition." In contrast, the proxy statute states: "A health care power of attorney may be revoked by the principal at any time, so long as the principal is capable of making and communicating health care decisions." This is arguably a higher standard, one more in accord with ordinary expectations about decision-making than is the very lenient standard expressed in the living will statute and in most revocation clauses generally. See the discussion of revocation standards in chapter 5.

### Pennsylvania
(Advance Directive for Health Care Act 1992)

A declaration may but need not be in the following form and may include other specific directives including, but not limited to, designation of another person to make the treatment decision for the declarant if the declarant is incompetent and is determined to be in a terminal condition or to be permanently unconscious.

### DECLARATION

I, _____, being of sound mind, willfully and voluntarily make this declaration to be followed if I become incompetent. This declaration reflects my firm and settled commitment to refuse life-sustaining treatment under the circumstances indicated below.

I direct my attending physician to withhold or withdraw life-sustaining treatment that serves only to prolong the process of my dying, if I should be in a terminal condition or in a state of permanent unconsciousness.

I direct that treatment be limited to measures to keep me comfortable and to relieve pain, including any pain that might occur by withholding or withdrawing life-sustaining treatment.

In addition, if I am in the condition described above, I feel especially strong about the following forms of treatment:

I ( ) do ( ) do not want cardiac resuscitation.

I ( ) do ( ) do not want mechanical respiration.

I ( ) do ( ) do not want tube feeding or any other artificial or invasive form of nutrition (food) or hydration (water).

I ( ) do ( ) do not want blood or blood products.

I ( ) do ( ) do not want any form of surgery or invasive diagnostic tests.

I ( ) do ( ) do not want kidney dialysis.

I ( ) do ( ) do not want antibiotics.

I realize that if I do not specifically indicate my preference regarding any of the forms of treatment listed above, I may receive that form of treatment.

Other instructions:

I ( ) do ( ) do not want to designate another person as my surrogate to make medical treatment decisions for me if I should be incompetent and in a terminal condition or in a state of permanent unconsciousness. Name and address of surrogate (if applicable):

Name and address of substitute surrogate (if surrogate designated above is unable to serve):

I made this declaration on the _____ day of _____ (month, year).

Declarant's signature: _____

Declarant's address: _____

The declarant or the person on behalf of and at the direction of the declarant knowingly and voluntarily signed this writing by signature or mark in my presence.

Witness's signature: _____

Witness's address: _____

Witness's signature:  _____

Witness's address:   _____

*Points of Interest and Analysis.*  Pennsylvania's recently enacted statute is short and sweet, but still employs a rather extensive checklist. The legislative purpose clause is interesting; it states that competent adults have a "qualified right to control decisions relating to their own medical care." The qualifications are put this way: "This right is subject to certain interests of society, such as the maintenance of ethical standards in the medical profession and the preservation and protection of human life." The origins of the right lie in technology's capacity to prolong life "beyond natural limits" and the possibility that life prolongation may be painful, burdensome, and undignified. The purpose clause also states, as quite a few states do, that the existence of advance directive statutes creates no presumption one way or another about the intent of anyone who has no directive.

Pennsylvania is one of only a few states to permit at least some minors to execute advance directives. Persons executing directives must be eighteen, or have graduated high school, or have married. Marriage is usually an emancipating condition; high-school graduation presumably indicates some degree of maturity. The statutory definition of "life-sustaining treatment" specifically includes artificial nutrition and hydration, even though it and other forms of life-sustaining treatment are listed separately in the model directive. More confusingly, the language of the directive is focused on treatment refusal, and the checklist of treatments is described as an addition, to be completed if the patient feels "especially strong" about any; but the directive also states that if a preference is not specifically indicated in the checklist, that form of treatment may be provided—which seems at odds with the baseline statement of the directive and could make it difficult to interpret the wishes of a patient who completes the directive otherwise appropriately but checks nothing. Perhaps this is why a lawyerly clause is included to explain that if "any specific direction" should be held invalid, that should not affect the validity of other directions that can be honored "without the invalid direction."

A provision addressing emergency medical services permits emergency personnel to honor an original of a statutory declaration upon notification of the "medical command physician." (Most statutory schemes instead provide a different form solely for out-of-hospital settings but do not then require the notification step.) There is also a pregnancy clause that, like New Hampshire's, permits treatment withdrawal when live birth will not be possible or continued treatment will be harmful or painful. Pennsylvania's language is far more unequivocal than New Hampshire's, however, in stating that unless one of these conditions obtains, life-sustaining treatment must be given to pregnant women. This is consistent with the legislative purpose clause but gives rise to serious constitutional questions. (Perhaps this is the reason a severability clause is included as well, making clear that if any portion of the statutory scheme is held to be unconstitutional, the rest shall remain in force as though the invalidated portion had never been included.)

## READING DIRECTIVES

Even this cursory examination of just a few statutory model advance directives has demonstrated the complexity and variety of the ways statutory advance directives facilitate identifying and honoring patients' choices. It now seems clear that a legalistic view of directives can only result in overwhelming confusion and that directives make best sense as documents of engagement, of moral persuasion (Weir 1994), a beginning of conversation and commitment. But what follows that beginning is crucial.

It is easy to make a persuasive case for the superior validity and guidance of a very complex, multifunctional advance directive. People who want to control their own medical decisions through advance directives are well advised to prepare comprehensive directives reflecting their preferences and reasoning. But this book is directed also to physicians and other caregivers who must interpret and implement directives. What help is knowing what a really good directive is if you are likely to see directives that are not so comprehensive or are quite different from what you consider useful guidance?

First and most important, caregivers have a vital role to play with all of their patients in advising them, before they are incapable of decision-making, about making good advance directives—or, at the very least, advising them to begin thinking about what they might want to happen if they become gravely impaired.

Second, both in giving that advice and in reading directives, caregivers must think beyond the advance directive forms given by statutory models. In a sense, caregivers attempting to interpret and honor advance directives are acting as proxy decision-makers for their patients, attempting to use all they know of their patients to interpret and apply their directives fully and fairly. They should advise patients to do more than what is found in statutes, and more importantly, they should not read and judge directives by statutory models. Directives that do not look the way living will statutes prescribe may nonetheless be perfectly valid for all intents and purposes. The fear of liability for implementing nonconforming directives is largely unfounded; so long as the directive gives its readers adequate guidance and assurance that it was written with understanding of its gravity and its consequences, most nonconforming directives will not even be challenged, and those that are stand a good chance of being found valid.

Recognizing that the model directives contained in living will statutes not only are never free from problems but also invite excessively legalistic thinking about treatment refusal, an extremely accomplished and distinguished collection of legal scholars and practitioners, the Legal Advisors Committee for Concern for Dying, some years ago drafted a model "Right to Refuse Treatment Act" (Legal Advisors Committee 1983), which does *not* contain a model directive. Instead, after defining some of the key terms it employs, the Act simply and clearly sets out the scope of the patient's power to write advance directives of both the instruction type and the proxy type and specifies very general minimum requirements for a directive's validity:

### Section 2.
A competent person has the right to refuse any medical procedure or treatment, and any palliative care measure.

### Section 3.
A competent person may execute a declaration directing the withholding or withdrawal of any medical procedure or treatment or any palliative care measure which is in use or may be used in the future in the person's medical care or treatment, even if continuance of the medical procedure or treatment could prevent or postpone the person's death from being caused by the person's disease, illness or injury. The declaration shall be in writing, dated and signed by the declarant in the presence of two adult witnesses. The two witnesses must sign the declaration and by their signatures indicate they believe the declarant's execution of the declaration was understanding and voluntary.

**Section 5.**

A declarant shall have the right to appoint in the declaration a person authorized to order the administration, withholding or withdrawal of medical procedures and treatment in the event that the declarant becomes incompetent. A person so authorized shall have the power to enforce the provisions of the declaration and shall be bound to exercise this authority consistent with the declaration and the authorized person's best judgment as to the actual desires and preferences of the declarant. No palliative care measure may be withheld by an authorized person unless explicitly provided for in the declaration. Physicians and health care providers caring for incompetent declarants shall provide such authorized persons all medical information which would be available to the declarant if the declarant were competent.

The straightforward, nonformulaic approach of this model act helps to make clear that a directive can take any form that makes the patient's wishes known and appears to have been prepared voluntarily and with understanding.

Most of the time caregivers will face statutory model advance directives, because that is what people think they have to write. These directives can present guidance problems for clinicians. Sometimes they, like the statutes they follow, say very little; in other places they are as elaborate and confusing as the complex, much-amended statutes that give rise to them. When a directive can be applied to the decision faced, there is, of course, no problem; nonetheless, the clinician acting in good faith should try to supplement the directive's guidance with all of the usual means of learning about the patient, including conversation with family and friends, consultation with the patient's other physicians, complete familiarity with the patient's medical history, and the like.

These same means of learning about the patient must also be used, and are of considerably greater importance, when the directive does not appear to apply directly to the decision faced. A directive that seems to give little guidance must become the basis for the clinician's attempt to find decisional guidance—not the excuse for a failure to ascertain or to honor the patient's wishes.

How shall the clinician know when a directive should be honored? Perhaps it is easier to say when a directive should not be honored. First, if, after the clinician makes a good-faith effort to interpret it in the light of all other information, the directive does not provide reasonably clear guidance for the decision faced, it will not be possible to implement it.

Second, and related, if it is so incomplete or radically inconsistent as to call into question the presumption that the patient had decisional capacity and deliberately intended it to be effective, it should not be implemented.

Third, if persuasive external evidence (from family, friends, etc.) is so in conflict with the directive as to raise serious doubts about its validity when written, it ought not to be implemented.[23]

In each of these situations, when the directive cannot simply be honored, the caregiver should use the directive as some evidence of the patient's wishes in order to come to a decision based on the patient's wishes and medical judgment, with the help of the patient's family and friends or of a hospital ethics committee. If this is not possible, the caregiver should turn the problem over to another authorized decision-maker (e.g., to a court or a legal guardian). Every directive must be taken as far as it can be taken in good faith to discern the answers it is trying to provide. See chapter 5 for further discussion of this problem.

# 5

# Directions for Decision: When Documents Don't Do It All

By focusing on written advance directives, this volume is tackling the easiest part of the problem of medical decision-making.[1] Any caregiver who regards the patient's autonomous choices and preferences as important will find advance directives to be, at the very least, important guidance. Advance directive policy will undoubtedly help—has already helped—to inform the larger policy discussion. But because encouraging written directives cannot provide answers in every case, a brief discussion of decision-making in the absence of advance directives is appropriate here. It is also necessary to discuss some of the issues and problems that arise in implementing advance directives. Directives aren't ever just "on" or "off." Even before they are implemented, directives are always a source of information about the patient's wishes, a starting point for discussion, and evidence. When they go into effect, directives often need to be carefully interpreted and applied to the facts at hand. And even determining when they should be in effect can be less than straightforward.

Good-faith engagement with a patient's wishes by means of an advance directive is always challenging; indeed, this accounts for the ever-increasing popularity of proxy directives, which give caregivers a designated person to work things through with. Growing experience with implementation of directives has begun to make clear that the context of end-of-life decision-making has a profound impact on decisions made not only for patients who have directives, but also for those who do not. Thus, this chapter examines decision-making in the absence of directives, as well as some issues of interpretation.

Discussing what happens to patients without written directives helps those faced with writing, advising about, or reading and evaluating advance directives to understand them in the context of the legitimate concerns of others, thus making them easier to write as wanted and to read as intended. Advance directives let loose in the world are not marching orders but documents of engagement. As discussed in chapter 3, advance directives depend, in their writing and application, upon both the value of autonomy and the value of community. There will often be many people whose concern for the patient engenders their involvement when a decision needs to be made. There may be some patients whose directives are clear and complete and whose family, friends, and caregivers all agree in their support of the choices expressed therein. More often, perhaps, there will be questions. Clinicians should be prepared to contend with all the potential sources of evidence about the patient's wishes and best interests even in the presence of a directive. It will help, then, to know how much credit to give those sources.

## THE CONTEXT OF MEDICAL CHOICES

To make sense of advance directives, we need to understand the place they fill in the larger picture of medical decision-making, for no one can evaluate a directive without knowing both the consequences of honoring it and the consequences of determining it to be invalid.

Advance directives are often likened to wills—hence the popular name "living will."[2] But they differ from wills in crucial and little-noted respects (Francis 1989).

Most of us know a few things about wills. Most important, if we die without one, the state will dispose of our property according to an "intestate succession" formula established by law. Even though we may not know what the formula is, we probably know that it exists; moreover, we can readily find out what it is. We can decide whether we want to do something different from the formula and whether we are willing to go to the trouble of writing a will about it. We know that the formula also tells us what the state will do if we do write a will and it is ruled invalid. So we know what we risk by making a will that does not provide all the necessary indicia of validity or one that contains unconventional, challengeable dispositions.

We may also realize that the law of intestate succession is not an arbitrary formula. It names property dispositions according to a conventional social morality: Parents, spouse, and children are the principal beneficiaries. If we realize this, we will know that individuals can do almost anything they want with their property, so long as they clearly explain what they want to do and give reasons for departing drastically from the social norm (for example, for disinheriting all one's children in favor of an obscure charity administered through a Swiss bank account). Two values are at work here: First is the strong pull of the social order, as represented by the law that prescribes a formula for property distribution without a will, and, second and counter to it, great respect for individual choice, which must nonetheless prove its soundness by careful documentation. Everyone knows that many things can go wrong with a last will and testament; yet the overall scheme is simple, and its rules are straightforward.

In contrast, it is a significant problem for advance directives that we do not agree what will happen if you do not have one. American society is in the midst of struggling toward a moral consensus on this very question, and we may never reach it. We are not even sure what sort of consensus we should seek. Suppose that you have not made an advance directive and, comatose and terminally ill, you face being placed on a respirator. Should you be treated because, without written evidence of your preferences, the only reasonable thing to do is to treat you? Should you be treated because you did not express a preference in writing for nontreatment and therefore you must want treatment? Should evidence of your values and verbal statements govern the decision? Or should only your "best interests" be considered?

Requiring a written directive in order to withhold or withdraw treatment gives caregivers a clear and unequivocal action plan that appears to be based on respect for autonomy. According to this reasoning, patients who are motivated to refuse treatment may do so readily, simply by making an advance directive; therefore, if there is no directive, there is no desire to limit treatment. But this is not a fair assumption. To presume that only people with living wills do not want treatment imposes upon all patients a degree of foresight that may not be available to many people with unexpected illnesses.[3]

Indeed, it quite clear that many people without directives have well-developed preferences about end-of-life treatment (Layson et al. 1994). Why, then, does the number of persons with directives continue to hover under 20 percent of the U.S. population, despite the educational effects of the PSDA and increasing public attention to the problem (Brock 1994; Emanuel 1993)?

Chapter 4's discussion of the PSDA reviewed the reasons for concern that hospital inpatients, and the other clients and residents of health care facilities addressed by that legislation, may be the wrong populations to target for completion of advance directives. Many people have argued that outpatient and community education is a better focus. Still, in my view most state statutory advance directive documents contain their own barriers to execution. They require explanation and discussion, preferably with a health care provider as well as with the named health care agent. This takes time, and probably a portion of a physician visit. But time may not be as great a problem as the witnessing and notarization requirement.

It's likely that for every completed directive, there is another sitting around in someone else's papers, completely filled out except for the witnessing and notarization. Finding a notary and getting to the notary together with two witnesses who meet the statutory requirements can be a somewhat daunting task. Probably one of the best things institutions do to implement the PSDA is simply making notaries (and witnesses) more readily available.

This also means that people who go to lawyers to do their advance directives are more likely to complete one, since notaries are readily available in law offices (Emanuel 1994). These directives, however, are likely to end up in safe-deposit boxes with wills and other important papers, instead of being discussed and shared with caregivers and family, as they should, simply because that is the way lawyers tend to think.

We could perhaps force a flowering of foresight by legislating this scheme, mandating treatment if no directive exists; after all, it is true that knowing what will happen to your property without a will spurs people to make wills. But the law of intestate succession grew also out of a consensus about what most people wanted to do with their property, or at least a judgment about what good citizens ought to want—to give to the "natural objects of their bounty." Do we agree that people who have not made advance directives generally want treatment? Or that they should want it? It seems clear that we do not. We probably agree that in certain situations it is fair to presume that patients want treatment: for example, in the classic medical emergency. But where serious disability and short-term continuation of life are common treatment outcomes, we cannot claim consensus yet about what patients want (Danis et al., 1988). If we decided to force consensus by legislative choice, such a policy could be legitimated only by careful, serious, and explicit consideration of the advantages and disadvantages of such a move and its effects on the right to refuse treatment.

A beneficence-based decision to treat persons without advance directives because treatment is in their best interests is at least as difficult to support as the assumption that not having a directive is an expression of preference for treatment. Although this view seems plausible and in accordance with the ethics of the health professions, on closer examination it is difficult to grasp its meaning. We cannot say with consistency whether determining the patient's best interests is a medical or a nonmedical activity (Annas and Glantz 1986; *Canterbury v. Spence* 1972; *Cobbs v. Grant* 1972). We cannot state with certainty and generalizability who should make this determination or what should be considered in making it. Nor can we readily predict with certainty whether treatment or nontreatment will be the beneficent choice in a given case, however the prior questions have been decided.

The search continues for societal consensus about decision-making in the absence of advance directives, and the terms of the public conversation are beginning to change. Recently, in the *New England Journal of Medicine*, Dr. Marcia Angell proposed that persons reliably diagnosed as being in a persistent vegetative state be denied life-prolonging treatment unless they request it by directive or proxy (Angell 1994). She reasons that, as a result of advances in medical knowledge about PVS (Cranford 1991; Kinney et al. 1994; Multi-Society Task Force on PVS 1994), it is possible to state definitively that persons in PVS will not recover and cannot experience benefit (or burden) from their continued existence. Further, because the cost to society of maintaining persons in PVS is high in terms of both dollars and resources that could be expended elsewhere to produce benefits perceptible to patients, Dr. Angell argues that requiring persons who wish to be maintained on PVS to declare their wishes affirmatively is a just societal posture.

This intriguing and controversial proposal avoids the problems of attempting categorical best interests determinations by addressing a specific condition in which the patient is said by definition to have no current interests on which a best interests determination may be based. The problem of ascertaining the patient's best interests under other circumstances continues, and is discussed in more detail below.

Perhaps we will be able to agree on who should decide and on what factors should be considered. If so, patients without advance directives will have some idea of what will happen in general when a decision becomes necessary, even though they will still have no idea what will happen to them. Even the best possible knowledge, then, is precious little. Indeed, one of the foremost legal scholars in this field asserts the existence of a consensus about forgoing life-sustaining treatment (Meisel 1992). He names eight points of consensus, ranging from the existence of a right to refuse treatment to the preferred order of decision-making standards.[4] The consensus he sets forth is accurate enough, but quite general. Its existence is of great importance, but the guidance it can provide for individual cases is still minimal.

Moreover, patients who have written directives cannot necessarily protect themselves from being regarded as though they have not. Even under the PSDA, advance directives may not be discovered until it is too late, or may never be found at all. They may be invalidated, or they may not give guidance for the decision for which they are needed, or their language may require interpretation. In all of these instances, patients' caregivers, friends, and family will be unable to rely exclusively on the directive and will have to make decisions based, at least in part, on other decision-making principles.

## RECONSTRUCTING REFUSAL: SUBSTITUTED JUDGMENT

As we know from the emergency exception to the informed consent requirement (*Canterbury v. Spence* 1972, 788–89; Meisel 1979), physicians are presumed to act in their patients' best medical interests in advising, ordering, and performing treatment. When patients are unable to consent to treatment, physicians are sometimes permitted to proceed on the basis of their judgment of the patient's best interests, or they may serve as medical advisors to a court, a court-appointed guardian, or family members charged with making a decision in the patient's best interests (Baron 1978, 1979; *Superintendent of Belchertown State School v. Saikewicz* 1977). Treatment decision-making thus appears to present a neat dichotomy: If the patient is decisionally capable, do as the patient says; if not, do what the doctor says.

Treatment refusal complicates this simple scheme, however. The controversial decision-making doctrine known as "substituted judgment" (Annas 1979; Buchanan and Brock 1986; Harmon 1990; *In re A.C.* 1990; President's Commission 1983; Ramsey 1978; Tribe 1988, 1368–69), first developed to justify making disbursements of money from the estates of incompetents for the benefit of family members, came to be applied in cases where family members disagreed with medical decisions about treating incapacitated patients. According to this doctrine, a patient who cannot decide should be decided for by somebody else who acts as a true proxy, making the decision the patient would have made if able to decide.

On its face, this appears to be an entirely different standard from one that looks to the patient's best interests. The earliest medical applications of substituted judgment, however, explicitly pitted medical against psychosocial views of the patient's best interests, giving court approval for subjecting mentally retarded patients to the medical demands of major surgery to donate kidneys to siblings of normal intellect, on the basis that the retarded sibling would be more harmed by loss of a family member than by loss of a kidney (*Strunk v. Strunk* 1969).

The first case to apply substituted judgment to treatment refusal was the celebrated 1976 *Quinlan* decision (*In re Quinlan* 1976). Before her unexpected disability struck, Karen Quinlan had in casual conversation expressed opinions consistent with the desire to avoid life-prolonging medical treatment. Later these statements appeared to have some relevance to the decisions at issue when she was no longer capable of decision-making. They were, however, too vague for the Quinlan court to rely upon them as conclusive evidence of her treatment preferences. Thus, though the court reasoned that patients' treatment decisions were supported by the right of privacy, it could not find that Karen Quinlan had made a competent decision to refuse treatment.[5]

In order to make a decision on her behalf now, the court had to declare that incapacitated patients like Karen Quinlan held the same privacy right as did competent patients. The difference lay only in that incapacitated patients needed the assistance of a proxy to discover and declare the decision the patient would make if competent to do so. The court imagined a transient moment of lucidity for Ms. Quinlan in order to convey the nature of the decision that a proxy would be asked to make.

In the 1977 *Saikewicz* decision, where substituted judgment reached its full flower (*Superintendent of Belchertown State School v. Saikewicz* 1977), the transient moment of lucidity became a complete, rather than just a partial, fiction. Joseph Saikewicz had always been profoundly retarded and could not understand his circumstances. Whereas in *Quinlan* the court saw the proxy's task as that of reconstructing a prior decisionally capable self and determining its wishes about a current problem, the *Saikewicz* court was forced to imagine the existence of an unprecedented decisionally capable self suffering under unnatural constraints of irremediable ignorance. This was the only way it could determine what a temporarily aware and therefore entirely imaginary Joseph Saikewicz would face and what he would choose. If it did not perform this contortion, the court apparently thought it would be forced to treat never-capable persons differently from formerly capable persons in a way that would be fundamentally unfair. Perhaps it thought that according to the best interests standard, never-capable persons would always have to be treated.

Because personal values come strongly into play in end-of-life decision-making, the courts recognized that reliance on the best interests standard in cases like Karen Quinlan's might not be sufficient to take account of patients' values. There are obvious problems with using the substituted judgment standard instead, however, especially with patients like Joseph Saikewicz. Almost before the ink was dry on the *Quinlan* decision, courts and commentators began attempting to reformulate, rehabilitate, or replace it. Some of these efforts are discussed below. Still, substituted judgment can be a useful, if sometimes crude, decision-making tool, and many courts continue to apply it, requiring proxies to make "the decision the patient would make if competent." The influential Court of Appeals for the District of Columbia strongly affirmed substituted judgment as the appropriate decision-making standard in end-of-life decision-making (*In re A.C.* 1990), but the Supreme Court in *Cruzan* permitted Missouri to require the use of the subjective standard instead (*Cruzan v. Director* 1990).

## Who Decides?

The families of adult decisionally incapable patients were the first to seek decisional authority in treatment refusal cases. Parents, adult children, siblings and other relatives, and longtime friends have all, in various circumstances, been given authority to make substituted judgments for decisionally incapable patients. Court-appointed guardians have also been appointed to make substituted judgments when family and friends are unavailable or are thought to have a conflict of interest making them inappropriate proxies.

It is important to recognize that *no* relative of a decisionally incapable adult patient has any legal decision-making authority for the patient unless the patient has named that person as a proxy in a directive, or the court appoints that person as the patient's permanent or temporary guardian, or a state statute specifically conveys such authority. This seems puzzling at first. Physicians and other caregivers have always relied extensively on family members for information and decision-making. Moreover, many courts recently have emphasized that life-and-death decisions are properly private—that they should be made whenever possible by agreement between physicians and family and should not be judicially reviewed in every instance. That sounds like relatives are being given legal authority—and it also implies that patients who might prefer to have a friend or a lover as proxy will not be able to enforce their wishes if their families disapprove. But the crucial matter—the basis for decision—is yet to be addressed. Understanding the basis for decision will clarify how caregivers should view the decision-making role of family members and others.

## On What Basis?

A true substituted judgment is defined as what the patient would have wanted. Family and close friends are chosen as substitute decision-makers because of what they know about the patient. Their personal experience with the patient gives them access to information, direct and indirect, about the patient's preferences, values, character, habits, beliefs, desires, fears, hopes, and plans. It is precisely this information that must be assembled into a prediction on the patient's behalf.

Relying on close, interested parties to determine accurately what the patient wants has its risks. Interested parties may not be objective, confusing their own interests with those of the patient. In contrast, court-appointed guardians acting as surrogate decision-makers are substantially less likely to confuse patients' needs with their own. These guardians, however, must go out and gather information about the patient—information that family and friends already have. Court appointment of guardians also ensures that patients who are alone, without relatives or other "natural" advocates, can still have the benefit of substituted judgment.[6]

Recently courts and commentators have begun to realize with new clarity that reliance on judicial review of treatment decisions can be cumbersome, expensive, and time-consuming. Judicial review is also more likely to be abstract and "juiceless" and to result in conservative decisions (Burt 1988; Wolf 1990). Encouraging private decisional consensus where possible, perhaps with the help of a consulting ethics committee, is coming to be seen as more flexible, realistic, and potentially faithful to the patient's interests (Coordinating Council 1993).

Whether the decisional forum is public or private, the authority enjoyed by family members according to substituted judgment is only the authority to provide to caregivers good-faith input on the patient's putative choice—to provide *evidence*. That this authority is unappealable by default in many cases does not necessarily mean the family has the right to decide; it means only that the family is presumptively the best means of discovering the patient's choice. Therefore, if there is reason to doubt that the family is best for this purpose, the caregiver (or a court if necessary) must rely not on the family but on the best proxy, who could be a friend, neighbor, or lover.

Many adults may be better represented by friends than by family members rendered distant geographically, temporally, or generationally. The difficulty is that in the absence of a written directive, it may not be easy for a caregiver to discern that a family member is not the best proxy or that the family's choice reflects their own needs as much as it does the patient's interests. Some commentators (Dresser 1986; King 1991; Rhoden 1988, 1990) have suggested that this is not a bad thing—that rigid separation of patients' interests from the interests of their moral communities is artificial, potentially impossible, and not particularly realistic or productive. Thus, it is important that patients who wish to define their own moral communities and to distinguish their own wishes from the needs of their families write directives that can do so.

In the *Cruzan* decision, the U.S. Supreme Court permitted the State of Missouri to routinely disqualify family members as decision-makers for adults without advance directives, even when there was every reason to believe in the family's good intentions and in the accuracy of the evidence they brought to the decision. As a result, public and scholarly concern that families might sometimes overreach their role has been largely replaced by the realization that acknowledging families as "natural guardians" for their members makes for better outcomes in general than the alternative of decision-making by strangers (King 1991; Meisel 1992; Veatch 1993; but see Baron 1991). This shift in viewpoint has been marked by a considerable increase since *Cruzan* in the number of states with statutes governing surrogate decision-making in the absence of advance directives. As of mid-1995, half the states had passed such statutes.[7]

Such statutes list family members in an order of priority.[8] These family members are accorded by statute the authority to make decisions for the patient; this reinforces the authority of the family's knowledge of the patient and of the evidence the family holds about the patient's wishes or likely preferences. In these states it is especially important that individuals who would prefer a decision-maker other than immediate family execute an advance directive naming a health care proxy. The existence of such a statute, however, should not preclude any caregiver from expressing concern about the appropriateness of a proxy's choices—but only if there is good reason for concern. How best to use the available information in deciding for the patient should be discussed by caregivers and families working together.

When an advance directive exists, the role of family and friends changes. No longer primary sources of evidence, family and friends become clarifiers and supplementers of the directive unless named as proxies. Family and friends do have a role and an interest in the honoring of any directive; where possible, they should be involved in the directive's formulation, or at least alerted to its existence while the author is still decisionally capable and can discuss it. But families do not have the power to overrule or invalidate a directive because they disagree with it or are upset by it, and they should not be granted that power, unless it be by patients themselves. Only genuine, persuasive evidence from families that the directive should not be honored—for example, because it is fraudulent or because the patient was not decisionally capable when it was made—should be grounds for seeking consultation from an ethics committee or court.

## THE NEW BEST INTERESTS

The counterfactual contortions demanded by the substituted judgment standard in cases like *Saikewicz* have raised the question whether substituted judgment really has a place in many cases (Annas 1988, Dresser 1986; Harmon 1990; Rhoden 1988). Joseph Saikewicz's pain, fear, and resistance to blood transfusions and other aspects of his treatment just did not add up to a choice about treatment. Nor do patients with little or no accessible history present enough on which to base a genuine and distinctive choice. The introduction of substituted judgment permanently moved discussion beyond the dichotomy of the patient's choice or doctor's choice; but when information about patients and their preferences does not add up to enough to support a substituted judgment, it must be used in some other way.

Reexamining what the court did in the *Saikewicz* case led other courts, critics, and theorists to think more deeply about the best interests standard (Annas 1979, Buchanan 1979; Buchanan and Brock 1986; Capron 1984; Gutheil and Appelbaum 1983; Hunter 1985; President's Commission 1983; Hastings Center 1987). The results of these efforts have been expounded extensively in the literature and might be summed up in the following way: Patients make health care decisions in what they view as their own best interests. Their determination of their best interests comes from combining their own (nonmedical) beliefs and values, the physician's assessment of their best (medical) interests, and their preferences, feelings, and experiences. Thus, an advance directive or a true substituted judgment reflects the patient's best interests as the patient sees them. When a surrogate decision-maker tries to determine what the patient would have wanted, the decision-maker is determining the patient's best interests in this sense.

Joseph Saikewicz's beliefs and values were nonexistent or unknown. Medical opinion suggested that treatment could afford some chance of a short remission of his disease. Yet he responded to treatment with uncomprehending fear and pain that was harmful in itself and made treatment difficult and stressful. The court's reasoning about what he would have wanted could have been put this way: Because of his adverse response to treatment and his relatively small chance of a brief survival with the discomforts of treatment, it was in his best interests not to treat him.

This way of assembling the factors relevant to health care decisions on behalf of decisionally incapable patients has a satisfying consistency, as it places all information about the patient's preferences and probable choice on a continuum. A clear oral statement of the patient's wishes constitutes evidence equivalent to an advance directive. At the other end of the spectrum, an alone, unknown, comatose patient's future may be decided "objectively," solely according to medical judgment. In between, a "modified objective" standard can consider both "objective" medical information and "subjective" information about the patient's beliefs, values, and preferences, weighing each according to their persuasiveness. In 1976 the New Jersey Supreme Court refused to consider Karen Quinlan's conversations with friends about life-sustaining treatment in its decision about her because it rightly viewed them as casual, vague, and therefore not very helpful to its determination. But in a later decision introducing a modified objective standard of decision, the same court stated that it should have considered her statements, giving them only the weight they deserved, rather than disregarding them entirely because they were not decisive (*Matter of Conroy* 1985). And even more recently, taking up where *Conroy* left off, Dresser has called for careful, sensitive assessment of the subjective experience of incompetent patients in order to weigh the benefits and burdens of their treatment options fully and fairly (Dresser 1994a; Dresser and Whitehouse 1994).

Most courts now examine and weigh all relevant statements by patients, and most find them persuasive. A few courts—for example, those in New York State and in Missouri—set very high evidentiary standards and have ordered treatment in cases where apparently reliable evidence, including advance directives and decisions by named proxies, supported the removal of treatment (*Cruzan v. Harmon* 1988; *Evans v. Bellevue Hospital* 1987). Distressing as these decisions are to patients and their advocates, they are still a distinct minority. Moreover, reasonable decisions can still be made under such a "clear and convincing evidence" standard (*In re A.K.* 1989; *In re Guardianship of Browning* 1990), and courts and legislatures are free to select less rigid evidentiary standards or to empower families as decision-makers (Areen 1987; Gianelli 1990; *Cruzan v. Director* 1990).

## Acceptable Choice and the Quality of Life

Although it makes logical sense to employ this new best interests standard rather than substituted judgment in deciding on behalf of incompetent patients without advance directives, there is little reason to think that using different names will produce very different decisions so long as the process is carefully undertaken under either standard. Whether both standards are equally likely to result in unacceptable quality-of-life judgments is a more difficult question to answer. Judicially reviewed decisions do, however, incorporate a brake against the temptation to devalue decisionally incapable patients: There are some choices that neither medicine nor society currently accepts as being in a patient's best interest, even if the patient is permanently incapacitated. Patients may autonomously make these choices, of course; but if they have neither done so nor left persuasive evidence that they would, it may be appropriate for surrogate decision-makers to feel constrained not to make those decisions on their behalf. The range of choices acceptable under the new best interests standard will thus be somewhat narrowed, bounded by professional and societal consensus.[9]

Without a directive, many courts might hesitate to permit a proxy decision-maker to refuse standard treatments that would undoubtedly prevent the death of a patient not terminally ill or permanently unconscious—for example, antibiotics to cure pneumonia in a brain-injured but not comatose young adult. Artificial nutrition and hydration have been withdrawn from severely demented patients in some cases, where there is at least some evidence that the patient would have so chosen. Rebecca Dresser maintains that such decisions in the absence of directives rely excessively but covertly on the family's needs and interests and on quality-of-life judgments. She believes that although such factors have some place in decisions, their role can only be appropriately limited if they are clearly acknowledged and balanced against whatever interests in continued life and/or potential recovery the incapacitated patient currently enjoys (Dresser 1994a, 1986; Dresser and Whitehouse 1994). Nancy Rhoden takes a different approach, however, arguing persuasively for a presumption in favor of family choice when there is no directive (Rhoden 1988). And Robert Veatch advocates a reasonableness standard, which would acknowledge that reasonable decision-makers might make choices with which reasonable others disagree (Veatch 1993). This standard would permit surrogates some discretion in interpreting what is best for the patient. Veatch points out that "the common rhetoric" doesn't acknowledge the desirability of such discretion. Caregivers could further their own understanding by thinking in Veatch's terms, however: "Reasonableness" could help us to move from potentially endless wrangling over what's "best" to a more realistic posture about how health care decisions are and should be made.

## Food and Fluids for Vegetative Patients: The Limits of Consensus

The withdrawal or withholding of artificial nutrition and hydration from patients in persistent vegetative states represents the single most troublesome and disputed choice to be faced in the absence of an advance directive. It pushes the boundaries of moral comfort for the community for two reasons: Patients in persistent vegetative states are arguably not "terminally ill" (many are projected to have nearly normal life spans), and food and fluids, even delivered through sophisticated medical technology and therefore classifiable as "treatment," seem to have a symbolic, relational importance for caregivers and families that may make their nonprovision appear inhumane.

A few states have attempted to preclude patients from refusing nutrition and hydration by advance directive or from refusing any treatment when in persistent vegetative states, for the foregoing reasons. Most courts, on the other hand, have been willing to withdraw nasogastric or gastrostomy tubes from patients in persistent vegetative states whose families are able to present credible evidence in support of their claim that the patient would have wanted withdrawal. After *Cruzan*, a few states continue to require that evidence of the patient's wishes be "clear and convincing" in order to overcome the state's interest in preserving the lives of patients when they are not terminally ill. The trend toward restricting statutory directives has reversed, however, so that no state currently attempts completely to preclude withholding or withdrawing artificial nutrition and hydration (see chapter 4 for further discussion).

Ironically, continuing existence in a persistent vegetative state seems to be the archetypal situation that patients most wish to avoid ("I never want to be another Karen Ann Quinlan"). As more and more patients write directives and express wishes refusing artificially administered food and fluids and other interventions should they suffer from PVS, lingering reluctance to withdraw support from patients in persistent vegetative states is being overcome. This change is making decisions easier for victims of accident or sudden illness, such as Nancy Cruzan (*Cruzan v. Director* 1990) and Paul Brophy (*Brophy v. New England Sinai Hospital* 1986), who had no opportunity to write directives refusing artificial feeding. Indeed, commentators have argued eloquently that withdrawal of nutrition and hydration from patients in persistent vegetative states is appropriate and cannot be construed as euthanasia—even that it should perhaps become the norm (Cantor 1989, 1990, 1993; Angell 1994).

Clinicians should understand that "best interests" can have an expanded and comprehensive meaning that is able to account for the patient's individual character and choices to the maximum reasonable extent. If this new best interests standard is used for making decisions in the absence of a directive, clinicians, family, and friends may find the process of deciding for patients to be a little clearer—though not necessarily any easier.

## "MOTHER'S DAY SYNDROME" AND OTHER FAMILY PROBLEMS

How does one go about finding, and giving weight to, evidence about the patient's character and choices? Clinicians face many obstacles to the smooth resolution of treatment decisions. Perhaps the most mundane of these problems is lack of information about a patient. If sufficient information is not to be had, the temptation is to overvalue the few pieces of information available, whatever their nature or source. The solution is simply to remember to weigh all information appropriately, especially when there is little to go on. The less information the clinician has about the patient, the more important prognosis and general medical information become.

Equally common, and more troubling, is having too much information that is conflicting and contradictory. What should the clinician do, for example, when a patient, who may or may not have written an advance directive, is demented and of questionable capacity but is expressing choices? What if the choices flip-flop or the patient's decision-making ability appears to wax and wane? Whether there is a directive or not, how is the clinician to pin the patient's "real" choices down?

And what about the patient whose family is in conflict or the patient whose only child flies in from around the world after a twenty-year absence from the family and says, "Father would have wanted everything done!"? How should information from family members be regarded? May information from children thought to be exhibiting "Mother's Day syndrome"—that is, children who seem to be afraid that any treatment withdrawal would label them uncaring and ungrateful survivors—be discounted as motivated by guilt? Or must the family be obeyed in all cases?

As stated earlier, any time an advance directive is in the picture, all other evidence of the patient's wishes must be viewed in its light. If any evidence the clinician has calls the directive's validity seriously into question (e.g., forgery of a signature, witness testimony that the patient was decisionally incapable at the time the directive was signed), only then may other information override the directive. Family disagreement calls for extremely sensitive management of the situation by the clinician, but it simply cannot justify disregarding a patient's advance directive. When there is doubt, the clinician should seek the assistance of an ethics committee or a court to make the best possible decision, if there is no other way to resolve the conflict. Private consensus may be used to reach a decision in the absence of a directive or to interpret a directive without some outside consultation. The patient's autonomy requires that overriding the wishes clearly expressed in a directive should not be done lightly.

The patient with a directive should discuss it with family and friends when it is written. At the very least, family and friends should have notice of it so that they may prepare to respect the patient's wishes even if they disagree with them. Perhaps an advocate for the patient will emerge, or be named by the patient, and be able to engage friends and family in fruitful discussion of the patient's wishes. To the extent that physicians and other caregivers can facilitate any of these things, they must do so. Ultimately, however, caregivers need to remember that although they have responsibilities toward their patients' families, their responsibilities to their patients are overriding when there is a conflict. If the directive can be honored, it must be honored or turned over to one who will honor it. When there is a dispute in the family, the clinician who would otherwise honor a directive is not required to seek court approval before doing so simply because the family disagrees. Notice to the family of an intention to honor the directive is usually sufficient to permit the family to seek a court order if it wishes to do so.

Although family members are natural advocates for the patient, they have no automatic legal status as decision-makers. The parents of minors and court-appointed guardians for minors and legally incompetent adults do have legal proxy status. Proxies named in advance directives do, too, as do family members named by special statutes that apply when there is no directive—such statutes exist in about half the states now. When none of these procedures has given the family legal authority, the family of an incapacitated adult has an evidentiary role, like the physician's, in determining the patient's wishes. The family possesses, and must assemble and examine, information about the patient in order to help determine what decisions will be in the patient's best interests. If the family's interests conflict with the patient's, their information is not reliable. If the patient has written a directive, their information is less persuasive. If the patient's most natural advocate is not a family member but a friend or a lover, that person's evidence should be most persuasive, especially when he or she has been named by the patient.

When there is no directive or when there is a directive whose terms do not address the decision that is being faced, conflict in the family becomes more difficult to untangle. Caregivers must approach the decision as a court would, by assembling and weighing all of the evidence to arrive at a decision that appears to be consistent with this patient's best interests. Discussing this decision and the evidence and reasoning underlying it with family and friends is a necessary first step. This includes the very difficult task of raising with family members any concerns that their stances are unduly affected by their own grief and loss and the risk that their regard for the patient's wishes might therefore be compromised. Consultation with an institutional ethics committee may be helpful in examining complex situations.

Unless there are state laws in place giving to family members the authority to authorize termination of treatment for incapacitated adult patients in the absence of a directive,[10] there is, generally speaking, no legal requirement for the physician to seek a court's approval of a responsibly made decision about which the family disagrees (Areen 1987). But caregivers usually have far better access to legal resources, through their institutions, than families do. Caregivers should make sure that there is ample opportunity for discussion of the dilemma with the family, and the family should have the opportunity (perhaps even assistance) to seek a court resolution if it wishes, since the court is always available as the ultimate arbiter of who should properly choose for the patient. In making its determination, a court will assemble and critically examine the same sort of evidence as that already relied upon by the physician. Knowing this should help to reduce the physician's worries about involving the courts.

Courts in a growing number of states have declared their preference that decisions like this be made privately (Areen 1987, 1988; Coordinating Council 1993). Nonetheless, when disagreement persists, it may be necessary and is certainly appropriate to go to court for a final resolution. Ethics committees offer excellent forums for examination of these disagreements as well (Hunter 1985; King 1988). Though committees must not make decisions, they should facilitate open and comprehensive discussion and can help resolve conflict and confusion without court involvement.

One problem faced by clinicians and family who must make choices for patients when there is no advance directive lies in determining how much evidence is enough. When this question is posed to the courts, they address it in terms of the evidentiary standards employed in civil suits. The burden of proof has thus fallen upon those seeking to show that the patient without a directive would have wanted treatment stopped, in the face of institutions and clinicians seeking to continue it. The ordinary civil standard of proof is "by a preponderance of the evidence," that is, more likely than not. Courts in several states—for example, New York and Missouri (*Cruzan v. Director* 1990; *Cruzan v. Harmon* 1988; *Evans v. Bellevue Hospital* 1987; *In re A.K.* 1989)—have imposed a higher standard, that of "clear and convincing evidence," which is more than a preponderance but less than the criminal "beyond a reasonable doubt."

Caregivers have reasons to be concerned about the evidentiary standard applied in their states when disagreements about treatment in the absence of a directive reach the courts or when institutional policy favors treatment, because the effect of stringent standards of proof may be to presume that treatment is desirable, or desired, unless the patient's objections are "clear and convincing." Even if those objections fail to satisfy such a standard, however, the patient's best interests will not always require treatment, so that the existence of such standards still does not make clear what will happen when there is no directive. Patients and physicians in a jurisdiction whose courts apply the "clear and convincing" evidentiary standard will presumably be more successful in withholding and withdrawing treatment on the basis of an advance directive than without one, especially when the patient is not terminally ill or likely to die soon or when the treatment in question includes artificial nutrition and hydration (See *Cruzan v. Director*, 1990). Of course, whenever there is no advance directive, physicians in all jurisdictions have the obligation to assemble evidence of the patient's preferences and to apply their best medical judgment in determining where the patient's best interests lie.

## THE PROCESS OF DECISION

In sum, when directives are not available or not helpful, clinicians and others who would decide for the patient should determine the patient's best interests as the patient would see it. This means making use of as much evidence as is reasonably available about the patient's beliefs, values, preferences, and experiences,[11] as well as medical information and medical judgment. The credibility, relevance, and importance of all evidence must be assessed, and a decision must be reached on the basis of all of the evidence available. Conflicts within the family about decisions for the patient must be viewed in the light of the physician's duty to act in the patient's best interests. Where a state court or legislature has imposed a demanding evidentiary standard such as "clear and convincing evidence," the evidence available may not always meet this standard if there is no written directive, and sometimes judicial review may be advisable. Nonetheless, for physicians there is no essential difference between fulfilling the duty to the patient who has not written an advance directive and honoring a patient's advance directive. When a patient has conscientiously executed an advance directive, the physician's duty is simply that much easier to fulfill. Patients who have strong treatment preferences and patients who know or have reason to think that their families would make decisions for them that differ from those they would make for themselves will be much better assured of the decisions they want if they write directives—and if they discuss their directives beforehand with their families, their named proxies, and their physicians.

## "PLEASE DON'T EAT THE DAISIES!":
## INTERPRETING AND IMPLEMENTING ADVANCE DIRECTIVES

Physicians will in many cases find it easier to make end-of-life treatment recommendations and decisions for patients who have advance directives than for those who do not. Nonetheless, many difficulties and problems can arise in the process of interpretation and implementation. Research into when and why advance directives are followed or not followed commands great interest as hospitals try to evaluate their compliance with the PSDA. Some of the necessary research is beginning to appear. See, for example, Danis et al. (1991); Emanuel (1993); Layson et al. (1994); Mezey and Latimer (1993); Sabatino (1993); Special Supplement (1994); Weir (1994).

General reasons for deciding not to apply an advance directive to a particular decision are (1) the caregiver's or proxy's belief that withholding or withdrawing (or providing) a particular intervention does not reflect the patient's wishes as stated in the directive and (2) the caregiver's or proxy's belief that withholding or withdrawing (or providing) an intervention does not reflect the patient's best interests under the circumstances. The first situation may be quite common, especially since emphasis on standard statutory directives can wrongly discourage elaboration, refinement, or explanation of patients' choices. The second situation is problematic because patients may not have intended that others' views about their best interests be the standard of decision.

Problem #2 may be avoided in most cases if the patient can be explicit about the standard to be used by caregivers or by the proxy, but, as discussed in chapter 3, there may remain some situations in which the patient's expressed wishes conflict with caregivers' perceptions of the patient's current needs and interests. Problem #1 may be avoided in many cases by supplementing the statutory directive in a variety of ways, as previously discussed: with personal statements, "values histories," discussions with, and instructions to, caregivers and proxies, and the like—especially those attending to the goals of treatment and desired and disfavored outcomes, rather than merely requesting or refusing more kinds of interventions. It must be recognized, however, that not all problems of interpretation, implementation, and application of advance directives can be solved by such addenda. Advance directives that attempt to anticipate and head off every potential problem of interpretation will surely, by Murphy's law, attract some new problem that no one has thought of.

Moreover, the above-mentioned problems of implementation are by no means the only ones. Determining when the patient has lost decisional capacity, is terminally ill, or otherwise has become a "qualified patient" has its pitfalls as well[12]—as does the revocation issue, discussed below. If all possible problems were regarded discretely, they could quickly become overwhelming, and the process of honoring any advance directive could seem unworkable. Caregivers should come to realize, however, that these challenges are manageable by reference to the philosophy as well as the law of advance directives— that is, by addressing them within the context of a conscientious exploration of the patient's circumstances and all available evidence of the patient's choices and preferences.

## INTERPRETING REVOCATION

"And if I ever say I *do* want treatment, don't listen to me!" More and more frequently, the authors of advance directives are making declarations like this to their physicians, family members, and friends. People who seek to control their own future treatment decisions are becoming more sophisticated about the issues at stake and more aware of threats to that control. The possibility of revocation is one such threat; so are caregivers' concerns about honoring the directives of patients who are chronically diminished in their mental capacity but not completely unresponsive. Many people who are alive today can expect to live for long periods with mild or severe irreversible cognitive impairment. They may not be able to interact with their surroundings to a meaningful extent, and they may not be able to make decisions for themselves (Callahan 1987).

According to state living will statutes, all persons capable of giving a sign that is interpreted by someone as a revocation are considered to have revoked their directives. This wide-open revocation clause reflects a legislative preference for preserving life in the face of the irreversibility of directives—a discomfort that is often felt by caregivers, patients' families, and policy makers (Francis 1989). Yet many authors of directives, concerned that well-meaning interference with their competent choices may result from the application of these clauses, are seeking ways to avoid "involuntary revocation." They have been trying to make their directives into arrangements that will stay binding on the physician no matter what they say later. Although completely precluding a change of mind is both wrong and impossible, perhaps some partial protection against involuntary revocation could be a good thing for some patients.[13]

Consider the patient with chronic lung disease whose knowledge of her disease and familiarity with the experience of ventilator dependence in similarly affected relatives leads her to write a directive refusing, under any circumstances, to be placed on a ventilator.[14] She has discussed her decision thoroughly with her physicians and family; it is well conceived, well supported, and firm. During her first serious respiratory crisis, when she is frightened, in pain, and becoming obtunded, she is asked whether she would accept ventilator support, and she says yes.

It is not clear whether this patient has the capacity to make autonomous decisions, though she is apparently on her way to becoming incapacitated. As we know, advance directives become effective only when the patient becomes decisionally incapable, so in this example there is some question whether the directive has legal effect yet. But even if it does not, it clearly constitutes good evidence of the patient's views up to this point. Thus, whether this patient is decisionally capable or not, we must ask—just as we do in the classical "Ulysess contract," where Ulysses, tied to the mast of his ship and under the influence of the Sirens' songs, may or may not be decisionally capable—whether the patient's current wishes or her previous wishes should be honored.

We have already seen that to make sense of patients' rights to make autonomous decisions about their own health care, the standards used to measure the capacity for autonomous choice must be minimal standards (Danis et al. 1988; Faden and Beauchamp with King 1986). To encourage patients to exhibit high-level moral reasoning, have a coherent life plan and well-articulated values, and make forward-looking decisions that accord with a proper appreciation of all relevant facts and circumstances is to set standards that are vitally important as *guidelines* and *aspirations* (see chapter 2). But if these were *requirements*, so few people could meet them that health care decision-making would essentially be removed from the patient's control. Society permits apparently capable adults to make many important life decisions while under stresses and constraints of many kinds. There is no general requirement that decision-making be serene and pristine. Because there is no reason to treat health care decisions as fundamentally different from other decisions, to remove control of decision-making from patients by setting too high standards is unworkable and unfair.

It may nonetheless be thought prudent to require that the health care decisions accomplished by means of advance directives, because of their future-looking quality with its attendant increase in ignorance and uncertainty, be "more autonomous" than other health choices. This may also unfairly invalidate some directives. But advance directives that were not arrived at "more autonomously" are often less versatile, less easy for caregivers to understand and apply to the immense variety of clinical situations that may arise. If we wish to encourage patients to reflect a very high degree of decisional autonomy in their advance directives, even though they may not be required to, the problem of honoring revocations becomes even greater. Revocations of directives can exhibit high levels of autonomy, but they are often less autonomous than directives and may even not be autonomous at all.

As a general rule, the more recent of two autonomous decisions should be honored (Buchanan and Brock 1986). For advance directives, this means simply that a directive does not even become effective until the patient is decisionally incapable, since a patient with decisional capacity will be able to make an autonomous contemporaneous decision. Likewise, whenever an individual amends, updates, or even reaffirms a directive, a new autonomous decision is taking precedence over an old one. There is no hierarchy of autonomy among autonomous decisions (Faden and Beauchamp with King 1986). The decisionally capable patient can decide on an impulse to tear up a document executed with the greatest of gravity, and a reaffirmation of a directive may require very little thought but still be autonomously made.

Ulysses had his crew tie him to the mast of his ship so that he could hear the Sirens' song. He told his men to ignore him when he asked to be released, as he knew he would do when he heard them sing. Was Ulysses capable of autonomous choice when he begged his crew to release him to the Sirens' allure? If he was, the reasoning above would require his release. If he was not, should not his prior directive prevent his release? Perhaps—except that here is a living, breathing, talking subject pleading with his crew, and that is a hard thing to ignore (Dresser 1984; Winston et al. 1982). Similarly, in drafting living will statutes, legislators and policy makers felt they could not ignore any patient's attempt to revoke a directive because here the living person would be pleading not just to be released but to remain alive. Hence, all statutory directives have revocation clauses that permit anyone to revoke a directive anytime, and in any way, regardless of decisional capacity.

But should a nonautonomous choice that comes later always trump a directive? Consider the case of the woman who finally agrees to go on a respirator. If we put her on the respirator and she regains full clarity of mind and requests that it be discontinued, and we do so, we have merely subjected her to a period of discomfort that might have been avoided. We run several risks by this course of action, however. If this patient is successfully weaned from the respirator, her change of mind may make us less willing to honor her directive the next time it comes up. We may feel the need to reexplore with this patient all of her expressed choices and preferences, to see whether they have changed as a result of this one change of mind. If she then reaffirms all of her other desires for refusing treatments, we may not quite believe her unless she writes and solemnizes a new directive.

A bigger risk of this course of action is that the patient may not regain her full decision-making capacity. Whether she becomes permanently respirator-dependent or is weaned from the respirator, she may not regain her previous level of mental ability. Instead she may fall anywhere on a continuum from complete unresponsiveness to mild dementia, fluctuating in her abilities or fixed at one level. Wherever she falls on the continuum of capacity, we will not be able to consult her for effective decision-making guidance. What has become of her directive? Can we use it as evidence of her wishes? But it was revoked. Or was only one of its provisions revoked? How do we know she would not also revoke other provisions now if she could? Should we make a practice of asking patients of questionable capacity whether they want the very treatments they have refused in their directives? Even if we do not, should we question whether any information about such a patient's past life and wishes has any value or relevance now?

The question whether a revoked or partially revoked directive has value in future decisions about the care of the directive's author seems to have no better answer than that a careful evaluation of all of the circumstances is absolutely essential. The nature of the revocation is crucial, for a lot more can be learned from a decisive and spontaneous revocation than from an equivocal sound or gesture evoked from a seriously obtunded patient (Francis 1989). A genuine and reliable complete or partial revocation should make a directive substantially less meaningful.

Revocation also calls into question other evidence of values and preferences, whether from the patient or from the patient's family, that is consistent with the directive and therefore inconsistent with its revocation—thereby potentially making decision-making after revocation of a directive even more problematic than it is when no directive was ever written. A possible solution is to construe all revocations as narrowly as appears possible under the circumstances. For example, a patient who revokes a refusal of ventilator support cannot necessarily be assumed to desire CPR. Decisions that appear to fall outside the scope of the revocation should be examined in light of all of the evidence ordinarily available about the patient's wishes, including consideration of the revocation itself. Decisions that appear to be substantially affected by the revocation are more appropriately decided by the new best interests standard—a reasonable consideration of medical judgment in light of the patient's values—than by simply doing everything in every case.

The decisional process after apparent revocation will be tricky, demanding, and controversial. Caregivers should not duck the challenge contained in decisions after revocation by switching to a life-at-all-costs policy, except where it is clear that this is what the patient intended by revocation; it is unlikely that all revocations have this intended meaning.

Moreover, we cannot know for certain, in the case of the patient who revokes and does not regain decisional capacity, whether the revocation would stand if we could ask that patient again, magically and temporarily restored to capacity (as the court imagined Karen Quinlan when the substituted judgment standard was born). It is easy to imagine our ventilator patient saying, "Well, yes, I *did* revoke my directive; but I was confused and panicky then, and now, after that experience, I am clearer than ever about what I want." Imagining such reasoning for a patient who cannot now decide is consistent both with a declaration and with its revocation and seems called for when the evidence appears overwhelming that the patient's revocation was "uncharacteristic." Yet such considerations appear to make it nearly impossible for a decision-maker to stop oscillating between two poles: relying on the values expressed in a directive or giving greater credibility to the revocation and its implications.

Decision-makers who honor revocations will be stuck in that difficult oscillation. It seems unavoidable, and all that can be said is that they must honorably try to extricate themselves and their patients from it.

## REVOCATION AND THE FUTURE FACTOR

For the patient who pleads not to be listened to, there may be another solution: establishing carefully limited circumstances under which the apparent revocation of an advance directive should not be honored for some patients. This possibility returns us to the problem of the future factor—in a new guise, to be sure, but it is the same problem. Can caregivers rely on a patient's autonomous prior choice when some interpretations of the no-longer-autonomous patient's current interests would conflict with that choice?

Throughout this book it has been emphasized that the degree of autonomy patients are required to demonstrate, in making medical decisions generally and in writing advance directives in particular, is not higher than the basic minimal autonomy we all require of others in society when it comes to any significant self-regarding decisions in their lives—decisions, for example, about marriage, career, making investments, buying a home. It is just as vital for physicians to permit patients who are well informed and acting freely to make decisions emotionally or impulsively or idiosyncratically, if that is their desire, as it is for physicians to encourage and support their patients in making scrupulously reasoned decisions that express their long-held values. Physicians can and should do both these things without contradiction. The statement "You have a right to do this, but you are wrong to do so" embodies the physician's relationship to the patient who disagrees with medical advice—even when the patient's choice risks death.

Nonetheless, in order to be of genuine use to clinicians in making the choices patients want, advance directives should demonstrate a higher degree of reflection and foresight than patients' contemporaneous medical decisions must display. Thus, though greater decisional autonomy is not required for writers of advance directives, it will usually be present in a good directive.[15] Patients who are highly concerned that their wishes be understood and honored are well advised to take great care in conveying those wishes, and will naturally do so. They are setting for themselves a voluntary standard of high autonomy in order to ensure their directive's effectiveness.

When these patients say, "If I seem to revoke, don't listen," they are implicitly claiming that the higher standard of autonomy reflected in their directives should outweigh the less autonomous revocations they are attempting to disown. Perhaps they are concerned that if they become demented as a result of Alzheimer's disease or other conditions in which the ability to communicate is less impaired than cognitive ability, they might *say* things that could be construed as revoking a directive—things that they do not now believe they could have the capacity to *mean*. These patients are claiming the right to value different actions, and changes in their moral identities, differently—claiming that they themselves should finally control the definition of their true selves and rejecting an unknown, uncharacteristic, and diminished self.

The essence of this claim is no different from the claim that advance directives are valid even though, when they are applied, the patient's circumstances are changed. As discussed in chapter 3, respect for the autonomy of decisionally capable patients with concern for their futures dictates that directives be honored, even when those patients have lost the current capacity to reaffirm the values on which their directives are based, precisely because those values are so important that the failure to honor them is a failure to respect the judgment and humanity of the decisionally capable patient. Patients who recognize the risk that their directives may not be followed have real concerns that their dignity will be violated and the meaning of their lives will be diminished if their choices are not followed, even though they also recognize that they may not fully perceive those violations at the time. It is undeniably troubling for caregivers to contemplate honoring a patient's directive when the now incompetent patient could perhaps remain alive and without significant pain for some years, and perhaps there are instances where many caregivers would argue that the patient, in his or her directive, made a wrong decision. The real question is whether that moral uneasiness should outweigh the loss of trust and the failure of respect for autonomy that would result from a general reluctance to view directives as meaningful once the patient's decisional capacity is lost.

The claim that patients' choices about their own values and their own definitions of their true selves should control decisions about their treatment once their capacities have been irreversibly diminished appears in its most problematic form when the rejected self, though diminished and lacking mental capacity, has some capacity to respond to the environment and appears to want treatment the former, rejecting self has refused. If the patients who choose a higher standard of autonomy in writing their directives make explicit their desire to disavow purported revocations made when they lack decisional capacity, physicians and others asked to follow directives exemplifying these claims might be better prepared to implement them in the face of revocation. After all, it is common, and commonly regarded as admirable, for individuals to set for themselves higher than minimal standards in many areas—in moral behavior, in artistic, athletic, or academic achievement, in business or professional goals. Individuals who set high standards for themselves generally expect that other people will understand their reasons for setting high standards and will cooperate with their obedience to them. Thus, for example, a patient who has chosen a rigorous physical and mental rehabilitation program to maximize recovery from a stroke should be able to expect his or her physician's support in sticking to that regimen even though it is more ambitious than the physician usually prescribes. The general notion of sympathy with patients' self-imposed self-images and goals is a familiar and comfortable one.

Applying that notion to directives and their revocation, however, has somewhat different consequences. A patient who wishes to preclude nonautonomous revocations of a directive should state explicitly, in writing and discussing the directive with caregivers, family, and friends, that the preparation of the directive reflects a high standard of autonomy, including careful reasoning, reflection, and foresight, and that any change in, or revocation of, the directive must exhibit a similarly high degree of autonomy in order to be valid. The directive should explain the reason for this unusual requirement— the author's high degree of concern for preserving these very important decisions and preferences against the risk that crisis, illness, and diminished capacity could result in apparent changes of mind. The directive should state the patient's awareness that such a requirement is unusual in light of the revocation provisions in most directives, and give assurances of the patient's full understanding and acceptance of the consequences of this requirement.

Given such assurances, a clinician should feel able to implement a directive in the face of a revocation that does not appear comparably autonomous. In practical terms, a directive with these provisions enables the clinician not to invite revocation from the patient of questionable capacity—that is, not to ask whether the patient wants treatments previously refused. Instead, when the physician doubts the patient's decisional capacity, the patient might be told, "We are doing X, and not doing Y, in accordance with your instructions"—thus giving the patient the opportunity to object but requiring the patient to be somewhat active in doing so. Patients who then object might be questioned about whether they understand that their objection is a revocation of the directive they drafted especially to preclude revocation. This discussion should reveal to the physician whether the patient currently has the decisional capacity to revoke that this special provision of the directive requires. And of course, if the patient assures the physician that he or she is making a highly autonomous choice in revoking the directive, the revocation should be followed; it should *not* be possible to preclude *all* revocations categorically.

This kind of inquiry is fully in accord with the general procedure that physicians should follow any time the patient has written a directive and a decision that is within the directive's province needs to be made. No directive takes effect until the patient has lost decisional capacity; but if the patient is functional and responsive to any degree, it may not be until the point of decision that the occasion arises to examine the patient's capacity.[16] Beginning this inquiry with a discussion of the existing directive can facilitate autonomous decision-making in patients of questionable capacity by reminding them of their own earlier thinking and placing their decision in a context of continuity with the past. This can readily be done in ways that do not pressure the patient's decision, either to conform to the directive or to repudiate it.

When the patient has documented and discussed a desire to minimize the likelihood of nonautonomous revocation, the clinician's role in this discussion is admittedly more difficult. It is certainly appropriate for clinicians to inform patients that they feel they cannot ignore apparent revocations, even though patients at the height of their capacity may really want that. The clinician who agrees to honor an "antirevocation" provision may face some very difficult decisions; patients cannot expect physicians to ignore every revocation, and the clinician will have to make individual judgments about the decisional capacity of patients seeking revocation.

Of course, even the most clearly and persuasively reasoned antirevocation provision, obeyed in good faith by a scrupulous physician and approved by a hospital ethics committee, might not survive legal challenge by a family member or other interested party. Public policy has good reasons for favoring ready revocation of advance directives. Nonetheless, highly motivated individuals who explicitly and specifically disagree with that policy as applied to themselves should have the opportunity to have their reasonable wishes honored by a willing physician.[17] If the advice herein is carefully followed, legal challenges are unlikely to be successful; but the prudent physician should be realistic enough to prepare to face legal challenge in such cases, and the reasonable patient must recognize and be prepared to live with the powerful moral and emotional barriers to acceptance of antirevocation clauses.

## CONCLUSION

The patient's right to make his or her own medical decisions is one-half of the working basis for the physician-patient relationship, regardless of the patient's current capacity to make choices. The other half of the basis of the relationship is the physician's duty to use professional skill and judgment in the patient's best interests. Taken together, these two central principles comprise the general standard of medical decision-making: the patient's best interests as the patient sees them. The physician's expert judgment is directed toward formulating an opinion about the patient's best medical interests and informing and advising the patient about the best course of action in the physician's opinion. The patient then has a moral responsibility to consider the physician's advice but will also consider personal nonmedical values, preferences, experiences, and beliefs as important decision-making factors.

When the patient lacks current decision-making capacity, both the standard of decision and the factors (from both physician and patient) that enter into the decision remain unchanged. There are, however, different decisional processes that can be used. One is the process of implementing an advance directive—whether an instruction directive or a proxy directive. If there is no directive, a substitute decision-maker—one not named by the patient in a document—is identified, formally or informally, to examine and decide on the basis of those same factors.

When not made available in a directive, these factors will be found in the patient's past expressions, current apparent preferences, and medical condition. The decision-maker may be a family member, friend, physician, court, or court-appointed guardian. Assistance and advice may come from other caregivers or even from a hospital ethics committee. Although advance directives are the best evidence of a patient's wishes, the same kind of evidence of patients' wishes is vital in every case.

If there is no directive, many decisions will accord with what the physician advises, largely for lack of other evidence of the patient's wishes. When there is a directive, however, and the physician hesitates for any reason to rely completely upon it, the standard of decision to be used still points to the directive. As a principal source of information about the patient, directives always have some role to play in determining what the patient would have wanted.

# 6

# The Forecast for Advance Directives: Indispensable or Superfluous?

> Because death is so profoundly personal, public reflection on it is unusual. . . . [H]owever, such reflection must become more common if we are to deal responsibly with the modern circumstances of death. (*Cruzan v. Director* 1990, 497 U.S. at 261, Stevens, J., dissenting)

Advance directives are popular these days. Patient advocacy groups, medical ethics think tanks, attorneys, and many health care institutions are promoting them to patients and providers as useful and even indispensable documents. Advocacy groups send subscribers wallet-size laminated "living will" cards containing toll-free numbers for a central registry that can supply callers with the full text of the patient's directive in emergencies. "Medic Alert" bracelets, ordinarily used to alert emergency personnel to a patient's health problems, have been designed to alert caregivers to the patient's refusal of hospitalization and treatment (see *In re Finsterbach* 1990; Arizona Living Wills and Health Care Directives Act, §36–3251C [1992]). Federal legislation has been passed requiring health care facilities to promote advance directives in order to receive Medicare and Medicaid dollars (Patient Self-Determination Act 1990). At the same time, however, institutions, caregivers and sometimes patients' families fight hard to continue care for decisionally incapable patients and to promote policies that preserve life and discourage the cessation of treatment before death. This stark opposition could be a sign of healthy diversity of values in a pluralistic culture; it could represent the adversary viewpoints necessary, as in a court of law, for distilling the proper perspective; or it could demonstrate collective ambivalence and confusion over what advance directives are all about.

## ADVANCE DIRECTIVES AND MORAL COMMUNITIES

Widespread promotion of advance directives has its dangers, perhaps the greatest of which is that directives will be perceived as documents that lay down the law and close the conversation (Johnson 1987; Weir 1994). This book has sought to demonstrate that, on the contrary, advance directives continue the conversation between physician and patient. The sharing of responsibility in the doctor-patient relationship precludes patients from simply demanding compliance with directives and frees clinicians from simply being either "compliant" or "noncompliant" with patients' demands, permitting them instead to be genuinely responsive to patients' wishes.

The idea that the physician-patient relationship should embody a continuing conversation and a sharing of the decision-making process (Brock 1991; Katz 1984; Szasz and Hollender 1956) is hardly a new one, and it has its critics, both among those who believe that such mutuality can too easily threaten the autonomy of patients (Baron 1987) and those who believe that patients are unable to participate equally in such a relationship (Ingelfinger 1980). Authors of advance directives have a particular stake in characterizing the physician-patient relationship in this way, however: Directives are help-seeking documents by their very nature. Directives ask for the cooperation of caregivers, family, and friends in honoring the wishes they express. Though some directives ask only that others refrain from acting while some clearly require actions, all directives nonetheless ask others to take a posture of assistance. In this way they create what Raymond Duff (1988) has called "moral communities." Patients who cannot leave the hospital against medical advice or assert their own rights for themselves must rely upon these created moral communities of decision to honor their wishes. We can, if we wish, use only the terminology of rights when talking about advance directives, but that language alone does not seem to capture the felt responsibilities of caregivers or to account adequately for all patients' needs for support and care at the end of life.

If we think of advance directives as creating moral communities, it seems almost inevitable that our view of the entire decision-making process within the physician-patient relationship must become richer and deeper. Like the housekeeper who polishes the silver only to find that in order to do the silver justice, the table must also be polished, the dining-room windows washed, and the new candlesticks set out, physicians who accept membership in the created moral communities of patients who write advance directives will soon see the need to begin their conversations with patients early in the relationship and to engage their patients as fully as feasible in the decision-making process in order to be prepared to do justice to the decisions that may come later and the directives that may follow.

When clinicians recognize that it is permissible for patients to write advance directives and therefore it is right to try to implement them, they must then confront a natural human reluctance to raise difficult questions with patients. But that is just half the problem. If directives are to continue the conversation, how can a clinician who meets a decisionally incapacitated patient and his or her directive at the same time know whether that conversation was ever begun?

There is an easy answer: All who encounter a directive must presume it is the product of an autonomous decision-making process. Even the briefest and barest of directives, if it has a signature, a witness, and some statement indicating the writer's seriousness of purpose and understanding of the consequences of honoring it, provides enough to support that presumption and therefore requires the clinician to try in good faith to apply it. If it cannot be applied to the decision at hand, that is because the language in the directive cannot be made to fit the facts and circumstances—not because the directive as a whole is somehow untrustworthy because the clinician faced with implementing it could not talk with the patient. Many directives may not be easy to apply to specific facts; but if the effort is made, and the directive is not discarded outright, it still stands as evidence that this patient had some concerns about end-of-life decisions, about oppressive treatment, about "dying well." Recognition of these concerns will help direct the clinician's further inquiry about the patient and the patient's wishes.

Moreover, as advance directives become more popular, more widely employed, and more familiar, more clinicians will talk with patients about their directives, and evidence corroborating the patient's wishes will be easier to find in the medical record, in the directive itself, in the appointment of a proxy, the report of family and friends, and statements from other caregivers who observed or took part in discussions while the patient still had decisional capacity. Clinicians will come to expect such evidence and to provide it routinely for the benefit of other clinicians who may encounter the patient and the directive. As doctors and patients communicate better and share medical decision-making, end-of-life decisions should become easier to make.

This vision is highly optimistic and perhaps only partially warranted. It is also possible that directives might never step fully into the system of medical records, physicians' orders, and institutional policies that control health care decision-making for most patients, remaining always just one of a number of competing and overlapping decisional priorities that need to be waded through by clinicians, or even becoming obsolete.

## ARE DIRECTIVES COST CONTAINERS?

How could this happen? Well, it could happen as a result of misunderstanding what directives are really all about. The argument of this book is that directives are really about patients' choices, a way of preserving patients' choices about certain important matters under certain adverse circumstances. But the very great majority of directives address themselves exclusively to refusing treatment. If it could be said that directives were really about refusing treatment, even about the "right to die," then it could be argued that directives will become obsolete as soon as we face enough systemwide cost containment pressure. After all, there is no need to refuse treatment that is not available or not offered.

Indeed, many factors other than patients' choices are beginning to influence the general views of both physicians and society about prolonged intensive end-of-life treatment. Cost containment pressures from government payers, from insurers, and from capitation-model health care delivery systems; the need to increase the supply of donated organs; concern for the just allocation of scarce resources (such as intensive care beds); and extensive public discussion of individual end-of-life treatment controversies are among the factors that appear to be moving us, however slowly, toward a social consensus about the moral impropriety of continuing treatment as far as it has heretofore been continued. There is no agreement about when is too far or about how much is too much; but in the future, substantial agreement may be possible about the appropriateness of stopping at some point short of obvious futility (Angell 1994; Meisel 1992; Veatch 1993).

If advance directives were simply a way of ensuring that patients are not "overtreated," they would become superfluous in a climate that discouraged overtreatment even in the absence of directives. Some clinicians might prefer this, finding it artificial to view advance directives in a way that purports to separate the patient's right of choice from clinical and policy judgments that less care is better. Day-to-day hospital practice presents a range of questions about treatment in which the matter of advance directives occasionally bobs up like a cork in the sea. It may appear to clinicians and others whose first concern is giving good care in the hospital setting that the easier and more logical approach to managing care in a highly complex setting is to develop and coordinate guidelines, policies, and procedures sanctioning less care for some patients in some illness categories. Thus, much attention is given to guidelines for termination of treatment for dying patients, do-not-resuscitate policies and practices, policies about "futile" treatment, the establishment of hospital ethics committees, and discussions of when nontreatment should be considered and for which patients, with the aim of bringing hospital practice into harmony with the recognition that doing less can be better (Angell 1994; Cranford and Doudera 1984; Engelhardt and Rie 1986; Hastings Center 1987; New York State Task Force on Life and the Law 1986, 1987, 1992; President's Commission 1983; Ross and Wegner 1994; Steinbrook and Lo 1988; Stell 1992; Teel 1975; Tomlinson and Brody 1988; and Weinberg 1988). The impact of existing policy, malpractice concerns, the involvement of nonphysician caregivers, even payment issues and turf disputes, all must be dealt with in order to accomplish that aim—and all help to dwarf advance directives as an issue. When the central question is how best to terminate treatment for a selected category of patients, advance directives are minor: nice things to have, but neither necessary nor sufficient, nor even the best way to terminate treatment.[1] There is even a new term—"advance care planning"—exemplifying advance directives as only one part of the picture (Special Supplement, 1994).

Whether advance directives save money is a question that many have asked in the last twenty years, but only since the PSDA has empirical research begun to produce any answers at all—and those answers so far appear to be wildly divergent, showing increased costs *and* decreased costs and creating more problems than they solve. Although it seems obvious that forgoing life-sustaining treatment at the end of life would be less costly than providing it, a moment's reflection demonstrates that savings will only be realized if death comes sooner and/or if the treatments not given are costlier than the comfort care and treatments that are provided instead. Thus, refusing treatment by itself cannot guarantee savings; the patient's age and diagnosis must also be considered. Moreover, having an advance directive doesn't always mean wanting—or getting—less treatment at the end of life; thus, encouraging people to have directives does not necessarily result in lower costs.[2]

If, however, advance directives are viewed not as one means of giving less care but as a primary means of accomplishing the primary goal of mutual decision-making—to serve the patient's perception of his or her own best interests—advance directives are not minor but crucial. Bringing hospital practice into harmony with patients' choices is conceptually different from a selective retreat from the medical-technological imperative in the name of better care, even though many outcomes will be much the same. If the patient's choice is central, caregiving relationships, policies, and practices will be geared to eliciting patients' choices. If there are to be limits placed on those choices by other important priorities and interests—such as cost containment, resource scarcity, and medical necessity—the conflict must be openly acknowledged and directly faced.

It is sometimes assumed that ethical caregiving and "death with dignity" always mean doing less for and to patients. Advance directives are associated with treatment refusal and the end of life; thus, there is a strong identification between the freedom of choice and the freedom to refuse treatment. Yet less care is not always what patients who wish to direct their care either want or need. As caregivers know, "death with dignity" implies as much emphasis upon the humane and supportive qualities of the patient's care as upon the termination of the lifesaving components of that care (Pickard 1993; Schiffer 1987).

Advance directives are the primary means of ensuring that as many treatment decisions as possible are made by the patient rather than by someone else, or by a trusted proxy rather than a stranger. Yet because they emerged historically in response to a medical-technological imperative that appeared to attempt to evade death, directives are easy to misconstrue as only means of refusing treatment.

The reasons given by state legislatures for enacting living will laws, as expressed in the preambles and general purpose clauses of those laws, often demonstrate this mixture of meanings. North Carolina's statutory purpose clause is a good example: "The General Assembly recognizes as a matter of public policy that an individual's rights include the right to a peaceful and natural death and that a patient or his representative has the fundamental right to control the decisions relating to the rendering of his own medical care, including the decision to have extraordinary means withheld or withdrawn in instances of a terminal condition" (North Carolina Right to Natural Death Act 1983, §90–320[a]).

This one sentence acknowledges three "rights": the right to a certain kind of death, the right to control one's treatment, and the right to refuse treatment, at least in the case of terminal illness.

Despite its popularity as a term (cf. Cohen 1991; *Cruzan v. Director* 1990; Meisel 1989), the "right to die" has always seemed an odd sort of right to have, since it amounts to a right to do something about which, in the long run, no choice exists. Defining some deaths but not others as "natural" is also semantically troubling: it would seem that either all deaths are natural because everyone's death is naturally inevitable, or no death could be natural in a hospital or when the patient is connected to monitors, IVs, or any other "unnatural" accoutrements of medical technology. The right to a *peaceful* death is perhaps easier to understand, but when it stands alone, we cannot tell whether it means that patients can require others to do things to make their deaths peaceful or merely require that others refrain from disturbing the peace of their deaths.[3]

The other two rights recognized by the North Carolina legislature are less ambiguous. Refusal of treatment is a fairly straightforward negative right, the right to be left alone. The right to control one's treatment is much like the right to informed consent: Patients have the positive right to receive information and choose among therapies, or the negative right not to be touched unless the positive right to choose has been honored.

## REQUEST DIRECTIVES

Is there some component of positive right associated with advance directives—the right to elect certain treatments or to have a certain kind of dying experience? Let us examine "request" directives where patients ask for what has been irreverently but vividly labeled the "full-court press." This request, though rarely encountered in written directives, is far from unheard of. Some Orthodox Jews and followers of Islam even have difficulty accepting "brain death" as death. Other patients, whether their motivations stem from belief in the sanctity of life or from fear of being disvalued by others when gravely ill, may choose to instruct their physicians to "do everything possible" (Gold et al. 1990; Zugler 1989). Family members of patients may be even more likely to ask that "everything" be done for them (Freedman 1993).

If directives are really more about patients' own choices than about refusing rather than receiving treatment, then it seems it should follow that affirmative request directives where extensive treatment is sought should be honored just as readily as the more common directives refusing treatment. Nonetheless, we may well question whether they should be viewed in exactly the same light as refusal directives, especially if we believe that society must move toward withholding and withdrawing care for patients in some cases.

This problem is often answered by observing that physicians cannot be compelled to do anything that is not in accordance with their medical judgment and, therefore, affirmative request directives and refusal directives may legitimately be treated differently. Refusal directives must be honored because patients may refuse any treatment, medical judgment notwithstanding; but some request directives cannot be honored without forcing physicians to act in derogation of their medical judgment, and such directives need not be honored (Brett and McCullough 1986; Morreim 1994; Schneiderman, Jecker, and Jonsen 1990; Tomlinson and Brody 1988, 1990).

This way of distinguishing between request directives and refusal directives defines them as embodying, respectively, positive and negative rights. To say that physicians (or anyone) cannot be compelled to act against their will is to say that they do not have positive duties, duties to act affirmatively to uphold a patient's positive right to treatment. Refusals are different because the duty they impose upon caregivers is only to refrain from acting. Traditionally, in legal and moral reasoning, negative rights are much easier to identify and enforce than positive rights and are seen as preferable in a society oriented to independence and autonomy. Positive rights—for example, the right to health care itself—are considered hard to define and potentially burdensome.

This distinction, though superficially valid, is ultimately unsatisfying as a justification for honoring refusal directives but not request directives because it implies that the physician's role in treatment refusal is a negative, hands-off posture. Every advance directive, regardless of its provisions, makes a limited positive claim on every attending physician who encounters it. First, the physician must read the directive and determine whether it can be applied to provide a decision under the circumstances. Second, if (and of course only if) the directive can be applied, the attending physician must implement it or pass it on to one who will. Failure to act on a directive that can be implemented is not by itself blameworthy; but it is unprofessional and morally wrong to ignore a directive or to refuse to implement it without making reasonable efforts to find a physician who will. This is true for instruction directives, which require the physician to determine whether they can be implemented under the circumstances, and for proxy directives, which require the physician simply to recognize the surrogate decision-maker and then either accept the surrogate's decision or pass it on. A directive is the vehicle for delineating the physician-patient relationship after the patient has lost the capacity to do so directly. There is either treatment by mutual agreement or termination of the relationship without abandonment, by passing the care of the patient to a willing other.

Withholding treatment, withdrawing treatment, and providing treatment are therefore all positive acts in a meaningful moral sense. The relationship between physician and patient is mutual and complex and thus, even while the physician is not free to act without the patient's consent, the physician's action is not one of bare agency for the patient. The physician is responsible for assessing the directive in good faith and then, if it can be implemented, doing so or passing it on. The patient's choice drives the physician-patient relationship, but everything the physician does in accordance with that choice—including nothing at all—is an exercise of the physician's moral agency as well. Directives require clinicians to take responsibility for them; passing a directive on to one who will implement it is a responsible action and should be felt as such. By the same token, implementing a directive is not mere compliance; it, too, is a responsible act.

When an entire medical staff refuses to withdraw respiratory support from a comatose patient or when the hospital has a policy against treatment withdrawal, the continuation of unwanted treatment can be recognized in law as battery, and the patient may be able successfully to sue for discontinuation of treatment and for damages from continued treatment. The Ohio decision *Leach v. Shapiro* (1984) was the first to explicitly acknowledge the patient's right to bring such a lawsuit,[4] though the characterization of unwanted treatment as battery has existed for centuries. According to this battery viewpoint, continuation of treatment, the failure to stop, is not distinguished from starting in the first place. Although there are currently many obstacles to success in such lawsuits, the issues are becoming clearer for courts and caregivers, and the political and financial prudence of honoring patients' treatment refusals is becoming clearer as well (Cantor 1993; Gasner 1992; Veatch 1993).

The physician also has the right to withdraw from any relationship so long as the patient is not abandoned.  Of course, the physician who seeks to withdraw from a relationship in which the patient seeks the withdrawal of treatment obviously wants to leave the patient with the mechanisms of life support in place; yet physicians who refuse to withdraw treatment commit battery just as much as those who institute treatment without authorization. The courts, however, generally permit a physician who objects to withdrawing treatment to pass the task on to a willing substitute, since by doing so the physician ensures that treatment is not continued even though someone else withdraws the treatment.[5] But what if there is no willing substitute? More and more often lately, treatment refusal cases have quickly become notorious, and physicians and institutions may be reluctant to become involved in notorious cases. If no physician within the institution will act and there is no place willing to accept transfer of the patient, may the physician or the institution be required to withdraw treatment?

The answer in the law so far is a hesitant yes. When the patient's rights and interests in withdrawing from treatment are weighed against the physician's and institution's interests in acting according to their own values, the patient's rights are paramount (Annas 1987; In re Jobes 1987; In re Requena 1986). But there are a number of open questions remaining; for example, what if the patient had timely notice of the physician's or the institution's policies against withdrawing treatment (Miles, Singer, and Siegler 1989)? And what if the patient's needs include the provision of palliative care and pain relief and other desired treatments in addition to withdrawing or withholding treatment (see, e.g., Gaylin and Fried 1980)? Must these needs too be met by some unwilling physician? [6]

Suppose a patient writes an advance directive wanting "everything" done in case of permanent coma and the attending physician firmly believes that doing everything is wrong. We seem to be requiring a great deal of withdrawal action from physicians who *would* do everything; why should we not similarly require physicians to leave life support in place, which does not seem to be as much to ask?

This is the same question raised in treatment refusal cases that examine the state's interest in maintaining the integrity of the medical profession. As we saw in chapter 2, the courts have found that the decision to refuse treatment is one that professional values can support. But are there some decisions to continue treatment that are beyond the pale of professional values (Morreim 1994; Schneiderman, Jecker, and Jonsen 1990)? If the answer is no, it appears to make it impossible for physicians to end relationships with patients, and we know that physicians are always free to end relationships so long as they do not abandon patients (Morreim 1994). Yet if there is nowhere else for the patient to turn, the law of abandonment might suggest that the physician cannot refuse to treat. This issue is arising with ever greater frequency concerning the patient's ability to pay. Certainly a patient who can afford continued treatment is highly likely to find some physician who will give it; but with the changing health care financing climate, insurers and other payers are becoming more reluctant to view all end-of-life care as "necessary" (Hall and Anderson 1992).

When the issue of payment for care enters the picture, the distinction between refusal and request directives is reasserted in a different way. Although the patient's right to the physician's respectful consideration of his or her directive is the same for both types of directive, many request directives also incorporate positive claims on resources that exceed those made by refusal directives and may also exceed the resources available. Thus, the central question to be asked about request directives is not whether caregivers should honor them but whether there are other interests present that can override the patient's request for continued treatment. If the patient's choice cannot always rule the decision-making process, whose can outweigh it? The physician's? The payor's? Society's? When a physician refuses to perform a procedure, is that refusal valid when based on medical judgment? On professional values? On personal values? May society ask the physician to limit treatment based on social or fiscal policy? May social policy prevent a willing patient and a willing physician from undertaking some care?

## MEDICAL JUDGMENT AND ADVANCE DIRECTIVES

Can medical judgment outweigh the patient's decision? It is difficult to define medical judgment, to determine whether it can or should be free from the influence of professional and personal values. Every decision about whether to begin the sixth resuscitation in twenty-four hours on a failing patient, whether to transplant a third or fourth or fifth liver into a child, whether to risk last-ditch surgery on an unstable patient or to treat another bout of Pneumocystis pneumonia in an AIDS patient—all these choices have components of personal values and risk assessment such that the *patient's* desire to make those last efforts, just as much as the *patient's* desire to forgo them, should be decisive. But physicians' values are implicated in these choices as well. Will we then require physicians to do what they believe to be harmful to the patient, medically futile, and wasteful?

No, we need not. Again we must examine the nature of the request that all advance directives make. "Do everything" cannot be read to require the medical profession to give care that is not medically indicated (Brett and McCullough 1986; Schneiderman, Jecker, and Jonsen 1990; Tomlinson 1993; Tomlinson and Brody 1988, 1990), unless society finds specific reason to disagree with the profession's assessment. This is likewise the case for directives refusing treatment. After all, physicians often think that withdrawing treatment is medically inadvisable. Recognizing the possibility of a clash of values, however, society has explicitly recognized the patient's right to withdraw "against medical advice."

Physicians faced with a patient's directive to "do everything" must be aware that their own personal values figure into their medical judgments and that it is precisely here where patients' differing values must be respected as far as possible. The physician who helps a patient draft such a directive or who has the opportunity to talk with the patient about it must take all such opportunities to understand the values underlying the patient's choice. Differences in views of the quality of life, the importance of suffering, the goals of treatment, and the meaning of "futile" all must be resolved in the patient's favor, whether the directive refuses treatment or requests it (Macklin 1993).

A directive that attempts to bind the physician to a specific list of treatments without permitting the exercise of medical judgment (e.g., "I want a liver transplant" expressed by a medically unsuitable candidate) cannot, however, be made binding upon any one physician unless the physician specifically accepts these terms—that is, unless the physician is willing to go along with the patient's attempt to make this directive no longer a directive but a contract. The patient who refuses to give consent for a DNR order need not be resuscitated if in the physician's judgment the resuscitation will not succeed (Tomlinson and Brody 1988, 1990). This is an instance where the patient's goal of prolonged survival cannot, in the physician's judgment, be met. Yet the patient who will survive after resuscitation, even briefly, maintains the right to choose that extension of life though the physician may disagree with that value choice (Macklin 1993; Tomlinson and Brody 1988, 1990; Zugler 1989).

## THE ASCENDANCE OF "FUTILITY"

The conflict between medical judgment and the requests of patients for continued treatment has been captured in academic and popular debate as the problem of futility. Although the term itself has been challenged (Tomlinson 1993), it has the advantage of being vivid, and there have been many arguments over its proper definition and application (Brody 1994; Kapp 1994; Truog, Brett, and Frader 1992).

More and more famous "futility" cases are becoming household names—most prominent among these the Helga Wanglie[7] and Baby K cases.[8] Despite all this attention, it is important to recognize that futility cases rarely involve advance directives—either instruction directives or proxy directives. Instead, usually there is no directive, and family members insist upon continued treatment for a loved one, on the basis of substituted judgment or their own characterization of the patient's best interests, in the face of physicians' argument that the medical benefits of continued treatment are nonexistent, outweighed by its burdens, or so slight, in comparison to its costs and to others' unmet needs, as to create injustice. It is important to understand and distinguish these justifications, which are too often lumped together. "Futility" ought properly to indicate only treatment's inability to achieve the goal desired. Issues of cost are not futility issues in any sense. The question whether preserving life is a benefit—a worthy goal—in a given case, when caregivers disagree with patients, their proxies, or their families, is a question of whose values take precedence. This conflict of values lies at the heart of the current futility conflict.

But why are these futility arguments not often happening over patients' own request directives or the decisions of their appointed proxies? There are several possible explanations. First, few patients to date have written request directives because few statutory advance directive forms offer the possibility.[9] Writing one's own request directive is bucking the trend. Moreover, some people may assume that request directives are unnecessary—that "everything" will automatically be done unless they have a refusal directive. But perhaps the most suggestive and controversial hypothesis is that patients' proxy decision-makers are more likely to request continued maximal treatment than are patients themselves.

Several reasons for this hypothesis come to mind. There is some evidence that proxies—especially family members not appointed by directive—do not consistently make the choices patients would make for themselves (Emanuel and Emanuel 1992; Seckler et al. 1991). It may be harder to refuse treatment for others than for oneself. It will certainly be harder for proxies who are called into service as decision-makers after the patient has lost capacity, without having discussed the patient's own beliefs, values, preferences and decisions directly with the patient when it was possible to do so. And it may be especially hard for patients' proxies to come to terms with the limitations of medicine. Unwarranted faith in technology and unrealistic hope and guilt can adversely affect decision-making by proxies as well as by caregivers—perhaps even more than by patients. The challenges of proxy decision-making are discussed further in chapter 5.

A thorough examination of the problem of futility is outside the scope of this book. For advance directives, however, the futility debate makes several important points. First, medicine's limits must be a part of the discussion between caregivers and patients about end-of-life decisions. Educating patients and families about what treatment can and cannot accomplish is part of the physician's task, according to the legal and moral doctrine of informed consent. Medical judgment, in this instance, is not a trump card for the physician to hide behind but something to explain. Both physicians and patients must overcome the historical legacy of medical triumphalism in order to come to realistic judgments together.

Second, caregivers must acknowledge that grief, fear, guilt, and even mistrust often influence patients' and proxies' requests for maximal end-of-life treatment, as well as their own decision-making (Kleissig 1992; Muller and Desmond 1992). Open discussion of sensitive emotional issues is difficult but often necessary to assure patients and their proxies that maximal *care* will continue even when treatment is withheld or withdrawn (Freedman 1993; Pickard 1993). Moreover, such discussion must start early; it cannot await an open crisis of disagreement.

The ascendance of futility as an issue has been characterized by some scholars[10] as a kind of medical backlash against patient autonomy. The growth of the right-to-die movement could be viewed as shifting power from physicians to patients. By these lights, the futility problem is a medical bid to regain control through the invocation of medical judgment. Unfortunately, shared decision-making in health care can too often take on this tug-of-war character. Clarity about the meaning of "futility" can help. For example, it is useful here to distinguish[11] the patient's power to set the goals of treatment (a matter of preferences and values, at least in part) from the physician's authority to determine whether those goals reasonably can be met by treatment (a matter of professional knowledge and judgment). Such distinctions can help to address and clarify some very difficult and sensitive issues.

Making end-of-life discussion work well when patients or proxies are inclined to request maximal treatment and caregivers disagree may also involve others in the institution or outside it: social workers, counselors, spiritual advisers, and the like. This expansion of the patient's moral community of decision is an important recognition that end-of-life decision-making is not just medical decision-making. Instead, it takes place in the larger context of the patient's life and the lives of the patient's family and friends, and it must be responsive to them as well as to medical judgment. Medicine and society have begun to come to terms with this larger context for treatment refusal. When it comes to requesting end-of-life treatment, however, we are still at the threshold of the question.

## THE IMPACT OF SCARCITY AND COST

Is continuation of treatment at the end of life socially desirable? Discussions of financing and rationing have recently begun to turn explicitly toward this question (Callahan 1987, 1990; Churchill 1987; Dworkin 1993; Emanuel 1991; Engelhardt and Rie 1986). What happens to the role of advance directives when social policy favors limiting patients' access to scarce resources and costly treatments (Danis 1994; Emanuel 1987; Teno, Nelson, and Lynn 1994; Teno et al. 1994)? When the backdrop against which patients declare their choices changes, will our views of acceptable choices change as well?

We have already agreed about some things. Society can pass brain death statutes that are opposed by some religious groups. It can ration organ distribution so that a rich Johnny-come-lately cannot bump others off the transplant list. But societal power to do such things should be carefully circumscribed, its rationale should be explicit, its necessity should be demonstrated convincingly, and its restrictions should be the least onerous possible.

One of the most provocative issues raised by the new cost consciousness is the tension between individual rights and interests and the collective good. We have been particularly schizophrenic about this tension when it comes to health care (Callahan 1987, 1990; Churchill 1987; Danis and Churchill 1991; Mariner 1988). Indeed, it seems ironic that patients' rights proponents devote so much argument to overcoming caregivers' strong beneficent impetus to do as much as possible to preserve the lives of patients who do not view their own benefit as their caregivers do, while at the same time we are beginning to realize that at the social policy level, cost considerations are becoming powerful reasons to offer less treatment (Callahan 1987, 1990; Engelhardt and Rie 1986). We are floundering in the attempt to determine whether the very old, severely handicapped infants, or transplant candidates should have access to all the resources they want at public expense, while we still aggressively debate the wisdom of treatment refusal with individual patients.

Caregivers often fail to recognize the extent to which considerations of cost are inextricably woven into their own health care decisions about their patients. The simplest and most obvious sign of this intimate relationship is the ethical proposition that physicians may choose whom they will serve. A critical implication of this traditional professional prerogative is not merely the right to choose only insured patients or to refuse Medicaid patients but also to limit one's patient load to a number that makes it possible to serve well the patients one already has.

All good patient care has cost factors built in, in the form of time. Some minimum length of visit is necessary for good caregiving, as is a maximum number of patients seen per day. Very similar considerations govern institutional decisions about staffing of physicians and other health care personnel, the provision of ancillary services, and the filling of beds. A malpractice case that identified intensive-care unit overbedding as the cause of harmful neglect of an accident victim was merely the first step toward open discussion of the competing needs of patients. Such discussion necessarily entails a comparison of the likelihood and magnitude of benefit to each patient from each intervention—essentially a cost-effectiveness comparison (Engelhardt and Rie 1986).

Yet acknowledging the integral role of cost in all health care decisions does not answer the question whether advance directives should have cost containment functions. Some patients refuse treatment in order to spare their families from the financial ruin that can attend catastrophic illness. This can be a valid and autonomous choice, however tragic such a choice may be.

Many state living will statutes, however, contain clauses that prohibit health insurers from making the execution of an advance directive a condition of insurance coverage. Most such statutes also contain clauses declaring that the death of a patient who refuses treatment by means of an advance directive shall not be considered suicide for any purpose—including denial of life insurance awards, which do not pay benefits for suicides. Thus, two very different sorts of attempts by insurers to save money through advance directives are forestalled by such clauses. On the other hand, persons who have written advance directives refusing treatment have for some time been maintaining that insurers should be free to offer lower rates to them by virtue of their advance directives,[12] just as many insurers now offer discounts to insureds who do not smoke, are not overweight, have exercise regimens, and take other preventive health measures.

The recognition that failing to implement an advance directive may increase the cost of care at the end of life (see the discussion of the PSDA in chapter 4) has begun to suggest to patients and families a new legal means of ensuring that caregivers follow directives or pass them on to others who will. Traditionally, patients who are treated successfully despite their refusals of care have not been particularly successful in their lawsuits for unauthorized treatment—not because they had no claim (they do; see chapter 2) but because they could claim no damages, the costs of the treatment being more than offset by the successful results. But because life-prolonging care can easily run into thousands of dollars per day, a few courts have begun to show themselves willing to hear argument that a patient who does not want treatment should not have to pay the bill for it.

When a hospital or nursing home delays unreasonably in honoring an advance directive or terminating supports for a patient declared dead, it is possible that under some circumstances at least, the patient's estate may be excused from payment of the portion of the expenses unreasonably incurred (Cohen 1987; Weir and Gostin 1990). What constitutes a reasonable delay is not settled but should be determined by the amount of time necessary to take reasonable and timely action to ascertain the validity of the advance directive and the diagnosis (Gasner 1992; *Grace Plaza v. Elbaum* 1993). Hospitals will need to institute policies and procedures to handle these cases with dispatch; they will also wish to give patients and their families notice of these policies and opportunities to discuss cases fully and freely so that the need for resort to the courts is minimized.

Insurance discounts for advance directives could also benefit patients when disagreements about termination arise. It can be in the insurer's interest to advocate for the patient when the patient's decision to terminate treatment is resisted by caregivers or institutions. If treatment is given despite the patient's objections, the insurer is less likely to reap the cost savings anticipated by the policy discount. With the insurer on the patient's side and with the growing risk of getting stuck with a big treatment bill, hospitals may soon see the need to take their responsibilities to patients as seriously when it comes to nontreatment as when it concerns treatment.[13]

The acknowledgment that advance directives can be used as cost containment devices by patients or by their insurers does not legitimate cost containment as a societal interest capable of generally overriding autonomous choice as expressed in advance directives. If cost considerations should be found to outweigh patients' directives in some circumstances, that calculus must be explicit and its necessity made apparent. There is no question but that we must develop a system of health care provision that is just and reasonable and that the cost of care must play an important part in any such system. Viewing advance directives as nothing but cost-cutting devices, however, does not further that goal.

The American system of health care delivery has as yet failed to confront squarely most of the important questions that arise about the provision of end-of-life care that is costly or in short supply (Callahan 1987, 1990). If the only issue were the ability to pay, it would be possible to distinguish readily between request and refusal directives. When request directives make positive claims upon resources, it is possible (though certainly not obligatory) to argue that these claims may be denied if they cannot be paid for. In contrast, the negative right asserted by a refusal directive may not be ignored, even though still requiring the expenditures associated with care for the dying.

Paying for care is not, however, the only issue. The scarcity of resources, the priorities of health planning, and the need to control costs could be advanced in justification of the argument that some care may be withheld from persons who want it, can pay for it, and could even derive at least marginal benefit from it. This argument is becoming one of the significant debates in health care reform, with a large volume of literature all its own. It is complex, controversial, and well beyond the scope of the discussion in this book (See, e.g., Callahan 1987, 1990; Danis and Churchill 1991; Morreim 1994; Dworkin 1993; Emanuel 1991; Englehardt and Rie 1986; Havighurst and King 1986). Its success would imply that patients' request directives could be overridden for the fiscal good of society or for the sake of other patients' claims to resources (whereas refusal directives, as we have seen, override state and medical interests asserted against them; see chapter 2). This book takes no position on whether such an argument should succeed, but only seeks to emphasize that any decision to set limits on patients' ability to receive requested treatment must be made and discussed only as a matter of policy imperatives rather than one of interpreting directives, so that the difficult questions underlying this critical issue may be directly addressed.

## MAKING ADVANCE DIRECTIVES MAKE SENSE

The only view of advance directives that is coherent and useful to health care providers recognizes that all types of directives—instruction directives and proxy directives, refusal directives and request directives—are equal in several respects. All directives provide patients with a way of continuing control over their own health care decisions, and in that respect the physician's duty is to attend to the directive and understand how it purports to guide decisions on the patient's behalf. All directives also provide physicians with the opportunity to refrain from implementing the directive so long as they pass it on to one who will do so. In this way the patient's right to make medical choices is balanced with the physician's freedom to choose whom to serve.

The decision not to follow a directive—that is, one that can in good faith be understood and applied—cannot be lightly made. Respect for patients and their rights and interests requires that such a decision be based upon careful moral deliberation. Only well-grounded and serious objections should suffice, and then only after as much discussion as seems necessary with patient, friends, family, colleagues, ethics committee, and so forth. Even physicians who have strong objections to the patient's choice must see to it that another physician agrees to honor that choice before they can withdraw. Even the most controversial directives—for example, directives refusing artificial nutrition and hydration—must be treated in this manner. Neither the type of directive nor the current social climate about end-of-life treatment affects these duties: Directives concern patients' choices, not the choices of physicians (Brett and McCullough 1986; Schneiderman, Jecker, and Jonsen 1990) or of institutions (Miles, Singer, and Siegler 1989) or even of society (Callahan 1987, 1990; Emanuel 1987; Weinberg 1988).

The important matter is determining what the directive says about the choice at hand. Perhaps most of the time, discerning what the patient wants will be easy. Either the decision faced will be specifically addressed in the directive or a designated decision-maker or other reliable friend or family member will be able to state the patient's preference with confidence. But many times, a decision that reflects the patient's wishes can only be arrived at by extrapolating from a general picture of the patient's beliefs, values, and preferences that is provided by the directive itself and conversation with the patient's family and friends. For the clinician whose relationship with the patient does not begin until after the patient has lost decisional capacity, this process may be very difficult. The problems posed by good-faith interpretation and implementation of patients' advance directives may well emerge as the most significant issue for caregivers in the wake of the PSDA, and as a new focus of empirical research.[14]

It is obviously preferable for physicians to discuss any directives as fully as possible with patients while they still retain the capacity to do so (Case Study 1992), and to encourage as much documentation of the patient's views as possible to help guide physicians who encounter the patient later. When that does not happen—and it will not happen as often as it should—it is the physician's responsibility to determine as clearly as possible the patient's views, without being overly influenced by his or her own personal and professional values or by popular morality.

This moral scrupulousness is demanding; but it is demanded by well-established and long-standing moral and legal convictions about patients and their choices. If this process does not bear fruit, only then may physicians look for guidance to other means of deciding for patients, using family values, "reasonable person" standards, and/or medical judgment to determine the patient's best interests.

The patient's duty in writing a directive is to strive to give others the best guidance possible. The consequence of failing to fulfill this duty is simply that physicians will find themselves unable in good faith to follow a directive because they cannot tell what following it entails.[15] Thus, a too narrowly drawn directive or vague statements of preference given to a designated proxy may unavoidably be affected by the physician's perception of what other people might do or what policy suggests they ought to do.

Despite all its good effects, the PSDA may compound this problem by discouraging patients from writing, and caregivers from taking seriously, directives that attempt to provide more information, guidance, and detail than the standard forms contained in state statutes. If would be a grave mistake for caregivers or institutions to welcome advance directives without being prepared to encourage, recognize, and use directives that provide better guidance than the standard forms.

We are being pulled in two directions at once in health care delivery. The tensions between individual rights and public policy interests are exacerbating daily as pressure mounts to save lives with multiple liver transplants, organ retrievals from anencephalic babies, fetal tissue transplants, and temporary artificial hearts, while surgeons bemoan the shortage of organ donors and Medicare and Medicaid patients suffer from their inability to afford the purchase of drugs and preventive care. We have more to overcome than just our desire to save the lives of those who do not wish to be saved; we must also face directly the possibility that we may need to refuse to save some who wish to be saved.

In doing so, however, we must avoid a very great temptation: to assume that the desire for the good death and the attempt to reduce unnecessary treatment and conserve costs are the same. When patients are given information and make choices, whether on the spot or by means of advance directives, those choices may indeed be the most cost-effective, but in most cases cost-effectiveness is not the patient's principal concern.

Even granting that what patients are offered to choose from is itself determined by both the medical profession's standards of good care and far-off public policy decisions about what resources will be made available, it is still the patient's choice that finally determines medical care. If—or, more likely, when—we must refuse some of what is chosen, in so doing we must not bypass the choice. The first step is to ascertain what the patient wants, or wanted, or would have wanted. Having acknowledged the patient's choice, we must honor it or pass it on, unless we have made a policy choice that overrides it. Only in this way will it be possible for caregivers to preserve their own sense of relationship with patients in the face of policy pressures that seem determined to undermine the intimacy of health care for our own good.

Advance directives ultimately demonstrate the true nature of autonomy. Much criticism has been leveled at the primacy of autonomy in medical ethics; many have argued that physicians who leave their patients to their own unaided exercise of autonomy in fact abandon them. This volume has attempted to navigate the narrow channel that all good clinicians must travel daily: Supporting and promoting the patient's exercise of autonomy without straying into either abandonment or paternalism.

Advance directives acknowledge that autonomy requires both responsibility, in thinking through choices and putting them in writing so they may be understood and honored, and community, in talking with others about choices and relying upon others to understand and honor them.[16] Advance directives also put the clinician's responsibility, the patient's responsibility, and the task of the patient's moral community in perspective. They embody decisions of the most deeply private and personal kind about experiences in which people are most truly alone; at the same time they acknowledge dependence on the help of others in the service of those singular choices. The moral community serves the individual; the individual discharges responsibility to the community by considering, declaring, and sharing the choices the community acts to honor. The balance to be effected is fine, in all senses of the word: delicate, costly, even noble.

The initial issues in advance directives concern our respect for the freedom of those who have the right to decide. But the further issues engage certain responsibilities to ourselves and to others, responsibilities that call on us to advise and be advised, to counsel and to be counseled, as we work out our notions about the ends befitting human lives. Until recently these questions have been obscured by the imperatives of a plot structure imposed by medical technology. Now they are in danger of being obscured by the imperatives of a moral philosophy insistent on the exclusive relevance of respect for freedom. But if there is such a thing as dying well—that is, dying in such a way that the narrative of our life is completed in a fitting way—then freedom can be well or poorly used. It is toward a discernment of that difference that we now need to move. Aristotle mused on an idea of Solon's that no one should be called happy until death. He asked whether we can call a life well-lived until we have seen and understood the manner of its ending. Advance directives enhance our ability to choose well regarding the end of life. Beyond respect for freedom, the coherence of lives well-lived over time and in community is at stake in our deliberation about advance directives. (Churchill 1989, 179)

This is a book not only for patients but also for clinicians, whose role in making sense of advance directives is different from that of patients. Recognizing that their role is to serve patients in the responsible making of critical choices about their medical treatment, clinicians, too, perhaps should think about what the good life and the good death are, about how many ways of making choices there can be, how many different choices can embody living well and dying well, and how we each can serve each other in our own ways of coming to decisions of great moment and in compassionately honoring those decisions during the time that remains for every patient.

# Appendix

# Advance Directive Statutes, State-by-State and Federal Listings*

Alabama Natural Death Act [1981], Ala. Code §§22–8A–1 to 22–8A–10 (1990).

Alaska Rights of Terminally Ill Act [1986, 1994], Alaska Stat. §§18.12.010 to 18.12.100 (1994).

Alaska Statutory Form Power of Attorney Act [1988, 1994], Alaska Stat. §§13.26.332 to 13.26.356 (Supp. 1994).

Arizona Living Wills and Health Care Directives Act [1985, 1991, 1992, 1994], Ariz. Rev. Stat. Ann. §§36–3201 to 36–3262 (1993 and Supp. 1994).

Arkansas Rights of the Terminally Ill or Permanently Unconscious Act [1977, 1987], Ark. Code Ann. §§20–17–201 to 20–17–218 (Michie 1991).

California Natural Death Act [1976, 1991], Cal. Health & Safety Code §§7185 to 7194.5 (West Supp. 1995).

California Durable Power of Attorney for Health Care Act [1984, 1985, 1988, 1990, 1991, 1992, 1993, 1994, 1995], Cal. Prob. Code §§4600 to 4779 (West Supp. 1995).

Colorado Medical Treatment Decision Act [1985, 1989, 1994], Colo. Rev. Stat. §§15–18–101 to 15–18–113 (1987 and Supp. 1994).

Colorado Patient Autonomy Act [1992, 1994], Colo. Rev. Stat. §§15–14–501 to 15–14–509 (1987 and Supp. 1994).

Connecticut Removal of Life Support Systems Act [1985, 1991, 1993], Conn. Gen. Stat. §§19a–570 to 19a–580c (Supp. 1993 and Substitute Bill 7244, signed June 29, 1993).

Connecticut Statutory Short Form Durable Power of Attorney Act [1990, 1991], Conn. Gen. Stat. §§1–43 to 1–54a (1988 and Supp. 1993).

Delaware Death with Dignity Act [1982, 1983, 1994], Del. Code Ann. tit. 16, §§2501 to 2509 (Michie 1983 and Supp. 1994).

---

* *Source:* Choice in Dying, Inc., 200 Varick Street, New York, NY 10014–4810, *Right to Die Law Digest*, September 1995.

District of Columbia Natural Death Act of 1981 [1982], D.C. Code Ann. §§6–2421 to 6–2430 (1989).

District of Columbia Health-Care Decisions Act of 1988 [1988, 1992, 1994], D.C. Code Ann. §§21–2201 to 21–2213 (1989 and Supp. 1994).

Florida Health Care Advance Directives Act [1984, 1985, 1990, 1992, 1994], Fla. Stat. Ann. §§765.101 to 765.401 (Supp. 1995).

Florida Durable Power of Attorney Act [1974, 1977, 1983, 1988,1990, 1992], Fla. Stat. Ann. §709.08 (Supp. 1993).

Georgia Living Wills Act [1984, 1986, 1987, 1989, 1992, 1993], Ga. Code Ann. §§31–32–1 to 31–32–12 (Michie 1991 and Supp. 1993).

Georgia Durable Power of Attorney for Health Care Act [1990], Ga. Code §§31–36–1 to 31–36–13 (Michie 1991).

Hawaii Medical Treatment Decisions Act [1986], Hawaii Rev. Stat. §§327D–1 to 327D–27 (Supp. 1992).

Hawaii Durable Power of Attorney for Health Care Decisions Act [1992], Hawaii Rev. Stat. §551D–1 to 551D–7 (Supp. 1992).

Idaho Natural Death Act [1977, 1986, 1988], Idaho Code §§39–4501 to 39–4509 (1993).

Illinois Living Will Act [1984, 1988], Ill. Ann. Stat. ch. 110 1/2, §§701 to 710 (Smith-Hurd Supp. 1993).

Illinois Powers of Attorney for Health Care Act [1987, 1988], Ill. Ann. Stat. ch. 110 1/2, §§804–1 to 804–12 (Smith-Hurd Supp. 1992).

Indiana Living Wills and Life-Prolonging Procedures Act [1985, 1993, 1994], Ind. Code Ann. §§16–36–4–1 to 16–36–4–22 (Burns 1993 and Supp. 1994).

Indiana Powers of Attorney Act [1991], Ind. Code Ann. §§30–5–1–1 to 30–5–10–4 (Burns Supp. 1992).

Iowa Life-Sustaining Procedures Act [1985, 1987, 1992], Iowa Code Ann. §§144A.1 to 144A.12 (1989 and Supp. 1993).

Iowa Durable Power of Attorney for Health Care Act [1991], Iowa Code Ann. §§144B.1 to 144B.12 (Supp. 1993).

Kansas Natural Death Act [1979], Kan. Stat. Ann. §§65–28,101 to 65–28,109 (1992).

Kansas Durable Power of Attorney for Health Care Decisions Act [1989, 1994], Kan. Stat. Ann. §§58–625 to 58–632 (Supp. 1993 and H.B. 2786, April 14, 1994).

Kentucky Living Will Directives Act [1990, 1994], Ky. Rev. Stat. Ann. §§311.621 to 311.644 (Michie Supp. 1994).

Louisiana Life-Sustaining Procedures Act [1984, 1985, 1990, 1991], La. Rev. Stat. Ann. §§40:1299.58.1 to 40:1299.58.10 (West 1992).

Louisiana Power of Attorney Act [1981, 1990], La. Civ. Code Ann. art. 2997 (West Supp. 1994).

Maine Uniform Health Care Decisions Act [1985, 1990, 1995], Me. Rev. Stat. Ann. tit. 18–A, §§5–801 to 5–817 (H.B. 182, signed June 30, 1995).

Maine Powers of Attorney Act [1986, 1991], Me. Rev. Stat. Ann. tit. 18–A, §§5–501 to 5–506 (West Supp. 1992).

Maryland Health Care Decision Act [1985, 1986, 1987, 1993, 1994], Md. Health-Gen. Code Ann. §§5–601 to 5–618 (1994 and Supp. 1994).

Massachusetts Health Care Proxies by Individuals Act [1990], Mass. Gen. L. ch. 201D (West Supp. 1994).

Michigan Power of Attorney for Health Care Act [1990], Mich. Comp. Laws, §§700.496 (West Supp. 1994).

Minnesota Living Will Act [1989, 1992, 1993, 1995], Minn. Stat. §§145B.01 to 145B.17 (West Supp. 1995 & H.B. 1450, signed May 27, 1995).

Minnesota Durable Power of Attorney for Health Care Act [1993], Minn. Stat. §§145C.01 to 145C.15 (West 1995).

Mississippi Withdrawal of Life-Saving Mechanisms Act [1984], Miss. Code Ann. §§41–41–101 to 41–41–121 (Supp. 1992).

Mississippi Durable Power of Attorney for Health Care Act [1990, 1993], Miss. Code Ann. §§41–41–151 to 41–41–183 (Supp. 1992 and S.B. 2830, signed March 16, 1993).

Missouri Life Support Declarations Act [1985], Mo. Ann. Stat. §§459.010 to 459.055 (Vernon 1992).

Missouri Durable Power of Attorney for Health Care Act [1991, 1992], Mo. Ann. Stat. §§404.800 to 404.872 (Vernon Supp. 1994).

Montana Rights of the Terminally Ill Act [1985, 1989, 1991], Mont. Code Ann. §§50–9–101 to 50–9–111, 50–9–201 to 50–9–206 (1993).

Montana Durable Power of Attorney Act [1974, 1985], Mont. Code Ann. §§72–5–501 to 75–5–502 (1993), as interpreted by Rights of the Terminally Ill Act, §50–9–103(4).

Nebraska Rights of the Terminally Ill Act [1992, 1993], Neb. Rev. Stat. §§20–401 to 20–416 (Supp. 1994).

Nebraska Power of Attorney for Health Care Act [1992, 1993], Neb. Rev. Stat. §§30–3401 to 30–3432 (Supp. 1994).

Nevada Uniform Act on the Rights of the Terminally Ill [1977, 1985, 1987, 1991], Nev. Rev. Stat. §§449.535 to 449.690 (1991, 1993 & Supp. 1993).

Nevada Durable Power of Attorney for Health Care Act [1987, 1991, 1993], Nev. Rev. Stat. Ann. §§449.800 to 449.860 (1991 & Supp. 1993).

New Hampshire Living Wills Act [1985, 1991, 1992], N.H. Rev. Stat. Ann. §§137–H:1 to 137–H:16 (1990 and Supp. 1994).

New Hampshire Durable Power of Attorney for Health Care [1991, 1992], N.H. Rev. Stat. Ann. §§137–J:1 to 137–J:16 (Supp. 1993).

New Jersey Advance Directives for Health Care Act [1991], N.J. Stat. Ann. §§26:2H–53 to 26:2H–78 (West Supp. 1994).

New Mexico Right to Die Act [1977, 1984], N.M. Stat. Ann. §§24–7–1 to 24–7–11 (Michie 1994).

New Mexico Uniform Health-Care Decisions Act [1995] (H.B. 483, signed April 4, 1994).

New Mexico Durable Power of Attorney Act [1989], N.M. Stat. Ann. §§45–5–501 to 45–5–502 (Michie 1993).

New York Health Care Proxy Act [1990, 1994], N.Y. Pub. Health Law §§2980 to 2994 (McKinney 1994 and Supp. 1995).

North Carolina Right to Natural Death Act [1977, 1979, 1981, 1983, 1991], N.C. Gen. Stat. §§90–320 to 90–322 (1993).

North Carolina Health Care Powers of Attorney Act [1991, 1993], N.C. Gen. Stat. §§32A–15 to 32A–26 (1993 & Supp. 1994).

North Dakota Uniform Rights of the Terminally Ill Act [1989, 1991, 1993], N.D. Cent. Code §§23–06.4–01 to 23–06.4–14 (1991 & Supp. 1993).

North Dakota Durable Powers of Attorney for Health Care Act [1991, 1993], N.D. Cent. Code §§23–06.5–01 to 23–06.5–18 (1991 & Supp. 1993).

Ohio Modified Uniform Rights of the Terminally Ill Act [1991], Ohio Rev. Code Ann. §§2133.01 to 2133.15 (Anderson 1994).

Ohio Power of Attorney for Health Care Act [1989, 1991], Ohio Rev. Code Ann. §§1337.11 to 1337.17 (Anderson 1993).

Oklahoma Rights of the Terminally Ill or Persistently Unconscious Act [1985, 1987, 1990, 1992], Okla. Stat. Ann. tit. 63, §§3101.1 to 3101.16 (West Supp. 1995).

Oklahoma Hydration & Nutrition for Incompetent Patients Act [1987, 1990, 1992], Okla. Stat. Ann. tit. 63, §§3080.1 to 3080.5 (West Supp. 1995).

Oregon Health Care Decisions Act [1977, 1983, 1987, 1993], Or. Rev. Stat. §§127.505 to 127.640 (Supp. 1994).

Pennsylvania Advance Directive for Health Care Act [1992], Pa. Stat. Ann. tit. 20, §§5401 to 5416 (West Supp. 1994).

Pennsylvania Durable Powers of Attorney Act [1982], Pa. Stat. Ann. tit. 20 §§5601 to 5607 (West Supp. 1994), *as interpreted by Pocono Medical Center v. Harley,* No. 3467 (Pa. Ct. Com. Pl. Monroe Co. Dec. 14, 1990).

Rhode Island Rights of the Terminally Ill Act [1991, 1992], R.I. Gen. Laws §§23–4.11–1 to 23–4.11–14 (West Supp. 1994).

Rhode Island Health Care Power of Attorney Act [1986, 1989, 1992, 1993, 1994], R.I. Gen. Laws §§23–4.10–1 to 23–4.10–12 (West Supp. 1994).

South Carolina Death with Dignity Act [1986, 1988, 1991], S.C. Code Ann. §§44–77–10 to 44–77–160 (Law Co-op Supp. 1993).

South Carolina Powers of Attorney Act (1986, 1990, 1992], S.C. Code Ann. §§62–5–501 to 62–5–505 (Law Co-op Supp. 1992).

South Dakota Living Will Act [1991, 1994], S.D. Codified Laws Ann. §§34–12D–1 to 34–12D–22 (Michie Supp. 1994).

South Dakota Durable Powers of Attorney Act [1977, 1979, 1990, 1992], S.D. Codified Laws Ann. §§59–7–2.1 to 59–7–2.8, 59–7–8 (Michie 1993).

Tennessee Right to Natural Death Act [1985, 1991, 1992], Tenn. Code Ann. §§32–11–101 to 32–11–112 (Michie Supp. 1994).

Tennessee Durable Power of Attorney for Health Care Act [1990], Tenn. Code Ann. §§34–6–201 to 34–6–214 (Michie 1991).

Texas Natural Death Act [1977, 1979, 1983, 1985, 1990, 1993], Tex. Health & Safety Code Ann. §§672.001 to 672.021 (1992 & Supp. 1995).

Texas Durable Power of Attorney for Health Care Act [1989, 1991], Tex. Civil Practice & Remedies Code Ann. §§135.001 to 135.018 (Vernon Supp. 1995).

Utah Personal Choice and Living Will Act [1985, 1988, 1993], Utah Code Ann. §§75–2–1101 to 75–2–1119 (Michie 1993 & Supp. 1994).

Vermont Terminal Care Document Act [1982], Vt. Stat. Ann. tit. 18, §§5251 to 5262, and tit. 13, §1801 (1987).

Vermont Durable Powers of Attorney for Health Care Act [1987], Vt. Stat. Ann. tit. 14, §§3451 to 3467 (1989 and Supp. 1993).

Virginia Health Care Decisions Act [1983, 1988, 1989, 1991, 1992, 1994], Va. Code §§54.1–2981 to 54.1–2993 (Michie Supp. 1994).

Washington Natural Death Act [1979, 1992], Wash. Rev. Code Ann. §§70.122.010 to 70.122.920 (West Supp. 1993).

Washington Durable Power of Attorney—Health Care Decisions Act [1989], Wash. Rev. Code Ann. §11.94.010 (West Supp. 1994).

West Virginia Natural Death Act [1984, 1991], W. Va. Code §§16–30–2 to 16–30–13 (Michie 1991 and Supp. 1993).

West Virginia Medical Power of Attorney Act [1990], W. Va. Code §§16–30a–1 to 16–30a–20 (Michie Supp. 1993).

Wisconsin Natural Death Act [1984, 1986, 1988, 1991, 1992], Wisc. Stat. Ann. §§154.01 to 154.15 (West 1989 and Supp. 1993).

Wisconsin Power of Attorney for Health Care Act [1990, 1992, 1993], Wisc. Stat. Ann. §§155.01 to 155.80 (West Supp. 1994).

Wyoming Living Will Act [1984, 1985, 1987, 1991, 1992, 1993], Wyo. Stat. §§35–22–101 to 35–22–109 (Michie 1994).

Wyoming Durable Power of Attorney for Health Care Act [1991, 1992, 1993], Wyo. Stat. §§3–5–201 to 3–5–213 (Michie Supp. 1994).

**United States:**

Patient Self-Determination Act, Pub. L. 101–508 §§4206, 4751 (Omnibus Budget Reconciliation Act, 101st Cong. 2nd Sess., Nov. 5, 1990); 42 U.S.C. §§1395 cc *et seq.*(1990).

**See also:**

Uniform Rights of the Terminally Ill Act [1985, 1987, 1989], §§1 to 18, 9B U.L.A. 96–115 (Supp. 1992).

Uniform Health-Care Decisions Act [1993], §§1 to 19, 9 U.L.A. 93–114 (Supp. 1994).

# Notes

## NOTES TO CHAPTER 1

1. By convention and for reasons of proof, advance directives are generally understood as *written statements*. Like informed consents, advance directives need not be in writing to be effective, but should be in writing to ensure that they are effective. Oral statements can be forgotten or misremembered, might not be disseminated to all the people who need to hear them, and are sometimes difficult to prove at all. Patients should be encouraged to put their wishes into written form—not necessarily into a legal document but into any form that is understandable and usable, such as a personal statement, a note in the medical record, or a letter to a chosen proxy decision-maker. Caregivers should recognize that these less "formal" advance directives can be valid. In addition, when a written directive is not available, patients' oral directives should also be recognized as potentially valid (though these will still have proof problems).

2. As of late-1995, Missouri is the only state whose living will statute requires the provision of artificial nutrition and hydration except in limited circumstances. No state with a health care proxy statute has a parallel requirement therein; Missouri permits health care agents to order withholding or withdrawal of this treatment. Eight states and the District of Columbia do not address this issue in either statute; another nine states address it in only one statute but not the other (Choice in Dying 1995). This lack of parallelism reflects the many changes in advance directive laws since 1990 and can create much confusion for caregivers and patients.

3. This example is taken from Schucking (1985), with modifications.

4. Choice in Dying, the National Council for the Right to Die, was formed in 1990 from the merger of Concern for Dying and the Society for the Right to Die. A national nonprofit organization with a long history, Choice in Dying works for the rights of patients at the end of life through education and training, publications, legal advice, the maintenance of a national Living Will Registry, and the distribution of advance directives that conform to the statutory requirements of every state. Their address is 200 Varick St., New York, NY 10014–4810; they also provide a toll-free number, 1-800-989-WILL.

5. Copies of the Medical Directive may be obtained from the Harvard Medical School Health Publications Group, 164 Longwood Avenue, Boston, MA 02115. For ordering information please write to: The Medical Directive, Dept. MD95, P.O. Box 380, Boston, MA 02117–0380.

6. The National Commission on Uniform Laws drafts model uniform legislation for states to enact in order to promote consistency nationwide on legal issues of potential variation and conflict. The Uniform Health-Care Decisions Act was designed to address uniformly the complexities arising from the post–*Cruzan* explosion of legal activity surrounding advance directives. The Commission first tackled health care decision-making with its 1982 Model Health-Care Decisions Act and later developed the Uniform Rights of the Terminally Ill Act (1985), which was adopted by a number of states and then revised in 1989 to include a proxy designation. All of those model uniform laws were superseded by the Uniform Health-Care Decisions Act (1994).

7. The booklet *Shape Your Health Care Future with Health Care Advance Directives*, which includes the Health Care Advance Directive form and instructions, is available through the AARP's Health Advocacy Services Programs Division, 601 E Street N.W., Washington, D.C. 20049. The ABA and AMA can also supply copies.

8. Popular knowledge of living wills centers on the refusal of treatment, but there is nothing to preclude the execution of a directive that requests treatment, whether routine or heroic. But whether such a "request directive" should carry exactly the same practical, moral, and legal authority as a refusal directive is a separate question (Brett and McCullough 1986; Morreim 1994). Request directives are further discussed in chapter 6.

## NOTES TO CHAPTER 2

1. In fact, the only reported criminal prosecution of physicians to date for withdrawing life-sustaining treatment from a patient was initiated by one of the patient's nurses after the patient's family resisted continuation of what was considered by the nursing service to be standard comfort care (turning the patient in bed and humidifying the patient's airway with a misting device). The charges against the physicians were ultimately dismissed (*Barber v. Superior Court* 1983).

2. For example, the development of anesthesia made consultation with patients during surgery impossible and incidentally caused many people to fear that physicians would perform procedures without their consent while they were unconscious (Pernick 1982).

3. For the most recent versions of the regulations, see Department of Health and Human Services (1993); Food and Drug Administration (1993). For their history, see Faden and Beauchamp with King (1986).

4. For example, the Declaration of Helsinki's informed consent requirement was considerably relaxed for what the WMA described as "therapeutic research," in which benefit to subjects was anticipated (World Medical Assembly 1964).

5. Thus, until the mid-twentieth century (*Brown v. Hughes* 1934; *Fortner v. Koch* 1935), any treatment considered "experimental" carried grave liability risks for the physician (*Carpenter v. Blake* 1871; *Slater v. Baker and Stapleton* 1767), and even now it is not clear, because of the courts' desire to protect patients, whether patient and physician may make a contract about unusual or unorthodox treatment—for example, to deliver cheaper, cost-saving care.

6. Even a recent controversial California decision stating that doctors are not required by the informed consent doctrine to give their patients statistical life expectancy information affirms the important general principle that the purpose of informed consent is to facilitate autonomous decision-making by patients (Annas 1994).

7. See Areen et al. (1984, 1112–1117); Burt (1979). See also the two films made about Dax Cowart's experience, *Please Let Me Die* and *Dax's Case* (made by Cowart himself), both available from Choice in Dying, 200 Varick Street, New York, NY 10014–4810.

8. When the patient refuses treatment, the integrity of the medical profession cannot require that treatment be continued. The issue is more complex whenever caregivers feel morally and professionally uneasy about continuing requested supportive care in the face of the patient's refusal of definitive treatment. Finally, when the patient requests particular treatments that the physician believes are not medically justifiable, the conflict of values is clearly drawn. Chapter 6 discusses the problem of futility and request directives in detail.

9. Of necessity, many determinations about a patient's capacity are made at the bedside by physicians—sometimes but not always with the assistance of psychiatric, neurological, or psychological expertise. Because decisional capacity is task-specific, a global determination of lack of capacity, such as that provided by a mental status examination, cannot necessarily show that the patient cannot make a given decision—especially if the determination of incapacity is made before the need for decision arises. Therefore, global determinations of incapacity should be considered preliminary and should either be reexamined at the time a decision is needed or used to provide evidence in a judicial proceeding to determine the patient's capacity (except where the emergency exception applies). Though some commentators have argued that the courts should always be consulted for determinations about patients' decisional capacities, except where statutes permit otherwise, by custom many such determinations are made by attending physicians without judicial review.

In essence, decisional capacity—"competence"—in the context of health care decision-making means the ability to give an informed consent, that is, the ability to give a consent that is intentional, based on understanding, and free from control by others. Setting the standards for understanding, voluntariness, and intention means determining how much of these attributes is necessary. Legally, decisional capacity is a *minimal* threshold standard, below which it is not reasonable to honor the patient's choices because the patient is not sufficiently capable of making them. Moreover, decisional capacity is task-specific—that is, patients may be competent in some ways and not in others, and therefore capable of making health care choices but not financial decisions or of making minor or familiar decisions but not of grasping complex technical information for other decisions. Finally, decisional capacity is not fixed but may wax and wane with the patient's condition. Decisions made during a "window of capacity" should be honored during incapacity.

Thus, standards of capacity must establish minimum threshold levels of decisional ability and must be specific, both temporally and in the ability being measured. Testing for that capacity takes many forms, each of which has some weaknesses and some strengths.

The *presence of decision* is sometimes offered as a test of decisional capacity. This test requires only the expression of assent or dissent. Such a test is insufficient, because it does not necessarily reflect the patient's ability to understand and to decide freely. It may mask any number of cognitive or psychological disorders and is likely to result in many false positive determinations of capacity. It can even give rise to false negative determinations, where anything from language barriers to massive motor-neural disorders could prevent the communication of a decision.

The patient's *understanding* of the decision faced is sometimes tested as a way of gauging capacity as well as a way of determining whether the patient has grasped the basic issues disclosed by the caregiver and has some sense of why they, and the decision faced, are important. The most common means of testing understanding is to ask the patient to repeat information back to the caregiver "in your own words." Sometimes more standardized, written multiple-choice questionnaires are used.

There is a risk of false negatives in this test, because it is unavoidably biased in favor of the caregiver's definition of "understanding." Moreover, it must be carefully applied to ensure that it does not become a test of the patient's recall. Since this test deals only with understanding and not also with the patient's reasoning process, however, its principal risk is that caregivers may overestimate the degree of understanding sufficient for patients to make informed choices. It is probably the best test, if carefully used.

Another test, frequently used, is examination of the patient's *decision-making process*—that is, asking patients to explain the basis for their choices, and evaluating their reasons and their reasoning. If a patient has not considered a decision fully enough or taken all of the important considerations into account in making it, the patient will be judged lacking in decisional capacity. This test runs a high risk of false negatives, as it clearly favors decision-making processes that resemble those of whoever is evaluating the process in question and it thus may be biased against cultural, social, and religious differences in decisional priorities.

Finally, the *decision* itself has been known to serve as a test of decisional capacity. This test is also substantially biased. Whether the patient makes the "right" choice may be as much a matter of legitimate differences in viewpoint as of defects in decisional capacity, resulting in false negatives caused by value conflicts. Like the test for presence of a decision, this test could also give rise to false positives, since a patient with no capacity to understand the situation could still announce the "right" choice.

## NOTES TO CHAPTER 3

1. The only exception is when a choice directly and unavoidably injures others, so this may not be true in some instances when the patient is pregnant.

2. But see also chapter 5's discussion about limiting the power to revoke directives if the writer so chooses.

3. For an answer to this argument, see the dissenting justice's opinion in the *Conroy* case (*Matter of Conroy* 1985).

4. It seems safe to assert that most people who plan for their aging and retirement think a great deal about maintaining their own sense of dignity during the changes of circumstances that accompany aging—including the possibilities of diminished income, social contact, activity, mobility, and health. Because concerns like dignity are so important to our planning for the future, it seems fundamentally wrong to deny their validity where the future holds extreme disability. See Dworkin's (1986) discussion of "precedent autonomy." See also Cantor's parallel legal arguments (1989, 403–404; 1993).

5. For example, many statutory directives are written to apply only in terminal illness. Many others apply only in terminal illness and PVS. Such language does not, however, make it "illegal" to honor a directive by a patient who is not terminally ill or one who is severely demented but not in PVS (see discussion in chapters 2 and 4). Many patients add to statutory directives their own provisions about withholding or withdrawing treatment in advanced Alzheimer's disease and other circumstances of severely diminished capacity, provisions that may not technically match statutory directive language. Such additions can raise problems of interpretation as caregivers attempt to combine the parts into a whole.

6. Other difficult questions of interpretation can arise when the patient's reasons for refusing particular treatments are not known, making it problematic to apply a directive to circumstances not specifically mentioned in it. Knowing the basis for the patient's refusal is important and may be very enlightening (Roth, Meisel, and Lidz 1977). Nonetheless, it is always hard to be certain you have enough information to make an appropriate decision, and the resultant ambiguity may be most troubling. See chapter 5 for further discussion of the problems of honoring patients' choices.

7. See also the discussion of decisional capacity in chapter 2.

8. For further discussion of how much knowledge, consideration, and safeguards might be enough, see chapter 4.

9. A surprisingly common scenario arises when a patient facing surgery seeks the surgeon's agreement to withhold or curtail emergency treatment if complications arise during the procedure (Lederer and Brock 1987; Cohen and Cohen 1991). See the discussion of perioperative DNR orders below.

10. Choice in Dying reports that twenty-seven states had passed statutes authorizing out-of-hospital DNR orders as of June 1995; nearly half of those were passed in 1994. Some twenty other legislatures were considering such a statute. Some half-dozen states without statutes have regulations and other means of recognizing out-of-hospital DNR orders, for example, through medical directors' adopting them as standing orders for emergency medical personnel.

11. See the discussion of competence in chapter 2; see also Faden and Beauchamp with King (1986).

12. But see Jay Katz's thoughtful rejoinder to his critics on the patient's obligation to explain (Katz 1994). Dan Brock (1991, 45) has also addressed this important and sensitive issue in a philosophical essay that concludes: "Shared decision making does not imply a value-neutral role for physicians; it requires of them a more delicate balancing. They must act as advocates for their patients' health and well-being, while also being prepared ultimately to respect patients' self-determination, even when they disagree with their patients' treatment choices."

13. Most state advance directive statutes do not permit the attending physician to serve as the patient's health care agent, presumably out of concerns about conflict of interest (financial or otherwise). This restriction, though understandable, may well serve to preclude the person who knows the patient's wishes best from implementing them. Patients who want their personal physicians to act as their agents can avoid the effects of this restriction in a variety of ways: (1) by naming a different agent and explicitly and specifically instructing that agent to follow the physician's recommendations; (2) by naming the physician as agent under circumstances where there will be a different attending physician; or (3) by ignoring it and naming the physi-

cian who is the attending physician, since using advance directive statutes is not the exclusive means of effectuating the right to choose.

Patients making this last choice must anticipate opposition from hospital counsel uneasy about deviations from state statutes. It may help to place certain things in writing in the document: (1) An acknowledgment that the patient is aware of the statutory restriction but understands that it is not legally binding; (2) an enumeration of the reasons for choosing the physician to act as agent (is the physician the best choice? the only reasonably available choice?) and an assertion of the conviction that greater risk is posed by not permitting the patient's chosen agent to act than by the theoretical possibility of conflict of interest; and (3) a statement that the patient and physician have talked together about the patient's wishes and the physician's role as agent, perhaps setting forth some agreed-upon safeguards, such as concurrence by other physicians, separate determination of decisional incapacity, or consultation with an ethics committee.

**14.** As Eric Cassell (1985) points out, patients nearly always make sense, even though the sense of what they say is not always readily apparent to doctors.

## NOTES TO CHAPTER 4

**1.** Although it appeared at first that only a contemporaneous expression or a written document (a living will, or instruction directive) could meet this standard, new evidence of Nancy Cruzan's conversations with friends and coworkers later formed the basis for the probate court's determination—without objection from the State of Missouri—that her artificial nutrition and hydration could be withdrawn.

**2.** Conscience clause statutes generally permit individuals and institutions to decline to participate in the provision of health care to which they have moral objections. Abortion is the most common example, although some states have passed conscience clause statutes about "futile treatment." To avoid the problem of abandonment, institutions must make such policies known to patients at or before admission, and individual caregivers must help to ensure that patients have access to other caregivers who will implement their advance directives. The federal regulations that implement the PSDA also require providers to give patients "a clear and precise statement" describing how services will be limited according to any conscience clause policy regarding advance directives and identifying the legal authority permitting the policy (Health Care Financing Administration 1995).

**3.** An extensive literature is developing on the PSDA—its problems, theoretical questions, issues of implementation, and areas needing research (see, for example, Special Supplement 1994; see also the cost literature cited in chapter 6). That discussion is outside the scope of this book.

4. Most advance directive statutes explicitly provide that they are intended to supplement, rather than replace or curtail, the common law (Gelfand 1987, 784 n. 202). See, for example, the language of legislative preambles in the statutes set out and discussed later in this chapter. Moreover, unless a statute or its legislative history explicitly provides that the legislature's intent was to change and to narrow the common law in this area, the chances are great that it would not be found to do so by a court, because the common law in this area is so well developed (see, e.g., *In re A.C.* 1990, 17–20). Several courts have so ruled, even without an explicit statutory provision to that effect; others have found statutory limitations on treatment refusal unconstitutional (e.g., *Corbett v. D'Alessandro* 1986; *In re Rodas* 1987).

5. See chapter 2's discussion of the legal basis for directives.

6. As of mid-1995, no state completely precludes by statute the refusal of artificial nutrition and hydration. Only one living will law—Missouri's—purports to require the provision of artificial nutrition and hydration (thirty-five states permit its refusal, and eleven states plus the District of Columbia do not explicitly address the issue). Missouri's health care proxy statute does, however, allow the proxy to refuse artificial nutrition and hydration on the patient's behalf if the patient has so indicated in the proxy appointment. No state proxy statutes limit the proxy's authority to refuse artificial nutrition and hydration, though fewer proxy statutes than living will statutes address the issue specifically.

Attempts to restrict treatment refusal during pregnancy are far more common: Thirty-four living will statutes and fourteen health care proxy statutes explicitly forbid withholding or withdrawing life-sustaining treatment in pregnancy. Only Arizona, Maryland, New Jersey, Florida, and Wisconsin explicitly permit treatment refusal during pregnancy in either type of advance directive statute. Living will statutes in eleven jurisdictions and health care proxy statutes in thirty-seven make no mention of pregnancy; thus, it appears that proxies are generally accorded greater decisional freedom by statute in this sensitive area (Choice in Dying 1994, 1995).

7. See the *Barber* case's discussion of the role of the criminal law in this area (*Barber v. Superior Court* 1983).

8. In *Randolph v. City of New York* (1986), a Jehovah's Witness refused blood transfusions and subsequently underwent a cesarean section. During an emergency hysterectomy that became necessary when the placenta could not be removed, an accidental laceration caused a massive hemorrhage. After unsuccessful efforts to control the hemorrhage, the physicians requested legal authorization for a transfusion, but it came too late to save the patient. When her husband brought suit for negligence, the court held that the patient's right to decide about her care outweighed the doctor's obligation to give necessary treatment, stating that it was unfair to penalize the physician for not ignoring the patient's wishes at the first sign of hemorrhage. It is hard to

imagine a stronger case than this for upholding the validity of an advance directive (which this patient's refusal of transfusion essentially was) even when the family disagrees.

9. After the United States Supreme Court's decision was announced, the Cruzan family sought a new hearing before the trial judge to offer new evidence of their daughter's wishes. The State of Missouri then sought and received dismissal as a party in the case, expressing confidence that the remaining parties, namely the Cruzans and Nancy Cruzan's court-appointed guardian, would properly apply the clear and convincing evidence standard (Gianelli 1990a). Because the new evidence was to consist of testimony from several of Nancy's former coworkers about oral statements she had made to them, the state's posture could be interpreted as conceding that oral statements can meet the standard (Gianelli 1990).

On December 14, 1990, in a brief opinion and order, Jasper County probate judge Teel found that Nancy Cruzan's prior oral statements to coworkers constituted clear and convincing evidence sufficient to support removal of her feeding tube. Judge Teel was the same judge who had originally ordered removal of Nancy Cruzan's feeding tube, which decision was challenged by the State of Missouri and resulted in the U.S. Supreme Court's ruling. This time, however, the State of Missouri did not challenge the court's decision, and state health department officials promised to comply with the order; ninety minutes after it was issued, Nancy Cruzan's gastrostomy tube was removed. She was expected to die within two weeks, while receiving comfort care and pain medication if necessary.

Nancy Beth Cruzan died peacefully in the early hours of December 26, 1990, amid a flurry of protests and last-minute legal efforts by right-to-life organizations. All of these efforts were rejected by both state and federal courts on the grounds that the petitioners had no standing, or legal interest, in Ms. Cruzan's case and presented no substantive grounds for intervention. An emergency petition was to have been submitted to the U.S. Supreme Court on the day she died.

Judge Teel's December 14 decision and its aftermath have made clear that in Missouri the clear and convincing evidence standard in this context may be met by oral statements, thus reducing the potential burden of such a standard on victims of sudden illness and injury and others who have not prepared written advance directives. Similarly, the Illinois Supreme Court has interpreted its own "clear and convincing evidence" standard as being met by oral statements (*In re Greenspan* 1990). Needless to say, in the vast majority of jurisdictions, which do not apply this high evidentiary standard, prior oral statements continue to be a principal means of ascertaining a patient's desires and views.

10. Many institutions and their legal advisors take a very cautious posture in this and other areas and would prefer that patients and their families

seek prior court authorization for nonconforming directives. This is an unreasonable posture (see articles collected in Gostin [1989] on the *Linares* case). Truly definitive judicial authorization is hard to come by, since the U. S. Supreme Court cannot hear all the cases we want it to hear, and certainly cannot hear them all in time for it to matter in many cases. Besides, when caregivers, patient, and family are in agreement except for "legal concerns," there is no reason in good conscience to indulge such disembodied concerns—especially because the moral underpinnings of advance directives are so strong (Meisel 1989). Finally, there is no justifiable assumption that a state law, especially in this controversial area, is constitutional unless proven otherwise. Legislatures often pass laws that they suspect or know are unconstitutional. Recall former Massachusetts governor Michael Dukakis's 1988 refusal to sign a state statute prohibiting flag desecration because his legal staff advised him it was unconstitutional. He was widely criticized for failing to pass a statute that he knew would not withstand scrutiny. Critics reasoned that it was not the governor's job to make such judgments and denounced him for failing to "send a message" about what the Constitution *ought* to say. Thus, to assume that a state legislature has made a correct constitutional judgment is problematic (though, of course, legislatures must be regarded as having acted in good faith unless there is evidence to the contrary).

**11.** To say that advance directives evidence rather than constitute choice is not to weaken their moral or legal force; on the contrary, it affirms their flexibility and suggests ways of strengthening their effectiveness (Weir 1994; but see Buchanan and Brock 1986, 56–67).

**12.** Most statutes provide that the withholding or withdrawal of treatment according to a directive that substantially conforms to their terms shall not be considered the cause of a patient's death. This is also true for any valid treatment refusal under common law or the Constitution. Therefore, most state statutes go on to offer physicians limited liability protection. Many provide that physicians and facilities acting according to the statutory terms shall not be "subject to liability" or even "subject to any proceeding." This sounds like broad immunity until it is realized that nearly all states qualify that immunity by offering it only to physicians who act "in good faith" or "in accordance with reasonable medical standards." Thus, physicians accused of bad faith or bad judgment or failure to meet the conditions of the statute are still required to defend themselves in court.

**13.** Generally speaking, statutes specifically addressing reciprocity recognize advance directives as valid according to the laws of the state they come from. As of mid-1995, advance directive statutes in thirty states contain reciprocity clauses; the rest do not address reciprocity (Choice in Dying 1994, 1995).

**14.** In fact, only a few statutes provide that directives may be executed on behalf of minors. According to Choice in Dying, as of mid-1995 seven states permit parents to complete advance directives for their terminally ill children, and a few other states permit certain categories of "emancipated" or "mature" minors to write directives. Presumably this indicates legislative recognition that treatment refusal, like all other significant decisions made by minors, requires particularized attention to whether the minor in question is capable of autonomous decision-making under the circumstances; it is not just a legislative determination that minors cannot write directives. Moreover, since parents have legal decision-making authority for their minor children, parents are, in a sense, automatic health care proxies for their children, thus all but obviating the need for statutory proxies for minors.

**15.** Along with the expansion of statutory language from "terminal illness" and "life-sustaining procedures" to address PVS and artificial nutrition and hydration comes the problem of determining whether artificial nutrition and hydration should be included within the category "life-sustaining procedures" or treated separately in statutory directives. Some states explicitly address this problem and others do not. Some states set up a presumption that all persons want to receive artificial nutrition and hydration unless they specifically declare otherwise in a directive. The validity of such a presumption is at best problematic, and pregnancy clauses seem obviously unconstitutional (Note 1990). The thorough and repetitive language used in these statutes provides a good example of the failure of even the most exhaustively scrutinized statute to shut all possible legal loopholes, and could be taken as an object lesson in the desirability of good physician-patient communication and understanding as an alternative to exclusive reliance on the written word (Annas 1991).

**16.** See discussions of decisional capacity in chapters 3 and 5.

**17.** A rather tragic example of ambiguity in advance directive terminology arose several years ago in New York. Tom Wirth was diagnosed as having AIDS-related complex (ARC) and wrote an advance directive substantially identical to an advocacy group's model directive; a few months later, he was admitted to Bellevue Hospital in a stuporous condition and was found to have toxoplasmosis. His directive provided for withholding or withdrawing all of the treatments listed in that version of the advocacy group's model directive, including antibiotics, if "there is no reasonable possibility of recovering or regaining a meaningful quality of life." His directive also named his longtime friend and lover, John Evans, as his proxy; Evans attempted to refuse antibiotic treatment for the toxoplasmosis. The hospital resisted and a court agreed, reasoning that Wirth was expected to recover from the toxoplasmosis if treated and that it was therefore not clear that he considered his pre-toxoplasmosis state not a meaningful quality of life just because he had ARC. Because of this ambiguity, the court refused to recognize his proxy's claim that Wirth had meant he wanted no treatment unless he could recover from ARC (*Evans v. Bellevue Hospital* 1987).

The court's somewhat questionable reasoning on this and other issues in the case was not tested on appeal; Mr. Wirth never regained decisional capacity, and treatment was eventually stopped in accordance with his directive. To its credit, the court did ask that directives be as clear and specific as possible; in this case it is likely that if Mr. Wirth had added some explanatory material to his directive, making it more than just a copy of a model form, the disagreement that arose in this case might have been avoided.

**18.** This question is discussed further in chapter 5.

**19.** By mid-1995, only Massachusetts, Michigan, and New York lacked some form of living will statute (Choice in Dying 1994, 1995).

**20.** Before *Cruzan*, only about a dozen state living will statutes provided for the appointment of a proxy in their model directives (Society for the Right to Die 1988). In response to Justice O'Connor's concurrence in the *Cruzan* decision, more and more states have specifically enacted durable powers of attorney for health care decision-making. By mid-1995 all but two states—Alabama and Alaska—had health care proxy statutes.

**21.** Such court-appointed guardianships, often called "guardians of the person" (as distinguished from guardianships of property), are provided for by statute in every state and are often part of the duties of social-services authorities, who take responsibility for incapacitated patients without families.

**22.** In addition, physicians have pointed out that the statutory definition of "persistent vegetative state," as used in the Declaration, is considerably broader than most medical definitions and is therefore comparable to "severe dementia" in the proxy statute.

**23.** This does *not* mean that a directive should not be honored if the family disagrees with it. See generally the discussion of this issue in chapter 5. See also note 8 above.

## NOTES TO CHAPTER 5

**1.** It is beyond the scope of this book to address comprehensively the theory or policy whereby medical treatment decisions in default of advance directives are and should be made. There is a vast and growing literature on this subject; some important and comprehensive discussions are found in Buchanan and Brock (1986); Burt (1988); Coordinating Council (1993); Dresser (1986, 1994a); Hastings Center (1987); Layson et al. (1994); Lynn (1992); Meisel (1989, 1992); President's Commission (1983); Rhoden (1988, 1990); Ruark and Raffin (1988); Steinbrook and Lo (1988); Veatch (1993); New York State Task Force on Life and the Law (1992); and Weir and Gostin (1990).

**2.** The term "living will" was coined in 1969 by Louis Kutner (Kutner 1969).

3. It is important to recognize that the U.S. Supreme Court, when it permitted states to require clear and convincing evidence of a decisionally incapable patient's wish to refuse artificial nutrition and hydration (*Cruzan v. Director* 1990), did *not* thereby rule that persons without written directives have chosen treatment. The *Cruzan* Court left largely unspecified the means by which patients could meet their evidentiary burdens, left the states free to choose a less demanding standard of proof (as many already have), and made clear that the reason for imposing a standard that might result in failure to act in accordance with some evidence of the patient's wishes is not a presumption about what those wishes are but, rather, a desire to protect the best interests of decisionally incapable patients. A number of advance directive statutes and the PSDA similarly declare that not having a directive gives rise to no presumptions about the patient's wishes.

4. Meisel's points of consensus (and he is careful to emphasize that consensus is not unanimity) are as follows (Meisel 1992, 315):

(1) Competent patients have a common-law and constitutional right to refuse treatment.

(2) Incompetent patients have the same rights as competent patients; but the manner in which these rights are exercised is, of necessity, different.

(3) No right is absolute, and limitations are imposed by societal interests on the right to refuse treatment.

(4) The decision-making process should generally occur in the clinical setting, without recourse to the courts.

(5) In making decisions for incompetent patients, surrogate decision-makers should apply, in descending order of preference, the subjective standard, the substituted-judgment standard, and the best-interests standard.

(6) In ascertaining an incompetent patient's preferences, the attending physician and the surrogate may rely on a patient's advance directive.

(7) Artificial nutrition and hydration is a medical treatment and may be withheld or withdrawn under the same conditions as any other form of medical treatment.

(8) Active euthanasia and assisted suicide are morally and legally distinct from forgoing life-sustaining treatment.

5. This decision-making standard, also applied in *Cruzan*, is what Meisel calls the "subjective" standard of treatment decision-making (which is met by written advance directives or their oral equivalents) (Meisel 1992, 322–323).

6. See the debate about these issues in Annas (1979), Baron (1978, 1979), Buchanan (1979), and Relman (1978).

7. Choice in Dying listed twenty-four states and the District of Columbia as having such statutes as of mid-1995.

8. This order usually corresponds roughly to priority lists in state laws describing the degree of relationship between kin for purposes such as inheritance.

9. This reasoning parallels to some degree that of the Supreme Court in *Cruzan v. Director* (1990), though it would permit more nontreatment decisions than would the State of Missouri. According to this new best interests standard, the withdrawal of artificial nutrition and hydration has been accepted in a number of cases (*Brophy v. New England Sinai Hospital* 1986; *Delio v. Westchester County Medical Center* 1987; *In re Jobes* 1987; *In re Peter* 1987). Withholding treatment from a demented victim of a serious but treatable condition is a much more controversial proposition, even though competent patients like Dax Cowart, Elizabeth Bouvia (*Bouvia v. Superior Court* [*Glenchur*] 1986), William Bartling (*Bartling v. Superior Court* 1984), or Beverly Requena (*In re Requena* 1986) may autonomously refuse treatment.

Decision-making without advance directives will in many cases be difficult at best, because the issues are so complex, our convictions are so diverse, and legal guidance for many of the situations caregivers face is still quite imperfect. An example of an increasingly common dilemma is the elderly nursing home resident without an advance directive who has severe Alzheimer's disease and other chronic debilitating conditions, who is somewhat responsive to her environment and somewhat ill and unhappy, and who suddenly becomes acutely septic or develops a treatable pneumonia. Somebody—one or all of the members of the health care team, or one or all of the family members, who may be involved and caring or deeply divided— suggests not treating the patient with antibiotics so that he or she will peacefully die (Brown and Thompson 1979). Somebody else disagrees (Dresser 1994a).

Disagreement in cases like this can at least ensure that all relevant information about the patient's current experience, prognosis, and past preferences and values is considered. The willingness of family, friends, and caregivers to discuss disagreements openly greatly increases the likelihood of reaching a decision that all parties can accept as in the patient's best interests as the patient would view them (see, e.g., Tomlinson and Brody 1988). But there are no firm rules here, and none of the circumstances that make some cases "easy." No one clearly holds the decisional authority, and there is no terminal illness, no respirator in place, no do-not-resuscitate order to discuss. It is still likely that at least some such disagreements will end in anger, bitterness, and the courtroom.

10. Authorizing someone to make the decision requires a determination, or at least a presumption, that the person chosen will make the decision on the basis of the best evidence. Special statutes usually require some degree of

consensus among family members in order to protect against self-interested decisions by relatives, and courts will scrutinize the motives of would-be decision-makers for the same reason. In the absence of a legal proxy, then, disagreement between physicians and family requires careful scrutiny of the evidence and reasoning behind the opposing contentions, but the decision itself belongs to no one in particular. Although the family's approval under these circumstances is not required, hospital lawyers routinely advise obtaining approval from the family or from the court as a prudential matter.

Special statutes are, however, becoming more common. The Uniform Rights of the Terminally Ill Act in 1989 paved the way for the states by including a provision permitting withdrawal of treatment from terminally ill persons without advance directives upon consent of specified relatives, who are given in order of priority in an extensive list. About half the states and the District of Columbia now have such statutes, many of which were passed after *Cruzan*. The Uniform Health-Care Decisions Act (1993), which supersedes URTIA, also contains a priority list for surrogates; the decision-making power for surrogates is considerably broader than URTIA authorized.

**11.** One means of recording patients' preferences that does not amount to writing a directive is the "values history," which appears to be gaining popularity in long-term care settings (Cantor 1993; Lambert, Gibson, and Nathanson 1990).

**12.** For example, an elderly widow has a standard statutory combined advance directive and health care power of attorney naming a neighbor as her proxy. She is hospitalized with a moderately severe stroke; she cannot speak, and whether she understands what is said to her is unclear. She also cannot swallow, and gastrostomy tube feeding is recommended. Placing the tube requires a minor surgical procedure. Her physician of many years, who did not know about her advance directive but states that he knows her wishes very well, reports to the surgeons that he has attempted to obtain her consent for the procedure and she has clearly refused, shaking her head and pushing him away.

On first examination the question of this patient's decisional capacity may seem moot, since she appears to refuse treatment both in her directive and "live," as it were. But a closer look reveals potential problems. If this patient lacks decisional capacity, her mental state does not reflect the kind of serious incapacity generally linked with treatment refusal in statutory living wills. If, on the other hand, the patient is decisionally capable, she is a competent patient apparently refusing treatment. In the first instance, her proxy might be called upon to make the decision whether or not to place the feeding tube. In the second instance, her personal physician is taking the lead in interpreting her actions. Thus, *how* this patient's directive is interpreted and used and *who* has the primary responsibility for doing that are potentially in dispute here and must be carefully thought through and discussed with all involved parties before this patient's wishes and interests can be well served.

13. The Commission on Uniform State Law's new model statute, the Uniform Health-Care Decisions Act (1993), establishes two different revocation standards: one for revoking the designation of a health care agent and another for revoking all or part of an advance directive other than the designation of an agent (that is, an instruction directive). The designation of an agent must be revoked by a signed writing or by "personally informing the supervising health care provider." This is a relatively high standard for revocation. In contrast, living will–type provisions may be revoked "in any manner that communicates an intent to revoke"—the typical low standard for revocation. The difference might exist because in this model statute, patients can appoint agents to begin deciding for them immediately, while they are still capable of decision-making, whereas their instruction directives only become effective when they lack decisional capacity. But it also makes sense to set a high standard for revoking the authority of an agent, for two reasons. The Uniform Act's commentary notes that an individual seeking control over the patient could fabricate a revocation of agency granted to someone else and thereby assume control. A fabricated revocation of an instruction directive, however, could have the same effect. More important is to recognize that honorable agents have reason to work with caregivers to decide for patients on the basis of all available information. Too easy revocation of agency could prevent those persons best situated to act on the patient's behalf from doing so. Involuntary revocation of an instruction directive, on the other hand, is information that a responsible agent will be able to take into account in attempting to honor the patient's wishes.

14. I am indebted to Erich Loewy, whose presentation of a similar case at the Society for Health and Human Values annual meeting in Arlington, Virginia, in November 1987, helped to illuminate this problem for me.

15. See chapter 3 for further discussion of this important point.

16. This works both ways: Because the patient's capacity may vary, a new inquiry may be needed at the time of decision even if the patient is already thought to be incompetent.

17. There is clearly a risk here that this antirevocation maneuver will simply focus all of the most difficult questions on this clause rather than on the entire directive—without the benefit of the assurances and safeguards provided to the clinician by standard revocation clauses. The problem is undeniable. Nonetheless, there is also an undeniable need to address patients' strong desires on this very question. This is one way to do so. It is legally unproven; yet the moral underpinnings of advance directives suggest that it merits exploration.

## NOTES TO CHAPTER 6

1. For example, in the Hastings Center's comprehensive *Guidelines* (1987), advance directives account for just 8 of 139 pages of suggestions for policy and procedures. Moreover, some recent research and scholarship downplays even further the role of advance directives in treatment decision-making (Dresser 1994).

2. The literature in this area is growing rapidly. Representative scholarship, research, and surveys include Brock 1994; Chambers et al. 1994; Danis 1994; Emanuel and Emanuel 1994; Correspondence 1994; Schneiderman et al. 1992; Teno, Nelson, and Lynn 1994; Teno et al. 1994.

3. As Sherwin Nuland (*How We Die*, 1994), Margaret Pabst Battin (*The Least Worst Death*, 1994), and Tim Quill (*Death and Dignity*, 1993) all point out, the language of the right-to-die movement may tend to obscure the irreducible reality that dying is often frightening and painful. Peacefulness and control are morally necessary attributes of the patient's relationship to caregivers and technology. These terms, however, cannot necessarily be ascribed to the patient's physical experience, though their proper use can certainly be of great help in managing a difficult dying process.

4. Several cases since *Leach* have addressed the same issue. More cases are pending (Cohen 1987; Gasner 1992). Most recently, although a New York appellate court ordered treatment withdrawal for a nursing home patient with an advance directive (*Elbaum v. Grace Plaza* 1989), the state's highest court ruled, in a dispute over payment of the $100,000 nursing home bill incurred after the facility refused to honor the directive, that the nursing home had not exhibited bad faith, and required the patient's widower to pay (*Grace Plaza v. Elbaum* 1993). See also *Anderson v. St. Francis-St. George Hospital* (1992), in which an Ohio appellate court refused to recognize "wrongful living" but left open the possibility of successful battery and negligence claims by a patient resuscitated against his will.

5. Disputes will arise about the time lags incurred in finding a willing substitute—see discussion of cases in Cohen (1987)—but such disputes do not affect the essential point that the physician can avoid the charge of battery by properly withdrawing from the relationship, however "proper" is defined by courts. Many advance directive statutes also specify procedures for patient transfer, thus helping to set standards for appropriate termination of the physician-patient relationship.

6. There is no sense minimizing the difficulty of these cases. When Elizabeth Bouvia first went to court to assert her right to refuse food, she was viewed by the court as attempting to starve herself while demanding extensive supportive care and pain relief from the hospital, and she lost (*Bouvia v. County of Riverside* 1983). Later, however, she couched her need for pain relief

and her disinclination to eat in less confrontational terms and succeeded in protecting her rights (*Bouvia v. Superior Court [Glenchur]* 1986). One of the reasons for the persistence of the artificial distinction between action and inaction is that it permits us to avoid discussing euthanasia. Certainly there are many similarities between arguments in favor of euthanasia and those supporting treatment refusal and "death with dignity" (see, e.g., *Cruzan v. Director* 1990, Scalia, J., concurring; Engelhardt 1986; Rachels 1986). And much attention has been showered on the Netherlands' complex legal loophole that makes possible a policy of official inattention to certain carefully documented instances of voluntary euthanasia (Harper 1987; Scholten 1986; Singer and Siegler 1990). This volume takes no position on euthanasia except to point out (1) that there is great need for openness, procedure, and safeguards if any such policy is to be instituted and (2) that the medical profession's involvement in voluntary euthanasia must be examined with the same sense of honesty and responsibility that has attended the best debate about the profession's role in withholding and withdrawing treatment. This is not to say that the profession's conclusion should be the same on both questions. (For an introduction to the large literature on physician-assisted suicide, readers should look elsewhere; to scratch the surface, consider Tim Quill's excellent book [1993], or Battin's [1994].)

7. Helga Wanglie was an elderly woman who broke her hip and suffered long-term complications of the injury and its treatment. As a patient in a Minnesota hospital, she was permanently respirator-dependent and in a persistent vegetative state when the hospital sought to terminate her treatment as medically inappropriate; her family objected (Angell 1991; *In re Conservatorship of Wanglie* 1991; Miles 1991). Her case has been the subject of much commentary and controversy.

8. Baby K was anencephalic—that is, she was born without a brain and without the portion of her skull that encases the brain. She was unable to see or hear and had no higher brain function. She did, however, have a brain stem and spinal cord. From the time of her birth, her mother requested maximal treatment for her, including mechanical ventilation when she had difficulty breathing. The hospital where she was born sought judicial permission to decline provision of ventilatory support, but the court ruled that treatment was required (*In re Baby K* 1994; Annas 1994; Capron 1994). Baby K—Stephanie Harrell—died in April 1995, while receiving treatment at the hospital where she was born. She was two and a half years old.

9. The model for end-of-life decision-making has historically focused on securing the patient's right to refuse unwanted treatment. Most—but not all—of the few advance directive statutes that address the patient's interest in receiving maximal treatment qualify the request with a reference to accepted medical standards. See the discussion in chapter 4.

10. Most notably Ruth Macklin, in *Enemies of Patients* (1993, 166–186).

**11.** As Tomlinson and Brody (1988, 1990) did for DNR orders; see chapter 3.

**12.** Nothing about advance directives is free from problems. It has been suggested to me by Larry Churchill that such insurance incentives, even though they are not conditions of coverage, could compromise the validity of the antirevocation clauses discussed in chapter 5.

**13.** Although clinicians may not be fully aware of the complexity of these decisions until one begins to go sour, insurers already play an important role in many treatment withdrawal decisions, simply because they must decide whether or not to pay for the continuation of treatment. Payment decisions are made by insurers on the basis of expert opinion about the propriety of treatment, and if the propriety of treatment is disputed, the insurer's experts may carry much weight—especially when they support the family's attempts to have treatment discontinued. In a dispute involving the hospital and the physician and their malpractice insurers as well as the patient's family and the patient's health insurer, the patient's insurer can be a major source of financial support for the patient's position, since expert opinion is expensive. But it is far from clear that insurers and patients can remain allies if insurance discount plans raise payment issues more often in end-of-life treatment settings. Although the cost-saving capacity of advance directives is being sharply questioned, the extreme pressure for cost containment that is currently being felt could provide insurers with avenues for inappropriate intervention in implementation of advance directives.

**14.** The PSDA and the JCAHO accreditation requirements addressing it and other ethical issues for patients have had a substantial impact on the development of institutional policy on advance directives but little apparent effect on improving understanding of the meaning and significance of the ethical principles upon which directives are based. See the discussion in chapter 4.

**15.** For example, a recent study comparing patients' responses to one state's widely used short-form advance directive with their choices from a different list of specific interventions in a range of specific circumstances and conditions found that patients' instructions on the short form did not match particularly well with their more specific preferences (Schneiderman et al. 1992a). One problem with this kind of comparison—as with empirical research testing patients' end-of-life preferences generally—is that written language can be surprisingly impenetrable. It cannot be emphasized enough that even the "perfect form" (which these authors appeared to be looking for) should not be expected to stand alone. The most advance directive forms can do is begin and continue the conversation and help to equip others—caregivers alone or caregivers along with proxies—to choose well on the patient's behalf.

**16.** The parsimonious view of autonomy that fails to acknowledge this richness may at last be in retreat. See, e.g., Brock (1991); Childress (1990).

# Bibliography

## BOOKS AND ARTICLES

Amundsen, D. W.: 1978, "The Physician's Obligation to Prolong Life: A Medical Duty without Classical Roots," *Hastings Center Report* 8(4), 23–30.

Angell, M.: 1991, "The Case of Helga Wanglie: A New Kind of 'Right to Die' Case," *New England Journal of Medicine* 325, 511–512.

_____: 1994, "After Quinlan: The Dilemma of the Persistent Vegetative State," *New England Journal of Medicine* 330, 1524–1525.

Annas, G.: 1979, "Reconciling Quinlan and Saikewicz: Decision Making for the Terminally Ill Incompetent," *American Journal of Law and Medicine* 4, 367–396.

_____: 1984, "The Case of Elizabeth Bouvia," *Hastings Center Report* 14 (2), 20–21.

_____: 1986, "Women as Fetal Containers," *Hastings Center Report* 16(6), 13–14.

_____: 1987, "Transferring the Ethical Hot Potato," *Hastings Center Report* 17(1), 20–21.

_____: 1988, *Judging Medicine*, Humana Press, Clifton, N.J.

_____: 1990, "Nancy Cruzan and the Right to Die," *New England Journal of Medicine* 323, 670–673.

_____: 1991, "The Health Care Proxy and the Living Will," *New England Journal of Medicine* 324, 1210–1213.

_____: 1993, *Standard of Care: The Law of American Bioethics*, Oxford University Press, New York.

_____: 1994, "Asking the Courts to Set the Standard of Emergency Care: The Case of Baby K," *New England Journal of Medicine* 330, 1524–1525.

_____: 1994a, "Informed Consent, Cancer, and Truth in Prognosis," *New England Journal of Medicine* 330, 223–225.

Annas, G. J., and Glantz, L. H.: 1986, "The Right of Elderly Patients to Refuse Life-Sustaining Treatment," *Milbank Quarterly* 64 (Supp. 2), 95–162.

Annas, G., et al.: 1990, "Bioethicists' Statement on the U.S. Supreme Court's Cruzan Decision," *New England Journal of Medicine* 323, 686–687.

Appelbaum, P. S., Lidz, C. W., and Meisel, A.: 1987, *Informed Consent: Legal Theory and Clinical Practice*, Oxford University Press, New York.

Areen, J.: 1987, "The Legal Status of Consent Obtained from Families of Adult Patients to Withhold or Withdraw Treatment," *Journal of the American Medical Association* 258, 229–235.

_____: 1988, "Legal Intrusions on Physician Independence," in N. M. P. King, L. R. Churchill, and A. W. Cross (eds.), *The Physician as Captain of the Ship: A Critical Reappraisal*, D. Reidel, Dordrecht, Netherlands, pp. 54–57.

_____: 1991, "Advance Directives under State Law and Judicial Decisions," *Law, Medicine, and Health Care* 19, 91–100.

Areen, J., et al.: 1984, *Law, Science, and Medicine*, Foundation Press, New York, pp. 1112–1117.

Baron, C.: 1978, "Assuring 'Detached but Passionate Investigation and Decision': The Role of Guardians Ad Litem in Saikewicz-Type Cases," *American Journal of Law and Medicine* 4, 111–130.

_____: 1979, "Medical Paternalism and the Rule of Law: A Reply to Dr. Relman," *American Journal of Law and Medicine* 4, 337–365.

_____: 1987, "On Knowing One's Chains and Decking Them with Flowers: Limits on Patient Autonomy in 'The Silent World of Doctor and Patient,'" *Western New England Law Review* 9, 31–41.

_____: 1991, "Why Withdrawal of Life-Support for PVS Patients Is Not a Family Decision," *Law, Medicine and Health Care* 19, 73–75.

Battin, M. P.: 1994, *The Least Worst Death: Essays in Bioethics on the End of Life*, Oxford University Press, New York.

Beauchamp, T., and Childress, J.: 1994, *Principles of Biomedical Ethics*, 4th ed., Oxford University Press, New York.

Brett, A., and McCullough, L.: 1986, "When Patients Request Specific Interventions: Defining the Limits of the Physician's Obligation," *New England Journal of Medicine* 315, 1347–1351.

Brock, D. W.: 1991, "The Ideal of Shared Decision Making between Physicians and Patients," *Kennedy Institute of Ethics Journal* 1, 28–47.

_____: 1994, "Advance Directives: What Is It Reasonable to Expect from Them?" *Journal of Clinical Ethics* 5, 57–62.

Brody, H.: 1994, "The Multiple Facets of Futility," *Journal of Clinical Ethics* 5, 142–144.

Brown, N., and Thompson, D.: 1979, "Nontreatment of Fever in Extended-Care Facilities," *New England Journal of Medicine* 300, 1246.

Buchanan, A.: 1979, "Medical Paternalism or Legal Imperialism: Not the Only Alternatives for Handling Saikewicz-Type Cases," *American Journal of Law and Medicine* 5, 103–104.

Buchanan, A., and Brock, D. W.: 1986, "Deciding for Others," *Milbank Quarterly* 64 (Supp. 2), 17–94.

_____: 1989, *Deciding for Others: The Ethics of Surrogate Decision Making*, Cambridge University Press, New York.

Burt, R.: 1979, *Taking Care of Strangers*, Free Press, New York.

_____: 1988, "Uncertainty and Medical Authority in the World of Jay Katz," *Law, Medicine and Health Care* 16, 190–195.

Callahan, D.: 1987, *Setting Limits: Medical Goals in an Aging Society*, Simon and Schuster, New York.

_____: 1990, *What Kind of Life: The Limits of Medical Progress*, Simon and Schuster, New York.

Cantor, N.: 1989, "The Permanently Unconscious Patient, Non-Feeding and Euthanasia," *American Journal of Law and Medicine* 15, 381–437.

_____: 1990, "My Annotated Living Will," *Law, Medicine, and Health Care* 18, 114–122.

_____: 1993, *Advance Directives and the Pursuit of Death with Dignity*, Indiana University Press, Bloomington.

Capron, A. M.: 1974, "Informed Consent in Catastrophic Disease Research and Treatment," *University of Pennsylvania Law Review* 123, 340–438.

_____, 1984: "Ironies and Tensions in Feeding the Dying," *Hastings Center Report* 14(5), 32–35.

_____, 1994: "Medical Futility: Strike Two," *Hastings Center Report* 24(5), 42–43.

Case Study: 1992, "Whether No Means No," *Hastings Center Report* 22(2), 26–27.

Cassell, E.: 1985, *Talking with Patients*, vol. I, MIT Press, Boston, pp. 53–55.

Chambers, C., et al.: 1994, "Relationship of Advance Directives to Hospital Charges in a Medicare Population," *Archives of Internal Medicine* 154, 541–547.

Childress, J.: 1990, "The Place of Autonomy in Bioethics," *Hastings Center Report* 20(1), 12–16.

Choice in Dying: 1994, *Refusal of Treatment Legislation*, Choice in Dying, New York.

_____: 1995, *Right-to-Die Law Digest*, Choice in Dying, New York.

Churchill, J.: 1989, "Advance Directives: Beyond Respect for Freedom," in J. C. Hackler, R. Moseley, and D. Vawter (eds.), *Advance Directives in Medicine*, Praeger, New York, pp. 171–179.

Churchill, L. R.: 1987, *Rationing Health Care in America: Perceptions and Principles of Justice*, Notre Dame Press, Notre Dame, Indiana.

Cohen, C., and Cohen, P.: 1991, "Sounding Board: Do-Not-Resuscitate Orders in the Operating Room," *New England Journal of Medicine* 325, 1879–1882.

Cohen, E.: 1987, "Civil Liability for Providing Unwanted Life Support," *BioLaw* 2(6),499–503.

_____: 1991, "Terminal Care Decision Making," in A. Dellinger (ed.), *Health Care Facilities Law*, Little, Brown, Boston, pp. 657–740.

Comment: 1967, "Informed Consent in Medical Malpractice," *California Law Review* 55, 1396.

Coordinating Council on Life-Sustaining Medical Treatment Decision Making by the Courts: 1993, *Guidelines for State Court Decision Making in Life-Sustaining Medical Treatment Cases*, 2d ed., National Center for State Courts, West Publishing, St. Paul, Minn.

Correspondence, 1994: "Cost Savings at the End of Life," *New England J Medicine* 331, 477–479.

Cranford, R. E.: 1991, "Neurologic Syndromes and Prolonged Survival: When Can Artificial Nutrition and Hydration Be Forgone?" *Law, Medicine and Health Care* 19 (1–2), 13–22.

Cranford, R. E., and Doudera, A. E.: 1984, "The Emergence of Institutional Ethics Committees," *Law, Medicine, and Health Care* 12, 13–20.

Culver, C., and Gert, B.: 1982, *Philosophy in Medicine*, Oxford University Press, New York.

Danis, M.: 1994, "Following Advance Directives," *Hastings Center Report* 24(6), S21–S23.

Danis, M., and Churchill, L. R.: 1991, "Autonomy and the Common Weal," *Hastings Center Report* 21(1), 25–31.

Danis, M., et al.: 1988, "Patient and Family Preferences for Medical Intensive Care," *Journal of the American Medical Association* 260, 797–802.

_____: 1991, "A Prospective Study of Advance Directives for Life-Sustaining Care," *New England Journal of Medicine* 324, 822–888.

De Lugo, J.: 1868, *Disputationes Scholasticae et Morales, 6*, De Justicia et Jure, disputation 10, sec. 1, n. 30, trans. D. Cronin: 1958, "The Moral Law in Regard to the Ordinary and Extraordinary Means of Conserving Life," ThD dissertation, Rome, p. 64.

Dresser, R.: 1984, "Bound to Treatment: The Ulysses Contract," *Hastings Center Report* 14(3), 13–16.

_____: 1986, "Life, Death, and Incompetent Patients: Conceptual Infirmities and Hidden Values in the Law," *Arizona Law Review* 28, 371–405.

_____: 1994, "Confronting the 'Near Irrelevance' of Advance Directives," *Journal of Clinical Ethics* 5, 55–56.

_____: 1994a, "Missing Persons: Legal Perceptions of Incompetent Patients," *Rutgers Law Review* 46, 609–719.

Dresser, R., and Robertson, J: 1989, "Quality of Life and Non-Treatment Decisions for Incompetent Patients: A Critique of the Orthodox Approach," *Law, Medicine, and Health Care* 17, 234–244.

Dresser, R., and Whitehouse, P.: 1994, "The Incompetent Patient on the Slippery Slope," *Hastings Center Report* 24, 6–12.

Duff, R.: 1988, "Unshared and Shared Decisionmaking: Reflections on Helplessness and Healing," in N. M. P. King, L. Churchill, and A. W. Cross (eds.), The Physician as Captain of the Ship: A Critical Reappraisal, D. Reidel, Dordrecht, Netherlands, pp. 191–221.

Dworkin, R.: 1986, "Autonomy and the Demented Self," *Milbank Quarterly* 64 (Supp. 2), 4–16.

_____: 1993, *Life's Dominion*, Knopf, New York.

Emanuel, E.: 1987, "A Communal Vision of Care for Incompetent Patients," *Hastings Center Report* 17(5), 15–20.

_____: 1991, *The Ends of Human Life: Medical Ethics in a Liberal Polity*, Harvard University Press, Cambridge.

_____: 1994, "Commentary on Discussions about Life-Sustaining Treatments," *Journal of Clinical Ethics* 5, 250–252.

Emanuel, E., and Emanuel, L.: 1990, "Living Wills: Past, Present, and Future," *Journal of Clinical Ethics*, 1, 9–19.

_____: 1992, "Proxy Decision Making for Incompetent Adults: An Ethical and Empirical Analysis," *Journal of the American Medical Association* 267, 2067–2071.

_____: 1994, "The Economics of Dying—the Illusion of Cost Savings at the End of Life," *New England Journal of Medicine* 330, 540–544.

Emanuel, L.: 1993, "Advance Directives: What Have We Learned So Far?" *Journal of Clinical Ethics* 4, 8–16.

Emanuel, L., and Emanuel, E.: 1989, "The Medical Directive: A New Comprehensive Advance Care Document," *Journal of the American Medical Association*, 261, 3288–3293.

Engelhardt, H. T., Jr.: 1986, *The Foundations of Bioethics*, Oxford University Press, New York.

Engelhardt, H. T., Jr., and Rie, M.: 1986, "Intensive Care Units, Scarce Resources, and Conflicting Principles of Justice," *Journal of the American Medical Association* 255, 1159–1164.

Faden, R., and Beauchamp, T. L., with King, N. M. P.: 1986, *A History and Theory of Informed Consent*, Oxford University Press, New York.

Feinberg, J.: 1984, *Harm to Others*, Oxford University Press, New York.

Francis, L.: 1989, "The Evanescence of Living Wills," *Real Property Probate and Trust Journal* 24, 141–164.

Freedman, B.: 1993, "Offering Truth: One Ethical Approach to the Uninformed Cancer Patient," *Archives of Internal Medicine*, 153, 572–576.

Gasner, M. R.: 1992, "Financial Penalties for Failing to Honor Patient Wishes to Refuse Treatment," *St. Louis University Public Law Review* 11, 499–520.

Gaylin, N., and Fried, C.: 1980, "Case Study—Refusing an Amputation: Who Should Pay for the Extra Care?" *Hastings Center Report* 10(1), 23–24.

Gelfand, R.: 1987, "Living Will Statutes: The First Decade," *Wisconsin Law Review* 1987, 737.

Gianelli, D.: 1990, "The Last Battle? New Witnesses Agree: Nancy Cruzan Would Want Tube-Feeding Stopped," *American Medical News*, November 16, p.1.

_____: 1990a, "Missouri Reverses Position, Wants Out of Cruzan Case," *American Medical News*, September 28, p.1.

_____: 1993, "Many Say Doctors Aren't Living Up to Expectations of Living Will Law," *American Medical News*, May 17, p.1.

Gold, J., et al.: 1990, "Is There a Right to Futile Treatment? The Case of a Dying Patient with Aids," *Journal of Clinical Ethics* 1, 19–23.

Gostin, L.: 1989, "Family Privacy and Persistent Vegetative State: A Symposium on the *Linares* Case," *Law, Medicine and Health Care* 17, 295–346.

_____: 1991, "Life and Death Choices after *Cruzan*," *Law, Medicine, and Health Care* 19, 9–12.

Gutheil, T. G., and Appelbaum, P. S.: 1983, "Substituted Judgment: Best Interests in Disguise," *Hastings Center Report* 13(3), 8–11.

Hall, M., and Anderson, G.: 1992, "Health Insurers' Assessment of Medical Necessity," *University of Pennsylvania Law Review* 140, 1637–1712.

Harmon, L.: 1990, "Falling off the Vine: Legal Fictions and the Doctrine of Substituted Judgment," *Yale Law Journal* 100, 1–71.

Harper, T.: 1987, "Where Euthanasia Is a Way of Death," *Medical Economics*, November 23, pp. 23–28.

Hastings Center: 1987, *Guidelines on the Termination of Life-Sustaining Treatment and the Care of the Dying*, The Hastings Center, Briarcliff Manor, New York.

Havighurst, C., and King, N.: 1986, "Liver Transplantation in Massachusetts: Public Policymaking as Morality Play?" *Indiana Law Review* 19, 955–987.

Hippocrates, *The Art*, reprinted in S. Reiser et al. (eds.): 1977, *Ethics in Medicine: Historical Perspectives and Contemporary Concerns*, MIT Press, Cambridge, p. 6.

Hunter, K.: 1985, "Limiting Treatment in a Social Vacuum," *Archives of Internal Medicine* 145, 716–719.

Ingelfinger, F.: 1980, "Arrogance," *New England Journal of Medicine* 303, 1507–1511.

Johnson, S. H.: 1987, "Sequential Domination, Autonomy, and Living Wills," *Western New England Law Review* 9, 113–137.

Joint Commission on Accreditation of Healthcare Organizations:1994, *Accreditation Manual for Hospitals*, JCAHO, Chicago, Ill.

Juengst, E., and Weil, C.: 1989, "Interpreting Proxy Directives: Clinical Decision-Making and the Durable Power of Attorney for Health Care," in C. Hackler, R. Moseley, and D. Vawter (eds.), *Advance Directives in Medicine*, Praeger, New York, pp. 21–37.

Kane, F.: 1985, "Keeping Elizabeth Bouvia Alive for the Public Good," *Hastings Center Report* 15(6), 5–8.

Kapp, M.: 1994, "Futile Medical Treatment: A Review of the Ethical Arguments and Legal Holdings," *Journal of General Internal Medicine* 9, 170–177.

Katz, J.: 1972, *Experimentation with Human Beings*, Russell Sage Foundation, New York.

_____: 1984, *The Silent World of Doctor and Patient*, Free Press, New York.

_____: 1994, "Informed Consent: Must It Remain a Fairy Tale?" *Journal of Contemporary Health Law and Policy* 10, 69–91.

Kayser-Jones, J., and Kapp, M.: 1989, "Advocacy for the Mentally Impaired Elderly: A Case Study," *American Journal of Law and Medicine* 14, 353–376.

King, N. M. P.: 1988, "Ethics Committees: Talking the Captain through Troubled Waters," in N. M. P. King, L. R. Churchill, and A. W. Cross (eds.), *The Physician as Captain of the Ship: A Critical Reappraisal*, D. Reidel, Dordrecht, Netherlands, pp. 223–241.

King, P. A.: 1991, "The Authority of Families to Make Medical Decisions for Incompetent Patients after the *Cruzan* Decision," *Law, Medicine, and Health Care* 19(1–2), 76–79.

Kinney, H. C., et al.: 1994, "Neuropathological Findings in the Brain of Karen Ann Quinlan: The Role of the Thalamus in the Persistent Vegetative State," *New England Journal of Medicine* 330, 1469–1475.

Kleissig, J.: 1992, "The Effect of Values and Culture on Life-Support Decisions," *Western Journal of Medicine* 157, 315–322.

Kutner, L.: 1969, "Due Process of Euthanasia: The Living Will, a Proposal," *Indiana Law Journal* 44, 539–554.

Lambert, P., Gibson, J., and Nathanson, P.: 1990, "The Values History: An Innovation in Surrogate Medical Decision-Making," *Law, Medicine and Health Care* 18, 202–212.

Layson, R., et al.: 1994, "Discussions about the Use of Life-Sustaining Treatments: A Literature Review of Physicians' and Patients' Attitudes and Practices," *Journal of Clinical Ethics* 5, 195–203.

Lederer, D., and Brock, D. W.: 1987, "Case Study: Surgical Risks and Advance Directives," *Hastings Center Report* 17(4), 18–19.

Legal Advisors Committee, Concern for Dying: 1983, "The Right to Refuse Treatment: A Model Act," *American Journal of Public Health* 73, 918–921.

Lo, B.: 1990, "Assessing Decision-Making Capacity," *Law, Medicine, and Health Care* 18, 193–201.

Loewy, E. H.: 1987, "Treatment Decisions in the Mentally Impaired," *New England Journal of Medicine* 317, 1465–1469.

Lynn, J.: 1992, "Procedures for Making Medical Decisions for Incompetent Adults," *Journal of the American Medical Association* 267, 2082–2084.

Macklin, R.: 1993, *Enemies of Patients*, Oxford University Press, New York.

Mariner, W.: 1988, "Social Goals and Doctors' Roles," in N. M. P. King, L. R. Churchill, and A. W. Cross (eds.), *The Physician as Captain of the Ship: A Critical Reappraisal*, D. Reidel, Dordrecht, Netherlands, pp. 177–187.

Mathieu, D.: 1991, *Preventing Prenatal Harm: Should the State Intervene?* Kluwer, Dordrecht, Netherlands.

McCoid, A. H.: 1957, "A Reappraisal of Liability for Unauthorized Medical Treatment," *Minnesota Law Review* 41, 381–434.

Meisel, A.: 1979, "The 'Exceptions' to the Informed Consent Doctrine: Striking a Balance between Competing Values in Decisionmaking," *Wisconsin Law Review* 1979, 413–488.

_____: 1989, *The Right to Die*, John Wiley and Sons, New York.

_____: 1992, "The Legal Consensus about Forgoing Life-Sustaining Treatment: Its Status and Its Prospects," *Kennedy Institute of Ethics Journal* 2, 309–345.

Mezey, M., and Latimer, B.: 1993, "The Patient Self-Determination Act: An Early Look at Implementation," *Hastings Center Report* 23(1), 16–20.

Miles, S.: 1991, "The Case of Helga Wanglie: A New Kind of 'Right to Die' Case," *New England Journal of Medicine* 325, 512–515.

Miles, S., Singer, P., and Siegler, M.: 1989, "Conflicts between Patients' Wishes to Forego Treatment and the Policies of Health Care Facilities," *New England Journal of Medicine* 321, 48–50.

Morreim, E. H.: 1993, "Impairments and Impediments in Patients' Decision
    Making: Reframing the Competence Question," *Journal of Clinical Ethics*
    4, 294–307.
_____: 1994, "Profoundly Diminished Life: The Casualties of Coercion,"
    *Hastings Center Report* 24(1), 33–42.
Muller, J. H., and Desmond, B.: 1992, "Ethical Dilemmas in a Cross-Cultural
    Context: A Chinese Example," *Western Journal of Medicine* 157, 323–327.
Multi-Society Task Force on PVS: 1994, "Medical Aspects of the Persistent
    Vegetative State," parts 1 and 2, *New England Journal of Medicine* 330,
    1499–1508, 1572–1579.

New York State Task Force on Life and the Law: 1986, *Do Not Resuscitate
    Orders*, Health Education Services, Albany.
_____: 1987, *Life-Sustaining Treatment*, Health Education Services, Albany.
_____: 1992, *When Others Must Choose*, Health Education Services, Albany.
Note: 1970, "Restructuring Informed Consent: Legal Therapy for the Doctor-
    Patient Relationship," *Yale Law Review* 79, 1533.
Note: 1990, "The Constitutionality of Pregnancy Clauses in Living Will Stat-
    utes," *Vanderbilt Law Review* 43, 1821–1837.
Nuland, S.: 1994, *How We Die*, Knopf, New York.

Parfit, D.: 1984, *Reasons and Persons*, Clarendon Press, Oxford.
"Patients Ask: 'If Jackie Had a Living Will, Shouldn't I?'" *American Medical
    News*, June 13, p. 16.
Pernick, M.: 1982, "The Patient's Role in Medical Decision-Making: A Social
    History of Informed Consent in Medical Therapy," in President's Com-
    mission for the Study of Ethical Problems in Medicine and Biomedical
    and Behavioral Research, *Making Health Care Decisions*, vol. 3, *Studies on
    the Foundations of Informed Consent*, U.S. Government Printing Office,
    Washington, pp. 1–35.
Pickard, C. G.: 1993, "Beyond the No-Code Order," *North Carolina Medical Jour-
    nal* 54, 383–385.
Plant, M.: 1968, "An Analysis of Informed Consent," *Fordham Law Review* 36,
    639.
President's Commission for the Study of Ethical Problems in Medicine and
    Biomedical and Behavioral Research: 1982, *Making Health Care Decisions*,
    U.S. Government Printing Office, Washington.
_____: 1983, *Deciding to Forego Life-Sustaining Treatment*, U.S. Government
    Printing Office, Washington.

Quill, T.: 1993, *Death and Dignity: Making Choices and Taking Charge*, Norton,
    New York.

Rachels, J.: 1986, *The End of Life: Euthanasia and Morality*, Oxford University
    Press, Oxford.
Ramsey, P.: 1978, "The *Saikewicz* Precedent: What's Good for an Incompetent
    Patient?" *Hastings Center Report* 8(6), 36–42.

Relman, A.: 1978, "The Saikewicz Decision: A Medical Viewpoint," *American Journal of Law and Medicine* 4, 233–237.

Rhoden, N. K.: 1987, "The Judge in the Delivery Room: The Emergence of Court-Ordered Cesareans," *California Law Review* 74, 1951.

————: 1988, "Litigating Life and Death," *Harvard Law Review* 102, 375–446.

————: 1990, "The Limits of Legal Objectivity," *North Carolina Law Review* 68, 845–865.

Ross, J., and Wegner, N.: 1994, "Institutional Ethics: Hospital Practices and Policies for Denying Life-Sustaining Treatment," *Whittier Law Review* 15, 33–49.

Roth, L. H., Meisel, A., and Lidz, C. W.: 1977, "Tests of Competency to Consent to Treatment," *American Journal of Psychiatry*, 134, 279–284.

Ruark, J. E., and Raffin, T. A.: 1988, "Initiating and Withdrawing Life Support: Principles and Practice in Adult Medicine" *New England Journal of Medicine* 318, 25–30.

Sabatino, C.: 1993, "Surely the Wizard Will Help Us, Toto? Implementing the Patient Self-Determination Act," *Hastings Center Report* 23(1), 12–16.

Schiffer, Charles F.: 1987, "'DNR' Doesn't Stand for 'Do Not Respect,'" *Medical Economics* February 2, pp. 29–32.

Schneiderman, L., Jecker, N., and Jonsen, A.: 1990, "Medical Futility: Its Meaning and Ethical Implications," *Annals of Internal Medicine* 112, 949–954.

Schneiderman, L., et al.: 1992, "Effects of Offering Advance Directives on Medical Treatments and Costs," *Annals of Internal Medicine* 117, 599–606.

————: 1992a, "Relationship of General Advance Directive Instructions to Specific Life-Sustaining Treatment Preferences in Patients with Serious Illness," *Archives of Internal Medicine* 152, 2114–2122.

Scholten, H. J.: 1986, "Court Decision: Justification of Active Euthanasia," *Medicine and Law* 5, 169–172.

Schucking, E.: 1985, "Death at a New York Hospital," *Law, Medicine, and Health Care* 13(6), 261–268.

Scott, C.: 1994, "Resisting the Temptation to Turn Medical Recommendations into Judicial Orders," *Georgia State University Law Review* 10, 615–689.

Seckler, A., et al.: 1991, "Substituted Judgment: How Accurate Are Proxy Predictions?" *Annals of Internal Medicine* 115, 92–98.

Singer, P., and Siegler, M.: 1990, "Euthanasia—a Critique," *New England Journal of Medicine* 322, 1881–1883.

Society for the Right to Die: 1988, *Checklist Chart of Living Will Laws*, Society for the Right to Die, New York.

Soto, D.: 1582, *Theologia Moralis*, Tractatus de Justicia et Jure, bk. 5, q. 2, art. 1, trans. D. Cronin: 1958, The "Moral Law in Regard to the Ordinary and Extraordinary Means of Conserving Life," ThD dissertation, Rome, p. 51.

Special Supplement: 1994, "Advance Care Planning: Priorities for Ethical and Empirical Research," *Hastings Center Report* 24(6), S1–S36.

Starr, P.: 1982, *The Social Transformation of American Medicine*, Basic Books, New York.

Steinbrook, R., and Lo, B.: 1988, "Artificial Feeding—Solid Ground, Not a Slippery Slope," *New England Journal of Medicine* 318, 286–290.

Stell, L.: 1992, "Stopping Treatment on Grounds of Futility: A Role for Institutional Policy," *St. Louis University Public Law Review* 11, 481–497.

Stevens, R.: 1971, *American Medicine and the Public Interest*, Yale University Press, New Haven.

Szasz, T., and Hollender, M.: 1956, "The Basic Models of the Doctor-Patient Relationship," *Archives of Internal Medicine* 97, 585–592.

Teel, K.: 1975, "The Physician's Dilemma—A Doctor's View: What the Law Should Be," *Baylor Law Review* 27, 6–9.

Teno, J., Nelson, H. L., and Lynn, J.: 1994, "Advance Care Planning: Priorities for Ethical and Empirical Research," *Hastings Center Report* 24(6), S32–S36.

Teno, J., et al.: 1994, "Do Formal Advance Directives Affect Resuscitation Decisions and the Use of Resources for Seriously Ill Patients?" *Journal of Clinical Ethics* 5, 23–30.

_____: 1994a, "The Impact of the Patient Self-Determination Act's Requirement That States Describe Law Concerning Patients' Rights," *Journal of Law, Medicine, and Ethics* 21, 102–108.

Thomas, L.: 1975, *The Lives of a Cell: Notes of a Biology Watcher*, Bantam Books, New York, pp. 35–42.

Tomlinson, T.: 1993, "Refusing Demands for Attempted Resuscitation: Ethics and Hospital Policy," in R. Blank and A. Bonnickson (eds.), *Emerging Issues in Biomedical Policy: An Annual Review*, vol. 2, Columbia University Press, New York, pp. 44–56.

Tomlinson, T., and Brody, H.: 1988, "Ethics and Communication in Do-Not-Resuscitate Orders," *New England Journal of Medicine* 318, 43–46.

_____: 1990, "Futility and the Ethics of Resuscitation," *Journal of the American Medical Association* 264, 1276–1280.

Tribe, L.: 1988, *American Constitutional Law*, 2d ed., Foundation Press, New York.

Truog, R., Brett, A., and Frader, J.: 1992, "The Problem with Futility," *New England Journal of Medicine* 326, 1560–1564.

U.S. Congress, Office of Technology Assessment: 1987, *Life-Sustaining Technologies and the Elderly*, U.S. Government Printing Office, Washington, p. 40.

Veatch, R., and Callahan, D.: 1984, "Is Autonomy an Outmoded Value?" *Hastings Center Report* 14(5), 38.

_____: 1993, "Forgoing Life-Sustaining Treatment: Limits to the Consensus," *Kennedy Institute of Ethics Journal* 3, 1–19.

Waltz, J. R., and Scheuneman, T.: 1970, "Informed Consent to Therapy," *Northwestern University Law Review* 64, 628.

Wanzer, S., et al.: 1984, "The Physician's Responsibility toward Hopelessly Ill Patients," *New England Journal of Medicine*, 310, 955–959.

_____: 1989, "The Physician's Responsibility toward Hopelessly Ill Patients: A Second Look," *New England Journal of Medicine*, 320, 844–849.

Weinberg, J.: 1988, "Whose Right Is It Anyway? Individualism, Community, and the Right to Die: A Commentary on the New Jersey Experience," *Hastings Law Journal* 40, 119–167.

Weir, R.: 1994, "Advance Directives as Instruments of Moral Persuasion," in R. Blank and A. Bonnicksen (eds.), *Medicine Unbound: The Human Body and the Limits of Medical Intervention*, Columbia University Press, New York, pp. 171–187.

Weir, R., and Gostin, L.: 1990, "Decisions to Abate Life-Sustaining Treatment for Nonautonomous Patients: Ethical Standards and Legal Liability for Physicians After *Cruzan*," *Journal of the American Medical Association* 264, 1846–1853.

Winston, M. E., et al.: 1982, "Case Study: Can a Subject Consent to a 'Ulysses Contract'?" *Hastings Center Report* 12(4), 26–28.

Wolf, S. M.: 1990, "Nancy Beth Cruzan: In No Voice at All," *Hastings Center Report* 20(1), 38–41.

Wolf, S. M., et al.: 1991, "Sources of Concern about the Patient Self-Determination Act," *New England Journal of Medicine* 325, 1666–1671.

World Medical Assembly: 1964, "Declaration of Helsinki: Recommendations Guiding Medical Doctors in Biomedical Research Involving Human Subjects," *New England Journal of Medicine* 271, 473.

Zugler, A: 1989, "High Hopes," *Journal of the American Medical Association* 262, 2988.

## CASES, STATUTES, AND REGULATIONS

Anderson v. St. Francis-St. George Hospital (Winter), 83 Ohio App. 3d 221, 614 NE2d 841 (1992).

Application of President and Directors of Georgetown College, Inc. 331 F.2d 100, *petition for rehearing en banc denied*, 331 F.2d 1010 (D.C. Cir. 1964), *cert. denied*, 377 U.S. 978 (1964).

Arizona Living Wills and Health Care Directives Act [1985, 1991, 1992, 1994], Ariz. Rev. Stat. Ann. §§36–3201 to 36–3262 (1993).

Barber v. Superior Court, 147 Cal. App.3d 1006, 195 Cal. Rptr. 484 (Ct. App. 1983).

Bartling v. Superior Court, 163 Cal. App. 3d 186, 209 Cal. Rptr. 220 (Ct. App. 1984).

Berkey v. Anderson, 1 Cal App. 3d 790, 82 Cal. Rptr. 67 (1969).

Bouvia v. County of Riverside, No. 159780 (Cal. Super. Ct. Riverside County Dec. 16, 1983) (Hews, J.).

Bouvia v. Superior Court (Glenchur), 179 Cal. App. 3d 1127, 225 Cal. Rptr. 297 (Ct. App. 1986), *review denied* (Cal. June 5, 1986).

Brophy v. New England Sinai Hospital, Inc., 398 Mass. 417, 497 N.E. 2d 626 (1986).
Brown v. Hughes, 94 Colo. 295, 30 P.2d 259 (1934).

Canterbury v. Spence, 464 F.2d 772 (D.C. Cir. 1972).
Carpenter v. Blake, 60 Barb. N.Y. 488 (1871).
Cobbs v. Grant, 104 Cal. Rptr. 505, 502 P.2d 1 (1972).
Cooper v. Roberts, 220 Pa. Super. 260, 286 A.2d 647 (1971).
Corbett v. D'Alessandro, 487 So.2d 368 (Fla. Dist. Ct. App.), *review denied*, 492 So.2d 1331 (Fla. 1986).
Cruzan v. Director, Missouri Dep't of Health, 497 U.S. 261, 111 L. Ed. 2d 224, 110 S. Ct. 2841 (1990).
Cruzan v. Harmon, 760 S. W. 2d 408 (Mo. 1988), aff'd *sub nom.*
Cruzan v. Director, Missouri Dep't of Health, 497 U.A. 261 (1990).

Department of Health and Human Services: 1993, 'Protection of Human Subjects,' Code of Federal Regulations 45, §§46.101 to 46.409.
Delio v. Westchester County Medical Center, 129 A.D.2d 1, 516 N.Y.S.2d 677 (App. Div. 2d Dept. 1987).

Elbaum v. Grace Plaza of Great Neck, Inc., 148 A.2d 244, 544 N.Y.S.2d 840 (2nd Dept. 1989).
Evans v. Bellevue Hospital (Wirth), No. 16536 87, N.Y. Sup. Ct., N.Y. County (July 27, 1987); N.Y.L.J. July 28, 1987, at 11, column 1.

Food and Drug Administration: 1993, 'Protection of Human Subjects,' *Code of Federal Regulations* 21, §§50.1 to 50.48, 56.101 to 56.124.
Fortner v. Koch, 272 Mich. 273, 261 N.W. 762 (1935).
Fosmire v. Nicoleau, 75 N.Y.2d 218, 551 N.E.2d 77 (1990).

Grace Plaza of Great Neck, Inc., v. Elbaum, 82 N.Y.2d 10 (N.Y. Ct. App. 1993).
Gray v. Grunnagle, 423 Pa. 144, 223 A.2d 663 (1966).
Gray v. Romeo, 709 F. Supp. 325 (D. RI 1988).

Health Care Financing Administration: 1992, "Medicare and Medicaid Programs; Advance Directives," *Federal Register* 57, 8194–8204 (March 6, 1992).
Health Care Financing Administration: 1995, "Medicare and Medicaid Programs; Advance Directives," *Federal Register* 60, 33262–33294 (June 27, 1995).

In re A.C., 573 A.2d 1235 (D.C. Ct. App. 1990), *rev'g* 533 A.2d 611 (1987).
In re A.K., RJ1 No. 26796, N.Y. Sup. Ct., Warren County (Feb. 16, 1989).
In re Baby Boy Doe v. Mother Doe, 260 Ill. App.3d 392, 632 N.E.2d 326 (Ill. Ct. App. 1st Dist. 2nd Div. 1994).
In re Baby K, 16 F.3d 590 (4th Cir. 1994)

In re Conservatorship of Wanglie, No. PX-91–283 (Minn. Dist. Ct. Hennepin Co., July 1991).

In re Finsterbach (N.Y. Sup. Ct. Oneida County, June 12, 1990).

In re Greenspan, No. 67903 (Ill. Supreme Ct., July 9, 1990).

In re Guardianship of Browning, No. 74,174 (Fla. Supreme Ct. Sept. 13, 1990), *aff' g* 543 So.2d 258 (Fla. Dist Ct. App.), clarified No. 88–02887 (Dist. Ct. App. May 3, 1989).

"In re Jamaica Hospital," *New York Law Journal*, May 17, 1985, p. 15.

In re Jobes, 108 N.J. 394, 529 A.2d 434 (1987).

In re Melideo, 390 N.Y.S.2d 523 (N.Y. Supreme Ct. 1976).

In re Osborne, 294 A.2d 372 (D.C. App. 1972).

In re Peter, 188 N.J. 365, 529 A.2d 419 (1987).

In re Quinlan, 70 N.J. 10, 355 A.2d 647 (1976).

In re Requena, 213 N.J. Super. 475, 517 A.2d 886 (Super. Ct. Ch. Div.), *aff'd*, 213 N.J. Super. 443, 517 A.2d 869 (Super. Ct.App. Div. 1986) (per curiam).

In re Rodas, No. 86PR139 (Colo. Dist. Ct. Mesa County Jan. 22, 1987) (Buss, J.).

In re Westchester County Medical Center (O'Connor), 72 N.Y.2d 517, 531 N.E.2d 607 (N.Y. Ct. App. 1988).

Jacobson v. Massachusetts, 197 U.S. 11 (1905).

Leach v. Shapiro, 13 Ohio App. 3d 393, 469 N.E.2d 1047 (Ct. App. 1984).

Maine Uniform Health Care Decisions Act [1985, 1990, 1991, 1995], Me. Rev. Stat. Ann. tit. 18–A, §§5–801 to 8–817 (H.B. 182, signed June 30, 1995).

Maryland Health Care Decision Act [1985, 1986, 1987, 1993], Md. Health-Gen. Code Ann. §§5–601 to 5–618 (1994).

Matter of Conroy, 98 N.J. 321, 486 A.2d 1209 (1985).

McFall v. Shimp, 10 Pa. D. & C. 3d 90 (Allegheny Ct. Comm. Pleas, 1978).

Mohr v. Williams, 95 Minn. 261, 104 N.W. 12 (1905).

Natanson v. Kline, 186 Kan. 393, 350 P.2d 1093, *opinion on denial of motion for rehearing*, 187 Kan. 186, 354 P.2d 670 (1960).

New Hampshire Living Wills Act [1985, 1991, 1992], N.H. Rev. Stat. Ann. §§137–H:1 to 137–H:16 (1990 and Supp. 1992).

New Hampshire Durable Power of Attorney for Health Care [1991],N.H. Rev. Stat. Ann. §§137–J:1 to 137–J:16 (Supp. 1993).

North Carolina Right to Natural Death Act [1977, 1979, 1981, 1983, 1991], N.C. Gen. Stat. §§90–320 to 90–322 (1993).

North Carolina Health Care Powers of Attorney Act [1991, 1993], N.C. Gen. Stat. §§32A–15 to 32A–26 (1993).

Patient Self-Determination Act, §§4206 to 4207, 4751 (Omnibus Budget Reconciliation Act, Pub. L. 101–508, 101st Cong. 2nd Sess., Nov. 5, 1990); 42 U.S.C. §§1395 cc *et seq.* (1990).

Pennsylvania Advance Directive for Health Care Act [1992], Pa. Stat. Ann. tit. 20, §§5401 to 5416 (West Supp. 1994).

Pratt v. Davis, 224 Ill. 300, 79 N.E. 562 (1906).

Randolph v. City of New York, 117 A.D.2d 44, 501 N.Y.S.2d 837 (1986).

Salgo v. Leland Stanford Jr. University Board of Trustees, 317 P.2d 170 (1957).
Satz v. Perlmutter, 362 So.2d 160 (Fla. Ct. App. 1978), *aff'd with opinion*, 379 So.2d 359 (Fla. Ct. App. 1980).
Schloendorff v. Society of New York Hospitals, 211 N.Y. 125, 105 N.E. 92 (1914).
Slater v. Baker and Stapleton, 95 Eng. Rep. 860 (K.B. 1767).
Strunk v. Strunk, 445 S.W.2d 145 (Ky, 1969).
Superintendent of Belchertown State School v. Saikewicz, 373 Mass. 728, 370 N.E.2d 417 (1977).

Truman v. Thomas, 165 Cal. Rptr. 308, 611 P.2d 902 (1980).

Uniform Durable Power of Attorney Act, 8 Uniform Laws Annotated 74 (1982).
Uniform Rights of the Terminally Ill Act, §§1 to 18, 9B Uniform Laws Annotated 96–115 (Supp. 1992) [superseded].
Uniform Health-Care Decisions Act, §§1 to 19, 9 Uniform Laws Annotated 93–114 (Supp. 1994).
United States v. Karl Brandt, *Trials of War Criminals Before the Nuremberg Military Tribunals under Control Council Law No. 10*, Vols. 1 and 2, "The Medical Case" (Military Tribunal I, 1947; Washington, D.C.: U.S. Government Printing Office 1948–49).

# Index